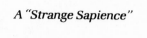

A "Strange Sapience"

A "Strange Sapience":
The Creative Imagination
of D. H. Lawrence

Daniel Dervin

The University of Massachusetts Press   Amherst, 1984

Acknowledgment is herewith made for permission to reprint material from the writings of D. H. Lawrence under copyright.

Viking Penguin, Inc.: *Aaron's Rod* © 1922 by Thomas Seltzer, Inc., renewed 1950 by Frieda Lawrence; *Apocalypse* © 1931 by the Estate of D. H. Lawrence; *Etruscan Places* (Viking Press, Inc., 1932); *Four Short Novels* (Viking Press, Inc., 1965); *Phoenix: The Posthumous Papers of D. H. Lawrence*, ed. Edward McDonald, © 1936 by Frieda Lawrence, renewed 1964 by the Estate of Frieda Lawrence Ravagli; *Phoenix II* © 1959, 1963, 1968 by the Estate of Frieda Lawrence Ravagli; *Fantasia of the Unconscious* © 1922 by Thomas Seltzer, Inc., renewed 1949 by Frieda Lawrence; *Sons and Lovers* © 1913 by Thomas Seltzer, Inc.; *The Collected Letters of D. H. Lawrence*, ed. Harry T. Moore, © 1962 by Angelo Ravagli and C. M. Weekley, executors of the Estate of Frieda Lawrence Ravagli; *The Complete Poems of D. H. Lawrence*, ed. Vivian de Sola Pinto and F. Warren Roberts, © 1964 by Angelo Ravagli and C. M. Weekley, executors of the Estate of Frieda Lawrence Ravagli; *The Complete Short Stories of D. H. Lawrence*, vol. 3, © 1933 by the Estate of D. H. Lawrence, renewed 1960 by Angelo Ravagli and C. M. Weekley, executors of the Estate of Frieda Lawrence Ravagli; *The Rainbow* © 1915 by D. H. Lawrence, renewed 1943 by Frieda Lawrence Ravagli; *Women in Love* © 1920, 1921 by D. H. Lawrence, renewed 1947, 1949 by Frieda Lawrence Ravagli; *Kangaroo* © 1923 by Thomas Seltzer, Inc., renewed 1950 by Frieda Lawrence.

Vintage Books, Alfred A. Knopf, Inc.: *The Plumed Serpent* © 1926, 1951 by Alfred A. Knopf, Inc.; *St. Mawr* and *The Man Who Died* © 1925, 1928 by Alfred A. Knopf, Inc., renewed 1953 by Frieda Lawrence Ravagli; *Mornings in Mexico*.

Grove Press, Inc.: *Lady Chatterley's Lover* (1957)

To my wife, Kate

Contents

Key to Titles   ix

Introduction   1

1   Fantasy   14

2   Reality   39

3   Symbol   48

4   Body   76

5   Play   111

6   Origins   127

7   Projection   148

8   Sun   166

9   Creative Selfhood   181

Appendixes

1: On Symbol Formation   203

2: On the Relation of Aggression
to Creativity and Sexuality   206

3: On Maturation versus Development   212

Notes   215

Selected Bibliography   231

Index   241

Key to Titles

A   *Apocalypse*

AD   *The Art of D. H. Lawrence*, Keith Sagar

AJ   *D. H. Lawrence's American Journey*, James Cowan

AR   *Aaron's Rod*

C   *The Crown*

CL   *The Collected Letters of D. H. Lawrence*, Harry T. Moore, ed.

CP   *The Complete Poems of D. H. Lawrence*

CSS   *The Complete Short Stories*, I, II, III

DN   *Dark Night of the Body*, L. D. Clark

EP   *Etruscan Places*

FF   *The Flying Fish*

FFU   Foreword to *Fantasia of the Unconscious*

FU   *Fantasia of the Unconscious*

HO   *The Hidden Order of Art*, Anton Ehrenzweig

JF   *D. H. Lawrence in Taos*, Joseph Foster

K   *Kangaroo*

LB   *Lawrence and Brett, A Friendship*, Dorothy Brett

LCL   *Lady Chatterley's Lover*

MD   *The Man Who Died*

MM   *Mornings in Mexico*

MW   *D. H. Lawrence: The Man and His Work*, Emile Delavenay

N   *D. H. Lawrence: A Composite Biography*, I, Edward Nehls

NI   *Not I, But the Wind*, Frieda Lawrence

NW   *D. H. Lawrence and the New World*, David Cavitch

P   *Phoenix*, "Love," 151 − 57; "Pornography and Obscenity," 170 − 87; "Study of Thomas Hardy," 398 − 516; "The Reality of Peace," 669 − 94

P2   *Phoenix II*

PE   *D. H. Lawrence, a Personal Record*, Jessie Chambers

PL   *The Priest of Love*, Harry T. Moore

PS   *The Plumed Serpent*

PT   *A Poet and Two Painters*, Knud Merrild

PU   *Psychoanalysis and the Unconscious*

QR   *The Quest for Rananim*, George J. Zytaruk

R   *The Rainbow*

RE   *Reflections on the Death of a Porcupine and Other Essays*

SL   *Sons and Lovers*

SM   *St. Mawr*

ST   *Studies in Classic American Literature*

SY   *The Symbolic Meaning*

T   *The Trespasser*

WL   *Women in Love*

WB   *Journey with Genius*, Witter Brynner

WP   *The White Peacock*

Let us accept our own destiny. Man can't live by instinct because he's got a mind. The serpent, with a crushed head, learned to brood along his spine, and take poison in his mouth. He has a strange sapience. But even he doesn't have ideas. Man has a mind and ideas, so it is just puerile to sigh for innocence and naive spontaneity. . . .

Man, poor, conscious, forever-animal man, has a very stern destiny from which he is never allowed to escape. It is his destiny that he must move on and on, in the thought-adventure. He is a thought-adventurer, and adventure he must. The moment he builds himself a house and begins to think he can sit still in his knowledge, his soul becomes deranged, and he begins to pull down the house over his own head. —Lawrence, "On Human Destiny" (P2, 623 — 29)

Introduction

... to make a permanent core ... a holy centre: whole, heal, hale.—D. H. Lawrence,
CL, 1031

I'll do my life work, sticking up for the love between man and woman.—D. H.
Lawrence, CL, 172

A psychoanalytic study of the creative process in D. H. Lawrence
can offer a distinctive contribution to his development into an
artist. Owing to two recent trends within psychoanalysis—investigations into the earliest periods of an individual's life, and a subsequent emphasis on normal development—it is now possible to
examine more closely the formation and evolution of the human
self. Out of primal fantasies and primal scenes, out of instinctual
drives, their repressions and displaced representations, out of
projection and reintrojection, out of primary harmony and primary chaos, a cohesive self emerges and begins to take shape in
a world of other selves. It is in this still-perplexing world of early
development that the formation of the artist also begins. Out of
what Lawrence calls "fierce incongruities" issues in a broad sense
the "strange sapience" of his art. To trace this unfolding is our
present purpose.

But to reach a more precise and profound awareness of this
writer's creative origins we must accommodate the interplay of
diverse tongues. In its own right, the still-evolving language of
psychoanalysis is often more richly evocative than scientifically
decisive; while the variety of tongues and tones through which
Lawrence spoke—visionary, polemicist, critic, intimate, yet always intensely imaginative—poses its own set of problems. Hence
a unified mode of discourse drawing on these distinct linguistic
worlds—a mode that sacrifices as little as possible to the prerogatives of either—is a goal that can only be approximated.

For example, when Lawrence in our epigraph contrasts the instinctive knowledge of the serpent with the thinking human, his richly evocative imagery of the serpent's crushed head, its brooding along the spine, and its poison in the mouth, connote a strange sapience which, like the unconscious, is radically different from man's conscious mind. The fact that the serpent's head is not really crushed, that it doesn't brood—and that its venom is not poisonous to its own species all suggest that Lawrence is using the figure to represent in nonhuman images a kind of mental life humans once shared and may yet recover—though in the present context he slights the primordial to emphasize the distinctly human destiny of the thought-adventurer. All the same, while reminding us here that we are "forever animal," he also celebrates the snake elsewhere as "one of the lords of life," a "king in exile" (CP, 349). And many other contexts make clear that Lawrence's own great destiny has been to rediscover through creative processes the instinctual sources of human life and to reorder the realms of the unconscious and the conscious. Yet the strange sapience of his own creative unconscious is distinctive enough to warrant the extended acts of attention that comprise these various chapters.

To enable the reader of the present text to perceive Lawrence through the peculiar focus of various psychoanalytic lenses, semantic compromises must be drawn between intrusive jargon and the lexical economy of that jargon as it is conceived within its discipline. *Objects*, for example, refer to persons, especially the first significant others of one's childhood, and thus also to subjective or partial perceptions of them. *Cathexis* may be better rendered not only as attachment to or emotional investment in those subjectively colored *objects*, but also in respect to oneself, as in narcissism. When their equivalent cannot be found, other technical terms will be defined and made clear in their context. Among post-Freudian psychoanalysts whose works have encouraged this project are Michael Balint, D. W. Winnicott, Anton Ehrenzweig, Hanna Segal, Lawrence Kubie, William Niederland, Margaret Mahler, and Heinz Kohut. For all their diversity they balance an interest in self and object-relations with the original theories of drive and defense—an important distinction to keep in mind.

A second distinction is evident in the first extensive psychoanalytic study of D. H. Lawrence. Both the strengths and liabilities of Daniel Weiss's *Oedipus in Nottingham* (1962) are cued by the title, for its outlook is circumscribed by the legitimate mainstream of 1950s American psychoanalysis, in effect a continuation of Freud's exploration of the Oedipus complex as central to human and cultural development. The analysts cited above may be further distinguished by their interest in earlier development, especially in the child-mother dyad (rather than the son-father complex), an area often nebulously or negatively referred to as pre-oedipal. Thus Michael Balint would replace primary narcissism with primary object-love; Margaret Mahler would emphasize ongoing phases of separation / individuation rather than the cataclysmic castration complex; and D. W. Winnicott would demarcate an intermediate sphere of experience called transitional, existing in the widening spaces between mother and child, a sphere that would include play, creativity, and many cultural products along a continuum that blends reality and illusion. These and other innovations—such as Niederland's that creativity entails self-injury and self-remaking rather than defenses against forbidden wishes contained in fantasies—hold a rich promise for a far more inclusive understanding of art and creativity.

The volume of psychoanalytic writing on creative personalities has always been disproportionately large, and by now this number is great enough to underscore general trends. My impression from many of these studies is that the most common underlying conflict is neither in the oedipal period nor concentrated in the traditional phallic or anal drive zones, but occurs around the end of the first year when issues of self-object differentiation come to the fore. That is why an increasing number of studies of creativity center on processes of object-loss, self/separation, and object-recovery, which Melanie Klein first singled out as the "depressive position." Creative urges cannot predate the sometimes anxious awareness of an absent object, nor can there be any grounds for mimetic representation before maternal separation engenders emotional spaces in the child's world. This is also around the time when the more primitive, discharge-prone mental processes—such as wish-fulfillment fantasy and hallucination—become amenable to symbol-formation with its ability to bind up, delay, and eventually redirect instinctual drives by providing internal representations.

Transitional phenomena, symbol-formation, and the first stirrings of creativity tend to come together toward the end of the child's first year and to coincide with the depressive position. This period within normal development is more positively referred to by Winnicott as "the stage of concern," and it is the one stage that figures most prominently in psychoanalytic studies of creative artists. Because the early mental processes are rooted in biological growth as well as in psychological ties, I must admit to being persuaded to persist with these developmental approaches rather than to follow what may be an equally promising modus operandi and one more seemingly suited to Lawrence's sensibility. I refer to the theories of C. G. Jung, whom Lawrence never attacked as he did Freud, though the relative disregard may have been the lesser compliment. Nonetheless, neither Jung nor Lawrence much cared for what they took to be Freud's scientific rationalism on the one hand and his apparent overemphasis on incest-motives on the other. Both men had protestant-based, quasi-religious views of man and the cosmos, and each in his own way set out to revise Freudian libido theory. They preferred myth to abstraction and found inspiration in their visits to the Pueblo Indians in Taos, New Mexico. During unguarded moments I find myself referring to Lawrence's great images and symbols as archetypal, and without a doubt Lawrence would have preferred Jung's interest in "living symbols" over Freud's seemingly simplistic reduction of symbols to overdetermined signs. Even if the contrast is unfair, Lawrence's life was a quest for living symbols, nothing less, and he succeeded to the extent that he found and revitalized them. Consider also his intuitive sense of the collective unconscious: "The human consciousness is really homogeneous. There is no forgetting, even in death. So that somewhere within us the old experience of the Euphrates, Mesopotamia between the rivers, lives still" (P, 298). Even though he found Jung "soft somewhere," there is also a strong mystical-occult side to Lawrence that Jung's own pursuits roughly paralleled (CL, 938). Jung's emphasis on the self and individuation as a reconciliation of opposites is also—let us admit it—a Lawrencean obsession.

Yet it can only be paradoxical that Lawrence was so absorbed in sexuality and sexual questions as to leave Jung far behind, and one hesitates to reduce the Lawrencean male and female to the warring components within our psychic mandala, though it is tempting. But in the end it is Jung's downplaying of the organic and the individual in favor of the alchemical and the generic, and Lawrence's determined genital striving no less than his early conflicts, that urge one to return to Freud's many-branched tree of psychoanalysis as the overarching shelter for this study, and to allow Jung, like the return of the repressed, to find his way back in.

We say that the human has originally two sexual objects: himself and the woman who tends him, and thereby we postulate a primary narcissism in everyone . . . the libidinal complement to the egoism of the instinct of self-preservation.—Freud, "On Narcissism"

"Spare me that word, 'narcissism,' will you? You use it on me like a club."—The writer Peter Tarnopol to his analyst in Philip Roth's My Life As a Man

To interpret Lawrence by the very system of thought he diametrically opposed (without quite comprehending) may be as unfair as it is to overlook the fact that from his struggle with psychoanalysis came his own psychological system, sometimes referred to as "pollyanalytics"—both Pollyanna and polymorphus. Moreover, one hardly wants to join the ranks of those who feel they know Lawrence better than Lawrence, infuriating as he can be; but his system is closer than one would think to psychoanalysis, especially to its recent developments. At the very least psychoanalysis can *in its own way* deliver one from the inimical self-regarding surface of the ego which Lawrence termed mental consciousness. It can also *in its own way*—by insight and working-through—put the individual in touch with the blood-consciousness of a self felt to be rooted in the body.

Certainly the artist should not be defined by his conflicts. Nor, on the other hand, should psychoanalysis be expected to define what art is, who the artist is, or how great his/her work is. These ideas are the categories "thrown off from life," as Lawrence would have it, "as leaves are shed from a tree, or as feathers fall from a bird" (PU, 46). But it is becoming possible psychoanalytically to see more clearly and more vitally *how an artist becomes*. This entails, however, a more inclusive and generous psychoanalytic approach than often obtains, and one that takes into account an unfolding developmental process from a dual perspective within the self and in its relation to others. The result should be to bring out more, rather than less, meaning. And what may initially appear as a form of reductivism may be more accurately rendered as the removal of the insentient and arbitrary divisions one imposes on the unknown to disarm and domesticate it.

Just as psychoanalysis first built its psychosexual phases out of bodily processes—oral, anal, phallic, genital—so Lawrence roots all experience and interactions with the "circumambient universe" in such bodily zones as the solar plexus, spinal, cardiac, and thoracic. The body in both instances is basic: a dynamic energy system as well as an entity that can be represented and conceptualized. Cowan's exegesis of this material has brought out several parallels which may work but which also need closer analysis. Lawrence begins with the startling assertion that consciousness arises in the "primal affective centre" of the solar plexus. From this active, sympathetic center, the "child is drawn to the mother again, crying, to heal the new wound, to re-establish the old oneness" (PU, 20—21). Because Lawrence describes the awareness at this phase as "I am I, the vital centre of all things" and "all is one with me," Cowan reasonably connects it with Freud's "primary narcissism" (AJ, 17). But note how Lawrence confuses the issues by speaking both of the mother, an object not known in the primary narcissism schema, and of a wound of separation, a condition no less alien to narcissistic bliss.

Lawrence then locates a center of resistance at the base of the spine, where the infant asserts himself and kicks away from mother; this Cowan correlates with the anal phase. But the polly- and the psycho-analytic parallels soon begin to break down, either because Cowan's Freudianism is too restricted, or Lawrence's system is too idiosyncratic. Yet we should not give up too readily, for Lawrence's theories are absolutely essential for a just treatment of his total work, not only because they provide the basis for an elaborate series of micro- and macrocosmic correspondences underlying and bolstering his creativity, but also because by itself, the primary-narcissism concept quickly turns reductive and maddeningly circular.

Primary narcissism might be given as the answer to the question (in a Pinter play), which asks, that "Apart from the known and the unknown, what else is there?" Although the term is not clinically derived, it does conveniently allow one to move on to other things, like secondary narcissism. At the same time, however, one cannot escape from an uneasy sense of question-begging, for if narcissism is technically defined as a libidinal investment in the self, primary narcissism seems to predate the emergence of a self to be attached to. More useful than verifiable, the term does address a cluster of primordial feelings of a quasi-mythical or oceanic order that persist and most likely go back to a period of extremely self-centered infancy.

Similarly, as narcissism was to be succeeded by personal ties, so would the child's autoeroticism yield to genital sexuality. But these pairs seem now to have been false opposites. And although today one hears about narcissistic disorders, one also learns about mature narcissism. Incentives to revise the concept apparently came both from the external pressures of shifts in patients and from needs within the field to clear up inconsistencies within the rapidly evolving psychoanalytic tradition. With this area still very much in a state of flux, little harm can be done by tilting the scales toward a neglected pioneer.

In England, Michael Balint was among the first to force a rethinking of primary narcissism. In his early papers he found that when his patients had reached a fairly advanced stage of deep transference, they always regressed to an "archaic pre-traumatic state" where they demanded certain primitive but modest gratifications. These were never satisfied in an autoerotic or narcissistic way, but were always "directed toward an object" (i.e., the therapist). If their needs were properly met (touching, holding, gift-giving, and so on), a "tranquil quiet sense of well-being" and a "new beginning" of growth toward wholeness often ensued. Balint formulated such regressed wishes as a need to be "loved and satisfied, without being under any obligation to give anything in return." This early condition he named "primary object-love," and considered both narcissism and active loving as "detours." "Primary love," as it came to be called, still appears to be narcissistic because "it does not recognize any difference between one's own interests and the interests of the object; it assumes as a matter of fact that the partner's desires are identical with one's own." Self-centered though it may be, a primitive sort of relationship with the environment exists.

This Edenic and idyllic state of primary love has probably been better rendered in the arts than in discursive texts. Consider the following passage as one evocation:

The sand was warm to his breast, and his belly, and his arms. It was like a great body he cleaved to. Almost, he fancied, he felt it heaving under him in its breathing. Then he turned his face to the sun and laughed. All the while, he hugged the warm body of the sea bay beneath him. He spread his hands upon the sand; he took it in handfuls, and let it run smooth, warm, delightful, through his fingers.... For the sun and the white flower of the bay were breathing and kissing him dry, were holding him in their warm concave, like a bee in a flower, like himself on the bosom of Helena.

This passage from *The Trespasser* was written by Lawrence in the summer of 1910 during the period of his first separation from his mother and his native village. He was then struggling as a young teacher outside London, and his mother's health may have already begun to fail, for she would not live out the year.

For his part, Balint depicts primary love as occurring before the infant perceives the mother as a whole person separate from himself and his needs. In his 1959 monograph, *Thrills and Regressions*, he rephrased his early ideas: "Primary love is a relationship in which only one partner may have demands and claims; the environment must be in complete harmony with the demands and enjoyments of the individual." Long before she is recognized as a subsisting person in her own right, the mother forms the infant's earliest living environment to which he is related from the very outset. In order to speak of this preobject environment, Balint draws on common-sense distinctions: objects (i.e., persons) are on the one hand targets of instinctual strivings, and on the other, firm and resistant shapes in the environment, but liquids and gases are not. "When attempting to include solids, liquids, and gases together, science and philosophy developed other words, such as substrate, substance, and matter." Literally and etymologically, *substrate* means "that which is spread under"; *substance*, "that which stands or is under"; and *matter* "derives from a common Indo-Germanic root denoting *mother*." Thus the infant's early environment contains substances as well as objects; and the "inescapable inference is that at one time there must have been a harmonious mix-up in our minds between ourselves and the world around us, and that our 'mother' was involved in it." This short-lived state of "primary harmony" between "subject and environment" is the basis for Balint's theory of primary love. It articulates Freud's "oceanic feeling" and is later approximated, according to Balint, through fairy tales, in states of ecstasy, and during orgasm.

For Lawrence, pristine consciousness relates directly through the solar plexus to the environment both as mother and universe. This sympathetic tie is one of primal love, not of primary narcissism; only in reaction does the secondary system of the spinal ganglion introduce resistance and repudiation, though both may have equal status. And even this "negative polarity" of singleness assumes the prior formation of an object against which one kicks, defines oneself, and at least partially separates from. For Lawrence, the theme of singleness came hectically to the fore during the turbulent war years, and receded somewhat thereafter. The later emphasis is always on connecting, or reconnecting after a painful break. "My individualism is really an illusion," he wrote in 1929 (A, 200). "I am a part of the great whole and can never escape." Moreover, the sun, which is so fundamental throughout Lawrence, operates as a life-giving *substance* for the individual. "In Mexico," he was to find, "the sun and air are alive, let man be what he may" (WB, 341). As one of his characters puts it, the vital principle in nature "soothes me, and it holds me up" (SM, 158). A clue to the importance of elemental substances occurs in his searing awareness before his mother's death that "nobody can come into my very self again and breath me like an atmosphere." But that remarkable response, and other notable passages in his letters where he proclaims his concern about what "the woman IS . . . inhumanly, physiologically, materially," illumine only part of his total emotional spectrum (CL, 282). Nonetheless, they do support the view that his imaginative resources were able to tap into that zone behind time when primary love may account for the sustaining sources of creativity and threatened maternal loss. But the total process is more paradoxical than logical. For in the long run, emotional losses only punctuate the necessary separateness which alone makes possible the writer's passionately desired rapprochement with the "great whole" of life.

The curse against all mothers . . .
It burns within me like a deep, old burn . . . —"She Looks Back" CP, 208

To speak of the "real" meaning disregards these principles [of overdetermination, multiple function, and ambivalence]. The fact that one has discerned further mean-ing, weightier meaning, more disturbing meaning, more archaic meaning, or more carefully disguised meaning than that which first met the eye or the ear does not justify the claim that one has discovered the ultimate truth that lies behind the world of appearances—the "real" world.—Roy Schafer, The Analytic Attitude, p. 7

We have begun to explore the formation of the self, the early world of the artist, and the development of creative processes within early relationships. Here, a breakdown of psychic functioning into three areas may be helpful:

(1) *Primary creativity* refers to the area of the self and its earliest efforts of constitution and reconstitution: narcissistic trans-formations.
(2) The *dyadic sphere* refers to the mother-child dual unity: pri-mary love.
(3) The *triadic sphere* refers to the child in his interaction with both parents: the oedipal stage and the triangulation of rela-tionships that follow.

A discernible bias toward "pre-oedipal" interpretations does not intend to discredit the oedipal stage so much as to place it on a continuum. Similarly, fantasy and symbol-formation are still valued not only because they reveal unconscious impulses (drive derivatives) and defenses, but also because they contain the earli-est mental representations of the mind's three areas. These psy-chic structures facilitate the present dual approach to creativity: not solely as a regressive, id-dominated, pleasure-bound activity, nor only as an active struggle with the morbid and pathological features of personality or culture, but as a dialectical process be-tween subjective and objective poles. As applied to Lawrence (in contrast, say, to Kafka), creativity is more analogous to therapeutic working-through than to catharsis, more akin to self-emergence than to circular-repetition, and so in the long run favoring matu-rity over the tenacious lures of childhood or the recurring grips of disease.

If this is a bias, it will at least prove to be a productive one. For example, Lawrence may have countered his fears of maternal envelopment by reproducing and enveloping his own universe of characters. We could isolate this process of defensive reliving, label it "identification with the aggressor," and designate an underlying drive of oral aggression as the "unconscious motive" behind the creative enterprise. But the search for the Ultimate Interpretation is futile, and the discovery of the ubiquitous is hardly a discovery anyway. Moreover, while demonstrating any given hypothesis, we would also be encountering a host of other drives, motives, and defenses clamoring for equal representation. To play favorites is to invite reductivism; to be democratically inclusive is to lose focus and risk analysis interminable. Although there is no decisive solution to this dilemma, we can uncover an ecology of the psyche, with its peculiar slopes, marshlands, shallows, and mouths, supporting lifeforms unique to each individual.

For me to stress Lawrence's striving to be whole (hale and healthy), along with his revitalizing the sex relation does favor certain motives over others, but formidable adversary forces need not be overlooked. Moreover, such an approach may delay anyone's rushing to affix categories, labels, or diagnoses, and, more positively, it may awaken the kind of sympathetic consciousness needed to make any analysis fruitful. If motive alone is not meaning but one of its shapers, then those motives which draw on, for example, narcissism and aggression, while seeking wholeness within the self and vital connections with others are appropriate both for creating works of art and for their psychoanalytic probing. More to the immediate point, such motives underpin the author's strange sapience.

The early chapters of this text explore Lawrence's inner world by providing a dialectical method for defining, in psychoanalytic terms, the creative process. The initial probing of motives through fantasy interpretation invokes a traditional psychoanalytic perspective. But a new tack is soon taken: *fantasy* distinguishes the subjective poles of creativity, *reality*, the objective poles. Although these extremes may be conveniently distinct, they are not starkly black and white: fantasy incorporates elements of the real world, and what we designate reality is in part created out of subjective distortions. As these polar concepts are defined, a working hypothesis about creativity is advanced. The chapter on *symbol* synthesizes these dualities; the chapter on *body* plunges deeper into the artist's subjective world. *Play* takes us back into the realm of childhood relationships and the intermediate sphere of experiencing that Winnicott has articulated as transitional. *Origins* follows a cue from Lawrence's word, "re-sourcing," to trace his own creative method through opposing versions of origins along the established subjective / objective axis. *Projection* plunges deeply again into the very problematic subjective processes that are both prior to and adapted by creativity. *Sun* continues their adaptive functions, and the final chapter on *creative selfhood* is a synthesis of the creative process as presently set forth. But in fact all the chapters may be taken as separate routes toward the center of creative energy.

This overview fosters a third potential bias, though not one vigorously argued: that Lawrence, in part owing to creativity's affinity with mastery and working-through, continued to grow and develop both individually and creatively—in brief, that his late works are also his best and most mature, because in some important way, he came through.

Although I am not alone in a certain practice among critics and "deep readers" of texts, some readers may be bothered by a tendency—hardly a method—to regard all of an author's texts, including letters, essays, and fictions, as comprising one complete Text. Of the hazards of this approach as well as the time-honored distinctions between fact and fiction, I am cognizant as well as respectful, if not strictly observant. Exculpating this tendency somewhat is the intensely personal quality of much Lawrencean fiction matched by the intensely imaginative quality of his nonfiction, owing in part to his capacity to thrust himself wholly into whatever piece of writing he was engaged in at the moment. I am also aware that although texts may be eloquent they don't exactly speak. Texts are not persons, and so have no on-going instinctual life to fulfill, no dream world to reveal, and no powers of free association to display. Yet I also know that persons do find meaning in a text over and beyond their own private encroachments, and that such meaning preexists and differs and invites various interpretations. That authors may also enclose in texts their deepest wishes, fears, and fantasies as well as their conscious perceptions also seems so incontrovertible as to be axiomatic. The blend of the subjective and the objective, which makes texts and our readings of them relatively real, returns us to Winnicott's transitional or intermediate sphere of experiencing. Language in and of itself places everyone in realms of culture and art where the objective blends with the subjective into personal visions of truth, tinged with illusion.

Portions of this study have appeared in the *Psychoanalytic Review, American Imago, Mosaic,* and the *Psychoanalytic Study of Society*. A version of the chapter on play was read before the American Psychoanalytic Association in December 1979. Although all of these pieces have been reworked and reshaped to fit this newer framework, I remain grateful to the interest and assistance accorded me along the way from Bryce Boyer, Harry Slochower, Marie Coleman Nelson, Leila Lerner, Sydney Pulver, and Evelyn Hinz. Without the close, patient, and informed readings of this book in early drafts by Dorothy McFarland and Murray Schwartz, I am certain it would never have been completed. To the University of Massachusetts Press I am profoundly indebted for the editorial support of Richard Martin and the admirable copyediting of Carol Schoen. For Mary Washington College's generous gift to the Press in support of this project, I am also especially grateful.

1
Fantasy

. . . the very ancient world was entirely religious and godless. While men still lived in close physical unison, like flocks of birds on the wing, in a close physical oneness, an ancient tribal unison in which the individual was hardly separated out, then the tribe lived breast to breast, as it were, with the cosmos, in naked contact with the cosmos, the whole cosmos was alive and in contact with the flesh of man, there was no room for the intrusion of the god idea. It was not till the individual began to feel separated off, not till he fell into awareness of himself, and hence into apartness . . . that the conception of God arose . . . —D. H. Lawrence, Apocalypse, *pp. 159 – 60*

1 Primary Harmony

Fantasy flows through the mind's channels, now visible, now submerged. At one extreme it may become so private and pervasive as to be delusion; at another extreme so public and refined as to be little more than sentiment. The former may affirm the perfected self in messianic terms, the latter may affirm the perfectability of man in political terms. Fantasy may reveal unfulfilled wishes as well as defenses against them, or it may serve adaptive and integrative functions. It may be centered on the self, concerned with the mother-child dyad, or be focused on triadic, oedipal issues. It may have passive or active aims; be erotic, hostile, ambitious; prepare for, accompany, or replace action. Depending on one's emphasis, a given fantasy in the creative process may be primal, and so a version of origins, as well as transitional, and so a bridge over the gulf of pure subjectivity to preexisting reality.

Fantasy can render familiar places unfamiliar, then turn right around and do the opposite. It can wind our personal clocks and set them ticking at various rates and in so doing dispose us to enter those other time-bound realms of experience peculiar to art. Despite its liabilities, the capacity for fantasy is on balance a powerful human asset inseparable from our greatest achievements, including those of art. But when Freud in his 1908 paper noted "The

Relation of the Poet to Daydreaming" and blazed the first psycho-analytic trail to the study of art, he realized even then, as others have emphasized since, that his ideas would most readily apply to mediocre art, the kind closest to wish fulfilment.[1]

To surmount this impediment various strategies have been instigated, and the present one has at least the advantage of being suited to the works of D. H. Lawrence, having in large part been derived from a study of them. The class of fantasies most amenable to creativity is designated as *primal*, since they are versions of human origins. Chief among them is the kind Freud described in 1909 as Family Romances. Subsequently Rank found mythological parallels in the birth of the hero (1914), while Kris (1952) and Greenacre (1957, 1958) elaborated its significance in the lives of creative artists.[2] This fantasy stems from the inevitable narcissistic wounds of childhood. The child who feels his original parents to be deficient in reciprocating his love finds relief for his painful feelings by believing himself to be adopted and the true son of more illustrious (royal, Olympian) parents who will soon restore his lost self-esteem. Most radically, it is a wish to revise one's origins in order to be born anew, but it is also a protean fantasy that can bear the hallmarks of virtually every phase of psychosexual development. In Greenacre's now classic formulations, the creative individual invests "peripheral objects" or "collective alternates" with great emotional significance and conducts a creative romance with the world. For Wordsworth it was Nature; for Shaw, the Life Force.[3] Simple at its nucleus, its variations are infinite.

Derivatives of some such cosmic romance are clearly felt behind Lawrence's need to reestablish vital connections with the universe. Moreover, the connection between the inspiring mother—who could "breathe [him] like an atmosphere" (CL, 70)—and his intense rapport with nature is a very close one: "We found some lovely big cowslips, whose scent is really a communication direct from the sources of creation like the breath of God breathed into Adam. It breathes into the Adam in me," he once exclaimed (CL, 552). The foundling theme becomes discernible in the fictions when one notices that the female characters have firm and detailed histories, whereas the males' origins are either elided or veiled in mystery. Ursula's genealogy goes back for generations in *The Rainbow*, whereas Birkin in *Women in Love* materializes fully grown. Similarly the galaxy of dark-skinned characters—including the Gypsy, the two Mexican revolutionaries, the Italian peasant in "Sun," and those flamelike bantams, Count Dionys and Mellors—have no family history to speak of. In *Sons and Lovers* Paul Morel is of course embedded in the coal-mining family which was Lawrence's own; but the biblical Paul (like Lawrence's David) evokes associations of a religious heritage, and—as in St. Paul's case—of dual parentage, Roman and Christian. Lawrence's friend Dorothy Brett would capture a similar dualism within Lawrence when she painted his features on Dionysus, the god of the vine, offering a bunch of grapes to Christ, the god of the crucifixion.

"I have always thought myself such an outcast!" confesses an early Lawrence character, both artist and lover. Then he reconsiders: "How can one be outcast in one's own night, and the moon always naked to us, and the sky half her time in rays? . . . the darkness is a sort of mother, and the moon a sister, and the stars children, and sometimes the sea is a brother: and there's a family in one house, you see" (T, 44). Here the sense of abandonment (outcast) is explicitly redressed by the creation of a second family, and as such it is the most naked and naive expression of the fantasy in the early writings.

Subsequently, Lawrence elevated these inclinations to a cosmic theory that owes more to astrology than to astronomy. "Sun and moon are dynamically polarized of our actual tissue, they affect this tissue all the time." The sun is not a "ball of gas," the moon is not a "dead snowy world" when they are imaginatively perceived in terms of emerging body-self consciousness (FU, 184). The sun is masculine and radiant heat, the moon is feminine and magnetic friction. They are the exalted progenitors of creation: the poles of the great life-death circuits, eternally destroying and reviving life. "Midway between the two cosmic infinities lies the third": the earth and individual life. "We, mankind, are all one family." We are polarized to the earth's center, but upon our death the "earth flings us out as wings to the sun and moon. . . . The inanimate universe is built upon the arch which spans the duality of living beings." In this process of eternal renewal "lies the great magic of sex" (FU, 188, 189, 214). In the sex act male and female are polarized and purified into their cosmic counterparts, and in every individual born of this union "burns the positive quick of all things." No orphan in this universe, man is the love-child of the cosmic parents, part of an eternal life-circuit of influences that owes more to the treasure-trove of occult fantasy than to the exactitude of science.

The subjective medium for these recondite macro / microcosmic correspondences is the Family Romance. At the very matrix of Lawrence's creative mind, it removed origins from their biological finality and, in freeing them up for imaginative revisions, made the impossible possible—namely rebirth. This important wish spurred Lawrence's recurrent utopian aspirations. These were in turn fed by his reading of modern anthropological reconstructions of the ancient world—which he narrowed down to a semi-fanciful "Egypt"—and by his own forays into the lost world of the Etruscans as well as into America's aboriginal past. Together those exotic realms confirmed for Lawrence the viability of a natural culture, one of organic wholeness. If the founding of a utopia represented a literal enactment of the wish, he also simultaneously entertained purely symbolic and individualistic varieties of rebirth as self-renewal.

On at least one occasion, he gave vent to this fantasy in nearly pure form. Near the end of his life, after the dreams for a specific utopian commune had been pretty much laid to rest and after he at least had his imagined ideals validated and fulfilled at a distance in the marvelous Etruscan art forms, he returns to the "poor, grimy, mean" Midlands of his origins. On a walk among the quarries, he comes upon a "little crystalline cavity in the rock, all crystal, a little pocket or womb of quartz, among the common stone." Through the crystal runs a "broad vein of purplish crystal" called Blue John. In this narrow and perhaps royal cavity he curls up "like an animal in a hold" and has a sort of dream-vision, which amounts to being born into another world. He is awakened by "strange men" with "formal, peaceful faces and trimmed beards, like old Egyptians." His heart "began to lift with strange, exultant strength," although throughout the episode he retains a dual consciousness—an outsider looking in on his own dream, as it were. He gazes down on his transformed town,

all yellow in the later afternoon light, with yellow, curved walls rising massive from the yellow-leaved orchards, and above, buildings swerving in a long, oval curve, and round, faintly conical towers rearing up. It has something at once soft and majestical about it, with its soft yet powerful curves, and no sharp angles or edges, the whole substance seeming soft and golden like the golden flesh of the city.

This shining organism with its rich substances he recognizes as the "place where I was born." It is (and is not) the "ugly colliery townlet of dirty red brick," for in superimposing the more majestic world of ancient Egypt onto his own common origins, he recaptures a semblance of primary harmony in which the early maternal organism is spread out before him as environment.

Led into this prelapsarian state, he encounters men "quite naked, and some young women, laughing together as they went . . . the rosy-tanned bodies were quite naked, save for a little girdle of white and green and purple cord fringe that hung around their hips and swung as they walked":

And they were comely as berries on a bush. That was what they reminded me of: rose-berries on a bush. That was the quality of all the people: an inner stillness and ease, like plants that come to flower and fruit. The individual was like a whole fruit, body and mind and spirit, without *split*. [Italics added]

As the "red sun was almost touching the tips of the tree-covered hills," music starts, and the square comes to life. "The men were stamping softly, like bulls, the women were softly swaying, and softly clapping their hands, without a strange noise, like leaves."

They were dancing the sun down, and dancing as birds wheel and dance, and fishes in the shoals, controlled by some strange unanimous instinct. It was at once terrifying and magnificent, I wanted to die, so as not to see it, and I wanted to rush down, to be one of them. To be a drop in that wave of life. ["Autobiographical Fragment," P, 817–36]

Oceanic, perhaps; symbiotic, no. Both ecstatic and articulate, this "fantasy of primary harmony," to use a phrase from Michael Balint, reproduces a sense of ideal equilibrium with the environment prior to the catastrophic split Balint refers to as the "basic fault." His geological figure is well suited to Lawrence's blended concept of psychic geography, hinted at in the prose passage from *The Trespasser* where the merging aim is more transparent (see Introduction, above).[4]

These evocations of primary harmony and subsequent utopian quests to reestablish its equivalent based on idealized cultures of prehistory, suggest something both lost and yet attainable. It is an ideal capable of revival through the persistent sense of primary love, putting the artist in touch with a world of felt wholeness prior to any disruptive trauma or break, to which the urgent quests and the dual consciousness nonetheless later testify. In fact so much of Lawrence's inner and external life is exposed in this one dream fragment that it could serve as a central port from which to launch several journeys: the compulsive return to the grave which is also the maternal womb; the bodying forth of a new beginning through the powers of the imagination; the transformation of memories from America and the Etruscan tombs; the expanded maternal presence as a holding or facilitating environment; the eidetic or heightened imagery of the Family Romance as a creative love affair with the world, permitting the regression to the prehistoric— always "Egyptian"—life embedded in nature; the eventual split; the cosmic reunion of heaven and earth; and the recapturing dance of sexuality. Perhaps Lawrence's most distinctive manner of representing this fantasy appears in his late painting of "Adam Throwing Back the Apple" of mental consciousness and thereby regaining paradise; but while Eve is there cheering him on, an astonished Jehovah is *not* driven off. The split between cerebral and visceral, between self and world, remains: the creation of art requires dual consciousness—a sapience that many might deem strange.

2   The Basic Fault

...another world, in which I can live apart from this foul world...—CL, 27 *September 1916*

When the Family Romance expands into a creative romance with the world, the fantasy appears to be a continuation of the mother's facilitating or holding environment. Lawrence's avowed aim in writing is nothing less than to recapture "the experience of the living heavens, with a living yet not human sun, and brilliant living stars in *live* space" which is as real and living as our bodies (P, 298). As the artist's medium or bridge for building correspondences between inner and outer reality, the Family Romance serves imagination, but more fundamentally it earns its keep by healing and mending psychic injuries. This assumes a prior disturbance which both Lawrence and Balint speak of in similar terms. For Lawrence the solar-plexus attraction of infant to mother aims "to re-establish the old oneness" which the "wound" of birth sev-

ered, like the above "split" of which the dreamer alone is aware.
For Balint, primary harmony was destroyed by what he early on
described as a "deep, painful, narcissistic wound," and later
changed to the "sense of a *fault* of our own doing, others' doing, or
cruel fate's." Subsequent consideration of Lawrence's self-styled
psychology—his pollyanalytic system of separate and opposed
layers of consciousness—will reveal a profound rift or fault running across the center of the self. But more immediately, we need
only mark his persistent vocabulary of "breach," "gap," and "split"
to describe his own conflicts, which are internal, whether they are
located within the self or between the self and others (italics
added below):

Now she was gone, and forever behind him was the *gap* in life, the tear in
the veil, through which his life seemed to drift slowly, as if he were drawn
towards death. There was something between him and them. He could
not get in touch. [SL, 407, 412]

. . . I don't feel there is any very cordial or fundamental contact between
me and society, or me and other people. There is a *breach*. And my contact
is with something that is non-human, non-vocal. [P2, 594—95]

His scenario of *Sons and Lovers* emphasizes a similar condition:
"As soon as the young men come into contact with women, there's
a *split*. William gives his sex to a fribble, and his mother holds his
soul. But the *split* kills him . . ." (CL, 160). "The trouble is, you see,
I'm not one man, but two," he told Jessie Chambers in the aftermath of his mother's death. "I am two men inside one skin." When
his sense of inner fission, fault, or splitting is rendered in a verbal
form, the key word is *break*, for the main business of his prose,
after *Sons and Lovers* and therefore after the catastrophic death of
the mother, is to depict this process in fictional displacements.
(The emotional import of *breaking* best reveals itself through the
smashed-doll episode, fully explored in the chapter on play, below, where that object of destructive play is revealed as the substrate for many characters.)

Balint characterizes the basic fault as taking place within a two-
person relationship, on a level prior to the oedipal, one which is
preverbal, all but inaccessible verbally, and is experienced by his
patients not as a conflict, complex, or situation, but as a *fault* with
its geological inferences intended, as "something wrong in the
mind, a kind of deficiency which must be put right." Lawrence's

psychological-minded readers have either isolated oral aggressive drives or dilated his already highly visible oedipal conflicts. This is perhaps unavoidable, in that without those drives and conflicts Lawrence would not be himself, but the result is to maintain things either on a simplistic instinctual base or on more manageable triadic levels which overshadow the less verbally available primitive world of emergent object relations. And these, Balint maintains, are not simply oral (with its paraphernalia of greed, sadism, dependency), but are also experienced within the previously outlined framework of primary harmony and basic fault. Thus the triadic, oedipal configuration which is already lucid in Lawrence's work may subtly support more primitive and more elusive levels.[5] For the basic fault, or something like it, is always there in the "wounds to the soul, to the deep emotional self," as expressed in "Healing," a late poem, and as uttered in his utopian cry for a "holy centre: whole, heal, hale" (CL, 1031).

3   The Utopian Projects

. . . an outcome of the mourning process following the loss of a significant object may be the reinvestment in an ideal.—George H. Pollock, "Mourning, Immortality, and Utopia"[6]

The Family Romance as a fantasy of primary harmony and as a means of bridging a rift between self and world can be most readily apprised in a series of utopian aspirations that Lawrence first referred to as *Rananim*. To place these quests in their proper sequence, however, we should specify the historical and personal ground from which such urges sprang. For in Lawrence's struggle to realize the fantasy directly, the artist in him is nearly eclipsed, and the fantasy itself veers treacherously near delusion.

There is ample evidence that Lawrence suffered a series of profoundly disruptive traumas, the most dramatic of which was the death of his mother in 1910. He was twenty-four years old and, as he wrote Garnett (11 March 1913), by no means fully "weaned" from the symbiotic bond. Another trauma was the catastrophic dissolution of his country during the First World War, a terror that nearly foreclosed his life as a writer at the very moment of its realization (see Paul Delaney's *D. H. Lawrence's Nightmare*). The far from stable personality structures which suffered these upheavals were formed in early childhood when Lawrence, contending with severe bronchial illness, was nursed by an overly involved and overly extended mother, herself torn among the demands of older children, another pregnancy, and a marriage her son would describe as one "carnal, bloody fight." This period of early childhood constitutes the first phase of traumas which conditioned and to some extent determined the course and outcome of the later two.

From those early events one infers that the emerging self was in a state of continual jeopardy, threatened from within by illness and from without by unstable adults. Death was never distant, and each recovery must have been akin to a reawakening to new life. With his own world experienced as an erratic cycle of birth, death, and self-regeneration, it is not surprising that the Phoenix became his archetype for the self. But this mythical figure, once it had been adapted and rendered by the imagination, is fantasy already bound: a realized symbol of wholeness and self-renewal. How the Phoenix and other composite symbols evolved and played variations on themes of birth and parentage is examined in the chapter on symbol; here we may simply liken the quest for Rananim to the Phoenix's quest for the tree in which to build its fiery nest of rebirth.

It would appear that each of the three turbulent periods in which Lawrence's self was placed in jeopardy sprang from a painful sense of losing, in turn, the very early environment-mother, the somewhat later personal-mother, and the more expanded cultural-mother. That is: (1) the threatened absence of the mother as a life-support system during the hatching-out of childhood; (2) the loss of the personal, sustaining relationship with the mother at her death; and (3) the collapse during the war years of Britannia, literary patroness and extension of the mother's value system.

If we can recognize certain parallel features among these three, then each in turn may illuminate the others. To get at the subjectively constant, or fantasy dimension, of these periods, we could infer that Lawrence told time, read history, and interpreted natural change not by such conventional means as the clock, the Idea of Progress, or the Theory of Evolution, but according to an internal Phoenix model reinforced by the external world of nature and sanctioned by the Family Romance which licensed a second birth within the cycle of humankind. Life for Lawrence—be it individual, national, or racial—is constantly flowing toward either decay and death or rebirth and renewal.[7]

Since the reader is likely to be most familiar with the last of these three periods, and since it is the one most fully documented, we will now turn to it. The months following England's decline into war find Lawrence a newly married man at work on both creative and theoretical projects to culminate in *The Rainbow*, "The Study of Thomas Hardy," and *The Crown* essays. He is still in his exuberant, "Look! We Have Come Through!" period. But he will look back on the first five months of the war as having been his "time in the sepulchre," as "if one wrote from a grave or a womb." And he will view the encroachings of war—e.g., a Zeppelin "like a bright golden finger" in the night—as signs of the Apocalypse. "It seemed as if the cosmic order were gone." And while his own soul is "fizzling savagely," the world around him has "burst, burst at last," and is dissolving into dust (CL, 314, 330, 366, 363).

As terrible as the actuality of the war was, even from Lawrence's safe distance, his responses to it are clearly overdetermined. For out of this same period he was also to conceive a new vision which drew on dreams and memory traces that appear to have emanated from those darker, timeless regions of his earliest mental formations. He claims a "new birth of life" and aspires to "give a new Humanity its birth" (CL, 314, 325). And although insisting he is "resurrected," he finds that "all the time I am struggling in the dark—very deep in the dark—and cut off from everybody and everything" (CL, 303, 330). A day or two of light and then the plunge again into "what utter darkness of chaos." He has beetle dreams, and fears the "terrible things that are real, in the darkness, and of the entire unreality of these things I see." Well into the spring of 1915, he is "fighting the powers of darkness." Less abstractly, he thinks, "It would do me so much good if I could kill a few people." Soon the existing order of life is reduced to a shell, a frame that must be smashed. Toward this end the war serves as a catalyst, though in the short run the war has unleashed the mob, the "pack," the "hydra" of the populace (CL, 331, 347).

His hatred of the masses—those "vermin who teem by the billions," "this horror of little swarming selves"—returns as a phobic aversion toward copulation (AR, 92; CL, 332–33). He complains of dreaming in the night of a "beetle that bites like a scorpion." He fears he will go mad, "because there is nowhere to go, no 'new world.'" He sees soldiers as "merging in a sticky male mass," or like obscene insects, "one mounted on another" (CL, 337, 456). Sexual aversions are blatant. Europe and England are a massive creeping "insect-teeming" hell, and their allies are "horrible obscene" rats. Worst of all is the alienation and growing feeling of being small and impotent, unable to affect the course of events, finally of being "cursed out." "I feel I cannot *touch* humanity, even in thought, it is abhorrent to me" (CL, 338, 448, 449). Correspondingly, Paul Morel after his mother's death "could not get into touch" (SL, 412).

To introduce a term to be used later, on a deeply unconscious level for Lawrence the war seems to have reawakened Primal Scene terrors over parental sexual activity and to have generated his defensive strategies of identifying with the threatened object (Britannia, mother) by conceiving new life within himself. Both the doctrine of blood-consciousness and the need for an allegiance of *blutbrüdershaft* come to the fore around the same time as the utopian projects. We can infer that Lawrence's ability to discover continually new objects of deep emotional attachment, yet always with some of their original flavor, bespeaks his ability to mourn and loosen former attachments as well as his difficulty in completing this process. But the magnitude of the crisis elicits a creative response that will not be circumscribed by art. In January 1915, he mentions a "pet scheme":

I want to gather together about twenty souls and sail away from this world of war and squalor and found a little colony where there shall be no money but a sort of communism as far as necessaries of life go, and some real decency. It is to be a colony built up on the real decency which is in each member of the community. A community which is established upon the assumption of goodness in the members, instead of the assumption of badness. [CL, 307]

Besides himself and his wife, Frieda, the members are to include John Murry and Katherine Mansfield, William Hopkin, Koteliansky, possibly E. M. Forster, Bertrand Russell, and his sometime mistress Lady Ottoline Morrell, a group that will form the nucleus of the community to "start a new life amongst us—a life in which the only riches is integrity of character" (CL, 311). "After the War, the soul of the people will be so maimed and so injured that it is horrible to think of." The "external good part" in a few must be preserved. It will be a "communism based, not on poverty but on riches, not on humility but on pride, not on sacrifice but upon complete fulfillment in the flesh of all strong desire, not in Heaven but on earth." The members will be reborn as "Sons of God," "aristocrats," or "Princes, as the angels are" (CL, 312); yet "they must be centered around a core of reality": i.e., their women (which "left the fate of Forster hanging" [MW, 259]).

This Utopia is to be *Rananim*, a word taken from a chant by Lawrence's Russian-Jewish friend, Koteliansky, apparently the chief collaborator in the project. The word derives from Hebrew and may mean either "rejoice," or "green, fresh, flourishing" (QR, xxxiv)—both of which would serve. The motto for the Order of Knights of Rananim is *Fier* ("fierce pride"); the badge is "an eagle, or phoenix argent, rising from a nest of scarlet, on a black background" (QR, 22; CL, 392–93). At first their refuge is to be a remote island, but it soon appears that the Russell faction would prefer that England be the island and thus stay put. Strife came early and inevitably. Lawrence rebounds with a revision which depicts the "new community in the midst of this old one, as a seed falls among the roots of the parent,"—or as the young Phoenix rises from its parent's ashes (CL, 314). At other times Rananim takes on the aspects of a rescue fantasy to save Britannia via her best young aristocrats.

As the scheme grows more grandiose Lawrence's ego appears to diminish and become more childlike. "Don't think *I* am important," he writes Lady Ottoline, after having just urged the destruction of the "old Moloch of greediness and Love of property and love of power." "But this thing which is of all of us is so important and splendid that the skies shiver with delight." Bumbling into politics, he writes Russell that any "vision of a better life must include a revolution of society." Democracy is finished, however. "There must be a body of chosen patricians," so he believes for awhile. The whole must culminate in an "absolute *Dictator*, and an equivalent *Dictatrix*" (those ideally adoptive parents of the Family Romance). Russell is to work out the details. But "a new constructive idea of a new state is needed immediately," Lawrence insists (CL, 324–26, 353, 354). Get anybody to help, even Shaw. Concurrently in his wildly rambling study of Hardy, he is groping toward a rebalancing of the "male and female principles" that involves a radically redefined holy Trinity with a phallic Paraclete (P, 490).

Due to misunderstandings over his idealistic intentions, his falling out with Russell, and the pressure of events ranging from the suppression of *The Rainbow* to the military's persecution of the Lawrences, the dream of Rananim languished. Yet Lawrence held stubbornly to it and hoped to found a colony in California, the Andes, or Florida. And even when he was on the ranch at Taos several years later the thought of community was revived. It was continually on his mind during the winter of 1922 – 23, which he and Frieda spent at Del Monte ranch with two Danish painters. This was a comparatively happy time for all of them, and Lawrence's hopes for starting a new life turned to Mexico. "When we have ourselves firmly established, then we can add one or two more of our friends at a time and let the thing grow slowly into full being, and the new life will grow and spread until it embraces the whole world" (PT, 251). The illusory nature of these ideals was captured by Frieda when she spoke of them as the Trinity: Lawrence, the Almighty Father; the Danes, the Son; and she, the Holy Ghost.

Clearly Frieda knew what time it was, and her sanity must have pruned the dangerously delusional shoots from the stalk of this powerful, enduring fantasy. For it was not until 1925 that Lawrence wrote, following Dorothy Brett's banishment from Oaxaca, "A life in common is an illusion, when the instinct is always to divide, to separate individuals and set them one against the other" (CL, 837). Collapsing along with Rananim was Lawrence's "militant ideal" of the hero: "The leader-cum-follower relationship is a bore" (CL, 1045). Paradoxically his friends were right from the beginning. The "new community grows in the midst of this old one": on English soil the seed falls. But the kernel of Lawrence's obdurate desire to establish an actual Rananim and to become a bona-fide leader of men would have to die many deaths before it could be laid to rest and be reborn in symbolic form. The organicism he discovered among the Taos Indians and Etruscans provided new clues, and the dream in the "Autobiographical Fragment" reveals both the wish's tenacity and the imagination's transforming power. But the new relationship between men and women which he had sought in Rananim had to await further humanization of its core fantasy before being realized as art. Then perhaps the new bond of sensual tenderness between the sexes could be represented. But even after Connie and Mellors have enjoyed their season of love, the utopian fantasy is revived once more in Mellors's final meditative letter. "If men wore red trousers," he muses, and "if they could dance and hop and skip and sin and swagger, they could do with very little cash."

And amuse the women themselves, and be amused by the women. They ought to learn to be naked and handsome, and to sing in a mass and dance the old group dances, and carve the stools they sit on, and embroider their own emblems. [LCL, 362]

The utopian project makes it clear that love between man and woman, no matter how good, is not good enough: a supportive environment, an organic community, are also needed. Jeffrey Meyers has likened Mellors's "homely plan" to the revolutionary "Men of Quetzalcoatl" who "weave clothing, rub themselves with red powder, drum and dance, and create a kind of William Morris ashram on the lake. . . ."[8] At its best it is a serious and altruistic wish, but a wish all the same, a daydream, because even while composing his pastoral novel and in the face of fatally deteriorating health, he harbored further Rananim hopes and fantasied a future journey: "I think, one day, I shall take a place in the country, somewhere, perhaps one or two other men might like to settle in the neighborhood, and we might possibly slowly evolve a new rhythm of life: learn to make the creative pauses, and learn to dance and sing together." So he diffidently wrote Rolf Gardiner, an English disciple, in 1926. But instead of going forth, as he hoped, "to meet one another, upon the third ground, the holy ground," he embarks on the third rewrite of his novel. And when he writes his friend again, it is in the second person: "You ought to have a few, very few . . . who would add together their little flames of consciousness to make a permanent core . . . a holy centre. . . ." But scarcely two months before his death, Lawrence imagined setting up a sort of Platonic academy at his New Mexico ranch: "An old school, like the Greek philosophers, talks in a garden—that is, under the pine trees. . . . Who knows!" (CL, 1230).

So much for the vicissitudes of the Rananim fantasy. Taken in isolation, the word spells failure: Lawrence did not implement his utopia. Taken in a larger context, the projects may be merely the unassimilated chaff left unground by his creative mills: what he could not found in the phenomenal world he created in his imagination—what he himself could not realize could be realized through the Phoenix process of his art. Rebirth for him as well as for those who encounter his work will have to be indirect—emotional if not physical, figurative if not literal.

4   The Other Side of Utopia

What more should be gleaned from this fantasy? Observing Lawrence from a purely behavioral perspective, one notes an apparent compromise. Lawrence was directly acting out his fantasy by traveling to Australia, Ceylon, Taos, and Oaxaca; simultaneously he was indirectly acting it out by delivering himself of creative visions, like *St. Mawr* and *The Plumed Serpent*, which both embodied and criticized the fantasy. Observed more closely from the perspective of psychic economy, one could conclude that the indirect release of the fantasy through the creative process served to modify and lessen the frustration over the failure of his messianic schemes.

It is likely that without his creative resources, Lawrence would have suffered a serious breakdown. Had he sought out modern psychiatric help during his nightmare period, his presenting symptoms might show up as dissociative reactions, free-floating anxiety, and entrenched phobias. Had he scorned such clinical categories and said, "I'll try analysis instead," a safe guess would be that had he peeled away his utopian fantasies, he would eventually have confronted a core of rage.

How this rage infiltrates his work during the middle period has been traced by several astute Lawrenceans who have discovered a spectrum of material clustering around the central image of the "devouring mother," a term Lawrence applied to Frieda in a 1918 letter (CL, 565). This aspect of the mother is variously cited: as the "mother-ogress, who destroys her son or daughter" (Hiller); as a "maternal cannibal" conveyed by "psychologically murderous parasitism" in "Paul's [Morel] fantasy life," as it is displaced from his mother onto Miriam and Clara (Kleinbard); via the Lawrencean "fox, the devourer of chickens [which] symbolizes the 'devouring' mother" (Bergler); through the dominating males in the leadership novels, who in overreacting to the threat of being destroyed by the devouring mother turn into devouring mothers themselves (Ruderman); and finally by the prevalence of vampire imagery in depicting the male/female relationships in *The Rainbow* and *Women in Love* (Twitchel).[9]

Other critics have drawn attention to the mythic dimensions of Lawrencean females—who personify Circe, Persephone, Magna Mater, Hecate, and Astarte—to encompass the procreative and destructive, the child-bearing and child-sacrificing aspects of woman.[10] The classical mythic sources—along with those from fairy tales, animal fables, and gothic fiction—provide a preexisting medium to which Lawrence's fantasies of destructive motherhood attach themselves and thereby allow him to initiate the complex reshaping processes of art. But the fact that the son's devouring wishes and merger fantasies are instinctually rooted is complicated by similar unresolved conflicts in the mother, whose echoing desires may dangerously legitimize or, one might say, *authorize* the very drives she should be helping him master.

Under the intensified intimacies of Lawrence's childhood, one would expect an intricate pattern of crisscrossing identifications. In *Sons and Lovers*, Mrs. Morel's tendency to seek from, as well as supply emotional nourishment to, her children, especially Paul, is expressed as the "two knitted together in perfect intimacy," and her "life now rooted itself" in his. Following her death, we read that for Paul "the realest thing was the thick darkness at night," and that he would talk to "barmaids, to almost any woman, but there was that dark, strained look in his eyes, as if he were hunting something" (SL, 410). Here are the first signs of that vampirism which will condition the relationships in the two novels to come. It is in the male / son axis rather than the female / mother that they first appear—although Mrs. Morel had warned Paul about Miriam's life-sucking propensities (SL, 160). In his careful reading of *The Rainbow* and *Women in Love*, Twitchel traces the evolution of the "female as vampire" fantasy from "Gertrude Morel, to Miriam Leivers, then to Anna, Ursula, Hermoine, and finally to Gudrun." In subsequent works he concludes that this figure disappears, and a healthier image of woman eventually appears, after a middle period of predatory maleness.[11] Such a reading corroborates the view that these images were projections which could in time be modified and assimilated. "Don't you think I get people in my grip?" Lawrence could ask his publisher in 1913 (CL, 186). But his subsequent prose loosened that grip, as his intensely subjective way of telling time blends with Frieda's realistic time sense and he ripens into the accurately self-styled insouciance of his final period. The sum of these readings points to Lawrence's availing himself of the creative process to effect a working-through of conflicts, a means as he himself knew, whereby "one sheds one's sickness in books—repeats and presents again one's emotions, to be master of them" (CL, 234).

Accordingly, in *The Rainbow* and *Women in Love*, Twitchel has astutely noticed that "Lawrence repeats again and again" a scene in which two young people meet and enter into what is described as a "battle for life itself." Vampire imagery intensifies the drama, and in most instances the males are the weaker parties: "praying mantises waiting to be devoured by the female after she has used them." The lamia figures may be blatant in these works because the instinctual drives are still displaced and supported by a repertory of culturally sanctioned fantasy. Yet, as the content of this insistent fantasy fades in the male-leadership novels, the conflict gradually becomes internalized as the men become cruel, predatory, and devouring in their own right. The line culminates in Mexico with Don Cipriano's bleeding knife, but it had begun with early drafts of Birkin (in the Prologue to *Women in Love*) running from "death to death" with the "eyes of a wolf" (P2, 93).

In marriages where the husband is unable to hold his own, Lawrence wrote:

The unhappy woman beats about for her insatiable satisfaction, seeking whom she may devour. And usually, she turns to her child. Here she provokes what she wants. Here, in her own son who belongs to her, she seems to find the last perfect responses for which she is craving. [FU, 157]

Taken as an analogue to his own family or to the plot of *Sons and Lovers*, this passage also shows how the devouring, oral-stage mother becomes the incestuous object for her child. Before he would develop his alternative theory of psychosexual development, Lawrence in 1918 acknowledged, "It seems to me there is much truth" in "this mother-incest idea"

that at certain periods the man has a desire to return into the woman, make her his goal and end. In this way he casts himself as it were into her womb, and she, the Magna Mater, receives him with gratification. This is a kind of incest. [CL, 565]

But even here Lawrence is thinking in a context of adult sexual relations, and when he sets forth his own pollyanalytic system he asserts that "there is no real sexual motive in a child," for the "great sexual centres are not even awake" (FU, 145). The real danger is supposedly the bond of spiritual, sympathetic love into which parents draw their children, a bond that stimulates the *thought* of incest and leads to that morbid form of mental consciousness Lawrence loved to harangue as "sex in the head."

But the point remains that he has connected the sexually frustrated wife with the devouring mother. In the child's mind, this threat is metamorphosed into the classic, downward displacement of the devouring mouth, via lamia's fangs, to form the dangerous and prohibitive *vagina dentata*.[12] This image is adaptive for the child insofar as it reinforces the incest taboo with threats of castration; it is not adaptive if the vaginal teeth are assigned to all future love-objects. Yet this is precisely the nature of the threat to "Aaron's rod" in the novel of that title, when he portrays his wife as using her harpy's beak against him. It is, so to speak, a bad oedipal marriage, as was the first marriage of the gamekeeper Mellors, who "had a big wound from old contacts," especially from his first wife who "would tear at me down there, as if it was a beak tearing me" (LCL, 102, 242). But while Connie is sexually frustrated, her appetites are not devouring, her mouth is not fanged, her vagina is not a beak, and so she can offer the prospect of mutuality and the peaceful stillness that succeeds vaginal orgasm rather than the excited friction of clitoral sex that had formerly stirred castration fears. In Lawrence's late works, Twitchel notes that the "process of energy transfer" and the issues of separation/merging are still felt. But the earlier, malignant forms of oral contamination have been substantially modified through assimilation and partial working through of conflicts.

The mother-ogress, the Persephone-Circe figures, and the lamia-harpy comprise fantasy material that may be subsumed into the obverse side of the Family Romance. Here the fantasy of divine origins undergoes a reversal: the life-giving goddess is replaced by a child-stealing witch in order to enact a demonic version of origins discernible in the pale, sickly son of the vampire-mother, Lamia. A black Family Romance, it remains dyadic with no paternal sexual role assigned; but hints of something self-damaging from a wounding relationship moderate the idealizations that are upheld in the original white version. Clearly, "the old, ghastly woman-spirit" that Lawrence evokes in *Sea and Sardinia* haunted his fantasy life long after his mother was safely in the grave. And despite his counterassaults he also knew, as Ruderman states, that only little boys believe mothers can be vanquished. The only mastery lay in self-understanding, a degree of which Lawrence achieved through creative work and his struggling with his turbulent personal relationships.

What does all this imply about our hypothetical analysis? Supposedly, while Lawrence would be struggling with rage fantasies, the analyst would find himself dealing with a devouring-mother transference-reaction. Crisscrossing this matrix would be paranoia, projected homosexual wishes, fears of maternal envelopment, and intense ambivalence preventing a fusion of libidinal and aggressive drives. If, for example, Lawrence should recall on the couch what he blurted at John Middleton Murry in 1915, "I hate your love, I hate it. You're an obscene bug sucking my life away," how might such affects be interpreted?[13] Listening with the analyst's third ear, one might sense the following forbidden wish: I want to suck on your body (penis). This homosexual wish of *I love you* is converted into its opposite of *I hate you* and projected as *you want to suck me*; then the homosexual transaction is further denied by making it obscene, inhuman, and so forth. But even more frightening than the homosexual urge—which Lawrence around this time was writing about through his self-character Rupert Birkin in the Cancelled Prologue to *Women in Love*—was the fear of the destructive force in the aggressive orality veiled in the allegation "suck my life away." The underlying fear of such primitive urges is world-destruction, and since much of the civilized world was at that time engaged in destroying itself, it is not surprising that Lawrence ruled out both patriotism and pacifism, for he perceived the war apocalyptically, as Armageddon, and cast himself in the savior-redeemer role as the founder of a nobler kingdom. In this utopian variation on the Family Romance, a final stage of reaction-formation would permit him to idealize and provisionally include John Middleton Murry along with selected others he exempted from a nearly total misanthropy.

In an attempt to escape their own destructive rage, it is no secret that revolutionaries, radicals, and idealists often heap scorn both on the common man and on the ordinary decencies and compromises of societal existence: note the plays of Molière and Ibsen, the lives of Robespierre and Trotsky, the general course of human history. Molière's thwarted idealist, insisting in vain that his fellowmen should always "be sincere, and never part / With any word that isn't from the heart," soon despairs not of his principles, which even he cannot apply when the moment of truth arrives, but of others: "Ah, it's too much; mankind has grown so base, / I mean to break with the whole human race." To preserve his own purity of purpose, he is "moved to flee and find / Some desert land unfouled by humankind." Similarly, during the war years Lawrence remarked that "it is only possible to live out of this world— make a sort of Garden of Eden of blameless but unfulfilled souls, in some sufficiently remote spot—the Marquesas Islands, Nuku-heva. Let us do that. I am sick to death of the world of man—had enough."[14] Liberty, Equality, and Fraternity are a "deadly hydra" (CL, 354). And before long he had either fallen out with or turned against each one of those blameless unfulfilled souls—including the Murrys, E. M. Forster, Bertrand Russell, Lady Ottoline, Cynthia Asquith, Koteliansky. Only Frieda remained when he at last set sail on his quests. Quoting Lawrence's words, "There are very many people, like insects, who await extermination," Paul Delaney extenuates such "genocidal rhetoric" by reminding readers that it came from a sick and desperate man, harrassed and mistreated by his fellow Englishmen, painfully uprooted and at the same time prevented from escaping the country. Nonetheless, Delaney concludes that "the idea of mass extermination became for him a key fantasy after 1915."[15] And so may it be included on the obverse side of the artist's creative romance with the world. Humanity has become the vampire beast that bars the gate to Eden: one must either "choke it before its obscene fangs drain one's vitality, or flee to a new world." If such a world cannot be found, then let it be created.

When desperate utopian fantasy dictates the creative process, the result may be a novel like *The Plumed Serpent* (1926). A certain kind of Family Romance fulfillment resounds through the grandiose projects and utterances of the right-wing revolutionary Don Ramon. Having called upon all Mexican people to embrace an ancient form of nature worship, he declares, "Then I, Cipriano, I First Man of Quetzalcoatl, with you First Man of Huitzilopochtli, and perhaps your wife, First Woman of Itzypapalotl, could we not meet, with pure souls, the other great aristocrats of the world?" (PS, 273).

This couple embody the earlier blueprint of a Rananim governed by a supreme dictator and dictatrix. (At first Lawrence's utopia was to be socialist; then a reversion against the masses summoned the need for authority which began as aristocratic but soon darkened and became more cruel until it resembled fascism.) Delavenay believed that Lady Ottoline was to be the dictatrix and Lawrence himself to be the dictator, though Lady Cynthia Asquith may also have been a candidate for the one and Bertrand Russell for the other (MW, 267). In any case, the Family Romance is present in the fluctuating needs to be under-idealized and ennobled parent-rulers, as either a privileged member of this new society or its quasi-divine founder.

Although Lawrence's letters suggest that the Rananim project floundered because others let him down, his novel more bravely explores internal incongruities. The utopian ideal is seen to breed another agenda which turns cruel and misanthropic. Under the new revolutionary order, the people's blood is soon running in the streets: the army has taken command and is making bloody converts to the new state religion, and Ramon's nasty little cohort is letting his knife drink deeply from the hearts of helpless captives. An upsurge of the devouring drives surging in the predatory male blackens the Family Romance, and the utopian dream is savaged before it can be realized. But while the novel fails to explore all the incongruities of its premises, it is honest in imparting through Kate Leslie's mediating consciousness an ultimate sense of malaise and irresolution.

5   Beyond Misanthropy

The violent split between love and hate which characterizes Lawrence's dualistic vision is fused somewhat in the celebration of tenderness and sensuality in *Lady Chatterley's Lover* (1928). Here the governing fantasy is the rescue variation on the Family Romance theme, and as the primal fantasies and their utopian offshoots have been relatively more concerned with the self and the mother-child dyad, the shift here is to the triadic. Connie is the noblewoman in the mansion on the hill, who is to be "rescued into love" by the obscure outsider, a gamekeeper of lowly lineage and no noticeable parentage.[16] The theme of adoption is portrayed by the rebirth of the lovers' organic selves, a transformation downward into Lady Jane and John Thomas. The sphere is that of private passion rather than political power. The obsession with blood brotherhood has been abandoned: Mellors is a lonely modest man whose prejudices resemble Lawrence's, and whose inflections resembled Lawrence's father. Yet the form is pastoral, with Edenic overtones evoking mankind's original Family Romance in the Garden; and the utopian impulses in their return to native soil are modified due either to the cathartic release from the earlier works or to a working-through of the underlying conflicts. After only two of his eighteen years with Frieda, Lawrence could write, "It is not so easy for one to be married. In marriage one must become something else. And I am changing, one way or the other." Some men, he wrote, are permanently split between flesh and spirit: they should have two wives. But he felt himself "becoming more and more unified" (CL, 264, 427 – 28).

As *Sons and Lovers* has consistently invited oedipal interpretations by reason of the explicit son-lover fusion in its title, so has *Lady Chatterley's Lover* invited interpretation as the final rendition of oedipal conflicts. This is symbolized both by the fusion of son and father in the inside-out anagram of "Mellors" from "Morel," and more subtly and decisively by Mellors's shameless *mining* of Connie's sex when he "smelt out the heaviest ore of the body into purity," and in so doing made a "different woman of her" (LCL, 297). In *Sons and Lovers* the struggle with incest involves the splitting of love-objects into virginal/sexual components, as Paul tries to love first spiritual Miriam, then earthy Clara, and "reaches the same impasse."[17] In the latter work Connie alone reunites the tender/sensual currents of love into a single whole. Clifford, the oedipal rival, is clearly defeated according to classic design, but neither Oedipus myth nor Oedipus complex is as simple as they are often made out to be. And even in *Sons and Lovers* the parental crime is not parricide but matricide, as Paul and Annie dose their mother's drink with morphia—the crime of Electra and Orestes rather than of Oedipus.

Not yet having bitten into the apple of Freudian consciousness—which Frieda would in time offer him—Lawrence anticipates it quite well when he echoes his mother's, "He hates his father. . . . It happened before he was born. . . . One night he put me out of the house" (PE, 138), with his own, "I was born hating" him (CL, 69). Clearly the two hatreds have gotten mixed together, the mother's interpenetrating the son's before it has had a chance to develop on its own. The oft-told family trauma of the pregnant mother's being locked out can be interpreted as a message to her son that he is heir-apparent to her queenly love as a consequence of the old king's tragic error. These royal terms are apt. And in the chapter on Origins, below, it will be shown that in all probability, it was during the course of that night that both the son's future oedipal mission and his Family Romance were in effect authorized.

The "strange smile" Jessie Chambers notices as Mrs. Lawrence gives her account rivets us to the classic oedipal viewpoint for a bit longer. Looking back on his childhood, Lawrence recognized the incongruities between his mother's ideals for her son and her own dreams. The ideal, which grew out of her "character-forming power" as autocrat of the hearth, was to have "humble, adoring, high-minded men" (P, 818). But she also began to have "secret dreams" of "some Don Juan sort of person whose influence would make the vine of Dionysus grow and coil over the pulpit of our Congregational Chapel." Then, having noted "we are such stuff as our grandmothers' dreams are made on," Lawrence decides that although it was his "turn to be the 'good son,'" it would be his "son's turn to fulfill the other dream." "Thank God," he adds, "I have no son to undertake the onerous burden." It was, instead, his children of the imagination who were to fulfill the onerous Don Juan burden of rescuing the woman from her Midlands and miners' world, while simultaneously struggling with the deeper task of sorting out filial desire from maternal will.

Géza Róheim noted wryly in 1934 that since the Oedipus drama contains such an uncensored version of the Oedipus complex, it is probably hiding something else.[18] He has been proven right many times over. Indeed there may be no better index to the growing sophistication within psychoanalysis than the development of commentary on *Oedipus Rex*, a profoundly condensed work that explores virtually the whole world of early childhood. The Sphinx, for example, is initially seen as the combined, coital parents, later as the "Strangler," or terrible mother of the oral-sadistic phase; a groundwork of homosexual conflict has been laid out between

Laius and his son; and perhaps most appropriate in the present context is Oedipus's murderous rage at Jocasta for having permitted the whole thing to happen. It is only after he has stormed, sword in hand, into her chambers and found her hanged that he turns his aggression inward and rips from her lobes the brooches with which he will gouge out his eyes. There is an interesting line of interpretation that disputes Oedipus's position as victorious son and focuses on him instead as dupe in Jocasta's scheme to revenge herself on her disappointing husband. Such sons are seen as carrying out "delegated missions."[19]

The principle is sound. Oedipal victories are inherently illusory. Mother is always spoken for and is almost always bound to have an ulterior motive for turning to her son. Hence *her will* contributes to his fate along with his inherently doomed instinctual strivings. There is something of this in Mrs. Morel's (and in her model's) turning to her children and directing them away from her husband.

Thus for Lawrence, the issue at the triadic stage is to disengage his oedipal/rescue fantasies from the mother's Don Juan dreams, just as at the dyadic stage he had to separate his wishes for fusion/ intimacy from the mother's devouring urges. Moreover, to become a lover of more than his mother, he must find a way to love and identify with his hated father. These activities can only occur out of the mother's sight; they are associated with the discovery and summoning of the dark gods, the pan-spirit, and all the allied fantasies of resurrected masculinity.

In summary, fantasy stocks part of the artist's workshop; and the Family Romance in particular expands the bounds of one's biological origins by intimating adoption into a line of exalted parentage:

(1)   Under optimal conditions this fantasy unfolds into a pervasive creative romance with the world; under stressful conditions, it fosters wishes for rebirth.

(2)   In Lawrence's case the Family Romance veered for a time into a utopian quest for a Rananim colony populated with an ideally reconstituted family.

(3)   The fantasy promoted a deeper quest for a kind of mythic and cultural re-sourcing that would take its cues from American Indians, ancient Egyptians, and the Etruscans, as embodi-

ments of a prelapsarian (i.e., preindustrial) organic wholeness. Such discoveries, whether made directly or indirectly
from anthropology and artifacts, hold the promise of rebirth
and adoption into a vital, dark-skinned community. Certain
reborn figures appear throughout Lawrence's works as a
Mexican revolutionary, an Italian peasant, an English gamekeeper, or a traveling gypsy, and are notably lacking in ordinary parentage.

(4) The fantasy fostered a cognitive style based on macro/micro-
cosmic correspondence between self and world (this to be
explored in the Body section).

(5) The fantasy evidently influenced his relationship with Frieda,
whose lineage as the "daughter of the ancient and famous
house of Richthoven" unduly impressed him and fueled his
transcontinental rescue operation of her from her stodgy
Midlands husband and their children (CL, 17 April 1912).

(6) The obverse side accommodated lamia, the mother of darkness and the maternal mirror-image of aggressive orality. The
adoption/rescue motif then gets replaced by abduction; the
welcoming embrace by a blood-sucking assault; deserving
love by undeserved hate, and so on. The figures are still idealized by reason of their preternatural powers. But whether
one's progenitors derive from a higher or a lower order, the
normal biological sequence of origins is denied and revised.

If we have scarcely done justice to fantasy, we must admit that
fantasy scarcely does justice to creativity. The Family Romance is
but one kind of subjective phenomenon, albeit fundamental for
the artist. When Freud suggested that the artist turned inward to
a fantasy world, it was preeminently that of the Family Romance—
already rendered in myth, fairy tale, fiction, drama, and poetry, but
capable of endless variation—to which the artist would be drawn.
But Freud also noted that the artist who had turned *away from*
a painful piece of reality would eventually find his way *back to*
reality, in part through the public acceptance of his art. Examining
how creative work issues forth from these subjective/objective dialectics will be the burden of future sections.

2

Reality

Because the source of all life and knowledge is in man and woman, and the source of all living is in the interchange and the meeting and mingling of these two . . .
—Lawrence, CL, 280

With our artist wrapped firmly around the subjective pole of creativity—a sort of totem pole of divine, semidivine, or demonic ancestors constituting his Family Romance—let us attempt to delineate the objective pole of creativity, that initially painful reality he turns away from and struggles back to. Our task is facilitated by establishing a link between the two poles—they are in effect connected by a basic concern with origins.

Primal fantasies are so called because they are responses to gaps in the child's knowledge about his own origins and about the adult sexual practices leading to them. Riddles of adult sexuality elude the child and are not fully understood until a series of ambiguous scenes have been witnessed or glimpsed, collateral observations in nature or art have been added, and along with fanciful speculations, all have taken a fairly ordered residence in his mind. These impressions, far from simply being expelled and replaced later on, may often relocate to other less obtrusive, more submerged mental quarters where they continue to exert distorting influences and perpetuate uncertainties or misgivings about the nature of human sexuality. In the ecology of the psyche apparently little is ever abandoned. Moreover, psychoanalysis suggests that the psychobiological emergence of the person is a dialectical process: the child who is biologically created by his parents returns the favor in due time by creating them internally. But "internalization" and "identification" are terms that seem too mild to account for the intensely emotional way children set about creating themselves through inwardly creating their relationships with parents. And the moment of truth in this process occurs when the child must come to terms with the one intimate relationship which has the power both to beget him and to exclude him. Here is Reality with a capital R.

Since the child tends to register his comprehension of sexual origins in terms of the bodily zone or psychosexual phase with which he is most involved at the time, it is possible to chart his primal fantasies about sex along a certain incline.[1] Thus the oral cavity may represent the earliest route for conception and birth (one recalls the Virgin's conception through the ear of the Word of God, the vampire's fanged kiss on neck or mouth, where the sexual component is all but absent). Freud's 1907 paper on the sexual theories of children emphasized the invisibility of female genitalia and the cloacal mode, one which the sight of copulating animals and the hatching posture of birds may reinforce for children.[2] In brief, these theories suggest that the unravelling of human origins has been a relatively late acquisition, both in the history of the individual and of the race. Meanwhile various distortions or pseudosolutions have bent, biased, and molded the child's mind into unforeseen, highly subjective directions.

A shift in emphasis from drive-zones to object-relations will allow us to further structure these fantasies. The earliest fantasy in this sequence might be the Phallic Woman, which, in attributing to mother the possession of a penis, allows the child to retain a sense of primordial unity and perfection. Here is a basis for the medusa, a source of androgynous ideals as well as those of Amazonian motherhood, and an etiology, according to Robert Bak, of fetishism.[3] In its more benign form it may be represented in Lawrence's mythic era when the tribe of humanity lived "breast to breast with the cosmos." In this version of origins, the mother is the parent, sole and supreme, and the modern male finds himself to be the "broken-off fragment of a woman," as Birkin nervously ponders in *Women in Love* (p. 192); in the sexual sphere she attacks and triumphs over the phallic hero with the "harpy's beak" of her vagina.

As noted, the Family Romance is a subjective revision of origins which, by allowing the maximum play of fantasy, clears vast spaces for the creative imagination to inhabit and take charge of. The primary service afforded here is to separate things lofty from things lowly. One's biological parents may do seemingly nasty and/or violent things in bed, which their child may witness while he is undergoing toilet-training and acquiring intimations of actions as good or bad and sexuality as clean or filthy. But the Olympian parents created in the child's mind to adopt him and replace the original set are blessedly free from the "obscene" practices to which our flesh is heir. So while separating what is perceived as lowly from lofty, the Family Romance in effect drops the veil of repression over human sexuality. Nevertheless, it advances beyond more primitive notions and implicitly validates the importance of the parental function. One could chart the progress of the dracula fantasy in the popular imagination as it shifts from a dyadic, mother-child tableau to more complex configurations that include triadic sexual adults, though still composed as it were by the child's subjectively colored oral-assaultive mode of instinctual awareness.

Freud divides the Family Romance into two phases. In the first or asexual phase, sexuality per se is denied and both parents are idealized. In the second or sexual phase, one's maternal origin is accepted while paternal idealization is fostered, although the rescue-fantasy variation introduces a further split between the fleshly and the spiritual mother. For example, the Andromeda who is rescued by the young Perseus may also stand for the male child's externalizing his feminine identification along the path of acquiring a masculine identity; or the myth may be a way of saving and so of giving back a life to the parents, thereby cancelling the debt of begetting.[4] These phases allow for increased degrees of sexual awareness, though they are still shaped by the child's mind and his phase-specific needs.

By now it may have occurred to the reader that the objective pole of human origins is simply adult sexuality as refracted in the prism of the child's mind. Some mastery of its meaning and some variation on its practice are the destiny of every growing child. Whatever else may be said about it, the act of copulation is real—not fanciful. The child's exposure to adult sexual acts or his fantasies about them is referred to in psychoanalytic literature as the Primal Scene—after Freud explored the phenomenon most thoroughly in the course of his work with the Wolf Man. We are led to ponder then whether the Primal Scene might also be the painful reality that the artist-to-be had originally turned away from.

Indeed, in several key respects the Primal Scene does qualify. It impresses on the child's mind that the two most important figures in his world have an emotionally intense relationship which has nothing to do with him or his needs. In this respect it is more frustrating than informing. The feeling of being excluded from things that matter greatly is precisely the kind of blow to self-esteem that would frustrate the need to feel one's love is duly reciprocated. This in turn would generate the wish to be an orphan/foundling who could be adopted by the sort of superior parents who would not stoop to such exclusive activities. In this manner, the child's natural quandaries about his origins can be deflected along a less disturbing route while tendering the semblance of a solution, though in the long run, the fantasy of mother as goddess is no more adequate than the apparent disillusioned conclusion that mother is a strumpet: one is simply less offensive than the other.

The painful piece of reality on the other hand may be *perceived* as the birth of a younger sibling or the behavior of a violent father. But the sibling is traceable to the same parental conspiracy, and the violent father may be partly the result of the child's tendency to perceive the parental act as an attack. Furthermore, whether or not the Primal Scene is directly witnessed, no child is free from fantasizing about it, and the overwhelming weight of clinical data acquired over many years and spanning diverse cultures testify that the consequences are disruptive.[5]

In coming to terms with the Primal Scene every child creates his own myth of origin. In many important respects, the manner in which he assimilates and masters the childhood distortions of the parental relation will deeply affect his own future as an adult destined for some variety of sexual loving. The artist, whatever he/she does as a private individual, appeals in part to our mature sense of reality by reason of the satisfactory ways in which the work resolves the quandaries of human origins. Unlike others, however, the artist attaches his/her origin's drama to a mythic-cultural tradition which provides built-in displacements and a certain guarantee of legitimacy. To a significant degree, it is through this means that he/she discovers a path back to reality.

We have noted Lawrence's capacity for using mythic, folkloric, or gothic imagery for screening oral-aggressive transactions. Vampire tableaus, in which the male bends over to attack a sleeping female or vice versa, readily lend themselves to Primal Scenes as distorted by infantile versions of sexuality as a violent attack. While this link is at least a structural one, it may have been something more for Lawrence. Though the evidence is insufficient, it can be affirmed that the vampire configuration is a demonic version of origins, an inversion of the Family Romance wish that most likely originates in a construction of adult-sexuality overdetermined by the child's excited orality. In *Sons and Lovers*, Paul's earliest memory is that of his father violently drawing blood from his mother's forehead and staining Paul's white shawl. This emblematic scene not only implicates Paul (and his author) in the sexual battlefield of the parents' marriage, but it also imprints him with an archetype of male and female in locked combat which he can no more avoid accepting than he can avoid struggling to overcome. Lawrence seems to be saying that here is a violent awakening into sexual consciousness which must be set alongside other idealized versions of origins. It is a traumatic baptism of blood and fire that threatens to annihilate him unless he masters it somehow, for while exposed to fragments of the parents' turbulent world, the child is nonetheless excluded from its substantial meaning. The confusions are radical: given the option of talking about milk, blood, or sperm, Lawrence will go for blood. He thereby injects a persisting ambiguity in the male/female relationship, as when he refers to "a transmission, I don't know of what, between her blood and mine, in the act of connection," or of the male being fertilized by the female (CL, 394, 291). Vampirism in any event leads away from understanding and mastery, deeper into the gothic woods of subjectivity. And fascinating as it may be to trace it as a lurid subtext in Lawrence's development, it is to his credit that eventually he worked beyond its morbid perimeters.

As Paul's name has a double birth, which will be examined later in the chapter on Origins, he also has a double baptism. First he is sprinkled as his mother "bowed over him, and a few tears shook swiftly out of her very heart" (SL, 36); this is the holy baptism of innocence. Immediately following is his initiation in the "carnal bloody fight" of his parents' marriage—his baptism of blood. The one points toward the Family Romance, the other to the Primal Scene. Hence, the adored infant, whom the mother calls "my lamb," implying the chosen of the Lord, now becomes sacrificial and interconnects with his mother's role of victim. Simultaneously, while the maternal tie is threatened, the terrifying violence of the male role raises almost insuperable barriers against mastery through identification. But obviously the whole scene is internalized, for in Lawrence's mind violence becomes so intimately associated with sex that virtually every scene of passionate lovemaking is preceded by a quarrel, a violation, or some symbolic form of bloodshed. This is as true in his fictional combats as in Frieda's well-documented bruises. The point, however, is not to take the above scene as explanatory or as a direct personal revelation, much less as exculpatory, but as a possible indication of how the infant readily perceives the parental relation as a violently disruptive act. And when the parents actually do quarrel and fight around their children as the Lawrences did, then reality reinforces fantasy and, oddly, serves to repress the erotic elements, which may also be dangerous in their way. Some readers may view it as narrowmindedly reductive to ascribe such formative importance to the parental relation; yet due to its enormous power over the child's emotional life it can hardly be overemphasized, regardless of how well it is repressed by most relatively healthy individuals.

The three most painful realities for Lawrence correspond to the three periods of traumatic upheaval mentioned earlier. It is readily evident how in his early childhood he had to contend with deficiencies in the body-image brought about through illness, teasing, or conflicted mothering. Just as decisively, in relation to the sexual/combative parents, he may have merely been one of the "in-betweens/little non-descripts," but he was also wounded in the crossfire (CP, 490). This uncontrollable reality, both humiliating and ever menacing, had to be revised in the only way possible—that of creativity—in order for Lawrence to break its hold over him before he could consolidate his own masculine identity, and eventually establish a reasonably mature sexual tie. It is mainly for these reasons that the Primal Scene is emphasized as the primary reality from which *this* artist, at least, turns, just as adult sexuality becomes the reality by which he charts his return, either directly through his libidinal ties or indirectly through his art.

The deeply felt loss of the mother epitomizes the impact of reality in the adolescent or second period. It marks the conclusion of an unconditional intimacy which fostered a virgin-goddess-mother brand of Family Romance. As noted, the regressive undertow of this loss was manifested in the devouring females who distort the sexual relationships in the novels that immediately follow.

The third shattering reality was the war itself, which Lawrence neither saw nor experienced first-hand, but suffered through as a sort of realized nightmare: as if the world were persecuting him by acting out his worst unconscious fears. His responses were wishes to escape and found a utopia out of a blend of panic, hysteria, and grandiosity, exacerbated by misanthropic urges that continually disrupted the idealistic projects. During this stormy period, wherein he drew blood as often as he was injured, inner and outer reality become hopelessly confused. He attacks himself in others, converts friends into enemies, and turns against the very ideals he had upheld the week before. Unable to sustain an allegiance with any cause or faction, he lashes out at all sides and denounces every position, including his own the week before. If there is any underlying emotional current in all this turmoil, it may be that his conflicted political postures are undercut by unassimilated sexual identifications.

The one consistent theme in his obsessions with attacking rats, obscenely mounting insects, teeming vermin, and so on, is a revulsion toward the act of breeding itself. The association is often quite clear between repulsive bestial behavior and human sexual behavior. In fact he never really turns against the natural world; it is only when he indiscriminately projects certain fears and phobias onto the nonhuman orders that they are rendered odious to him. It can be surmised that these revulsions sprang from childhood terrors centering on the Primal Scene. For example, he would like to be left alone with nature, but people creep in, "like bugs . . . fat men in white flannel trousers—*pères de famille*—and the familles—passing along the field-path and onlooking at the scenery. Oh, if one could have a great box of insect powder, and shake it over them, in the heavens, and exterminate them."[6] But he can no more change this reality than he can literally alter the role of the *père de famille* in his own begetting. Yet his art will precisely acquire the aim of revising the sex relation, of renewing it, and of placing his ideas at its center.

To summarize the theoretical points so far, the Primal Scene stands for the painful reality the artist turns away from; it keeps alive the concerns over origins that go into his work; it provides the prospect of mastery even as the alternative reality of the Family Romance is embraced; and, as recognition of the central importance of adult sexuality in human culture, it underlies the seal of maturity in the work of art. It also appears that as the artist works his way back toward the new vision of reality promised by his work, he does not so much abandon his various primal fantasies as enlist them as components: his stockroom of signs and images, his zodiac system for telling time, his bestiary, and his pack of tarot cards that guides our quests.

In this perspective the creative process is dialectical, swinging back and forth between the more objective and the more subjective poles of experience, which may function as regulators of creativity. This is an active process, a struggle; it is a grappling within a medium that is more aligned to working through than to dream-models, cathartic release, reliving, or other frequently mentioned defensive strategies with which various psychoanalytic investigations have tended to shackle art. In returning to origins, the artist initiates a spiraling process of self-remaking and object/environment/renewal in which others can participate and which distinguishes him/her from the original biological act and parental conflicts by which he/she was first constituted. But as he/she continues to draw on this process in certain mysterious ways, he/she wins for himself/herself and his/her work a measure of cultural legitimacy.

The dialectical approach to Lawrencean creativity addresses the unique standing of art in culture, one which is neither purely mental nor purely natural, neither all subjective nor all objective, but a blending of both in a special intermediate space that can be better defined hereafter. For the present we can post a few textual markers to show the likelihood that Lawrence was moving in directions consistent with those just outlined. Roughly speaking, the sequence runs from evasive ignorance to dark knowledge to luminous clarity:

(1) "The children had come, for some mysterious reason, out of both of them." ["Odour of Chrysanthemums," 1911]

(2) "Some things happen in life, and carry the body along with them, accomplish facts, and make one's history, and yet are not real. Mrs. Morel felt that her inner life denied her experience, said "It is a battlefield: my flesh is a battlefield where foreigners fight." [From an early draft of *Sons and Lovers*, referred to as Fragment 1, 1911]

(3) "Sometimes life takes hold of one, carries the body along. . . ."

[The same passage as it was shortened and slightly modified more positively in the published version, 1913]

(4) "Darkness and silence must fall perfectly on her, then she could know mystically, in unrevealed touch. She must lightly, mindlessly connect with him, have the knowledge which is death of knowledge, the reality of surety in not knowing."

"He knew her darkly, with the fullness of dark knowledge." [Ursula and Birkin, "Excurse" in *Women in Love*, 1919]

(5) ". . . softly he stroked the silky slope of her loins, down, down between her soft warm buttocks, coming nearer and nearer to the very quick of her. And she felt him like a flame of desire, yet tender, and she felt herself melting in the flame. She let herself go. She felt his penis risen against her. . . ." [*Lady Chatterley's Lover*, 1928]

In sum, everyone's primary reality is found in their parents' lives, their total lives including their sexual activities. This primary reality not only creates us but continues to shape our evolving sense of ourselves and the real world. The Primal Scene epitomizes and concentrates these processes, but it also lends itself to such indirect modes of representation as foster creativity. And for that reason, it pulls the artist in his work around the objective pole of origins. To know about sexual matters is one thing; to write about them significantly is another thing entirely. To come to grips with parental sexuality, especially when it is extremely conflict-ridden, is something else again. Lawrence had to engage all these realities.

To say that the Sphinx of parental sexuality conceals both one's origins and the germs of one's future sexual identity sounds so simple as almost to be a truism; yet paradoxically, the implications of so finite a statement are infinite.

3

Symbol

The strange potency and beauty of these Etruscan things arise, it seems to me, from the profundity of the symbolic meaning the artist was more or less aware of. The Etruscan religion, surely, was never anthropomorphic: that is, whatever gods it contained were not beings, but symbols of elemental powers, just symbols: as was the case earlier in Egypt. The undivided Godhead, if we can call it such, was symbolised by the mundum, *the plasm cell, with its nucleus. . . . To the Etruscan all was alive; the whole universe lived; and the business of man was himself to live amid it all. He had to draw life into himself, out of all the wandering huge vitalities of the world.—Lawrence,* Etruscan Places

He is a beast, a beast to mother, a beast to all of us. . . . —Lawrence in his youth referring to his father, in G. H. Neville's A Memoir of D. H. Lawrence, *p. 60*

1

When Lawrence was tragically near his own grave and knew it, he was drawn into the archaeological wonders of the Etruscan caves. While what he discovered there spurred him on to his final bursts of creativity, it must have also stunned him with an uncanny shock of recognition, for what he observed were prototypes of what he had been representing for many years in his own writings. "It must have been a wonderful world," he writes in admiration, "one thing springing from another, things mentally contradictory fusing together emotionally, so that a lion could be at the same moment also a goat, and not a goat." This figure happens to be a "queer galloping lion with his tongue out," and rising from his shoulders the "second neck of a dark faced, bearded goat":

The tail of the lion ends in a serpent's head. So this is the proper Chimaera. And galloping after the end of lion's tail comes a winged female sphinx.

There were different currents in the blood-stream and some always clashed. Bird and serpent, lion and deer, leopard and lamb. Yet the very clash was a form of unison, as we see in the lion which also has a goat's head.

The goat says: let me breed forever, til the world is one reeking goat. But then the lion roars from the other blood-stream, which is also in man, and he lifts his paw to strike, in the passion of the other wisdom. [EP, 66 – 69]

Elsewhere he comes upon hippocampi (fish-tailed horses) and "sea-monsters, the sea-man with fish-tail, and with wings, the sea-woman the same: or the man with serpent-legs, and wings.... Other common symbolic animals ... are the beaked griffins, the creatures of the powers that tear asunder and, at the same time, are guardians of the treasure ... lion and eagle combined...." They are fascinating, and Lawrence is fascinated by them, how much so we may fully appreciate only by considering his own composite symbols. "We can know the living world only symbolically," he is moved to conclude from his Etruscan discoveries. And perhaps we can only know the underlying coherence of Lawrence's living art by attending to his own great composite symbols: Rainbow, Plumed Serpent, and Phoenix. Whenever possible, the history of these symbols will be traced, located in Lawrence's works, common features noted, and an investigation conducted to ascertain their contribution to the creative process.

2

... for primal scene imagery is central to many socially important myths and rituals and contributes fundamentally to artistic productions.—Henry Edelheit[1]

When Freud first analyzed the Primal Scene in 1914, it referred to the child's witnessing of parental intercourse and later to his fantasies concerning it. More recently it has often been employed to encompass the total emotional life of the parents, as well as questions about human sexuality. Since the present concern is not rigorously clinical, the wider sphere of applications will prove more suitable. The Primal Scene has also been connected with the mythopoeic faculty, especially in regard to mythological composites, such as the Sphinx, Chimaera, Medusa, and to other configurations, such as the crucifixion and the bullfight. To these I would add the Caduceus (physicians' emblem), the Yin-Yang, and the Swastika. Drawing on Bradley's study, Edelheit refers to the Gilgamesh motif: a "common decorative detail in architecture," which is on the "heraldic theme [of] two wild beasts (in whom we recognize the parents) separated by a warrior (the child)," who later appears in the lion's skins (signaling identification).[2] Edelheit construes "the concept [as] structural rather than motivational," and accordingly it "may be understood as specific and characteristic aspects of the human mental organization." The concept's value consists not so much in its power to represent infantile material—though it unmistakably may do so—as in what it tells us about mental operations in a general way, and how the imagination may organize its energies and materials in a particular creative way.

Without traveling to Egypt, Lawrence could have discovered a fascinating assemblage of sphinxes and other composite beasts in the British Museum; and without reading *Dracula*, he could have found in Keats's poem *Lamia* a spellbound, "rainbow-sided" monster whose "head was serpent" but whose "mouth and fair eyes were woman's." Keats's Lamia, moreover, is visited by Hermes as a falcon "crown'd with feathers, fluttering light." Bending over her to break the spell and discover his own nymph, Hermes the falcon and Lamia the serpent, male and female, unite in a British prototype for Lawrence's Mexican Plumed Serpent. In other words, a legitimate array of cultural prototypes, whose structures and motifs having long since preempted personal motives, were available for Lawrence to draw on; but he would still do the selecting and shaping according to his own emotional and creative needs.

3

. . . no new thing has ever arisen, or can arise, save out of the impulse of the male upon the female, the female upon the male . . . this suffering, this delight, this imperfection. . . . —P, 444, 443

The Rainbow, the great biblical arch of hope sent by God after the flood, is Lawrence's first major symbol. In the context of his evolving theories of opposites, it is the interpenetration of light and darkness "when night clashes on day": the perfect but impermanent balance of consummation. In the Lawrencean Book of Genesis, "darkness is a vast infinite, an origin," that "has nourished us." This universal infinite darkness "necessarily conceives of its own opposite," "universal infinite light." When the "ray of ultimate light" enters the "womb of the primary darkness, . . . time is begotten," and man travels "across between the two great opposites of the Beginning and the End." We are the sum of these opposites and "exist by virtue of our inter-opposition" (C, 16, 7, 6).

But in depicting the dark-to-light, rainbow-process of growth in nature as a paradigm of human sexuality, Lawrence imposes a more violent scenario than the facts warrant:

Out of the dark, original flame issues a tiny green flicker, a weed coming alive. On the edge of the bright, ultimate, spiritual flame of the heavens is revealed a fragment of iris, a touch of green, a weed coming into being. The two flames surge and intermingle, casting up a crest of leaves and stems, their *battlefield*, their *meeting-ground*, their *marriage bed*, the embrace becomes closer, more unthinkably vivid, it leaps to climax, the battle grows fiercer, intolerably, till there is the swoon, the climax, the consummation, the little yellow disk gleams absolute between heaven and earth, radiant of both eternities, framed in the two infinities. [Italics added]

Dramatic in its own way, nature seems here to be enjoying a superimposed intensity. Clearly, Lawrence's concentrated prose conflates images and overdetermines meanings. For example, the iris is the colored center of the eye and the bright flowers in a bed of green spears, with both corresponding to the messenger of the Rainbow goddess and the Rainbow itself. But the iris here is also the fertilized egg of life and the eye of consciousness, whereas the Rainbow is a totality:

It is that which comes when night clashes on day, the rainbow, the yellow and rose and blue and purple of dawn and sunset, which leaps out of the breaking of light upon darkness, of darkness upon light, absolute beyond day or night; the rainbow, the iridescence which is darkness at once and light, the two-in-one; the crown that binds them both.

The Rainbow is the "supreme dark flow of the flame" of sexual union. It is the perfect balance of the fight both between light and dark within the individual, and between the sexual clash of male and female. The opposites who clash and come together in the sexual act confirm the opposites in the iris-flame center of the self born "between the two floods." In Lawrence's allusive, elliptical, and at times arbitrary correspondences, this self may be the literal self of the newborn infant or the renewed self of each sexual partner. Characteristically, Lawrence takes the generative nature of sexuality as a springboard for regenerative aims.

As an arch, wedding earth to the heavens, the Rainbow is implicit in his discussion of religious art and architecture; yet he never relinquishes the sexual aspect. The "column must always stand for the male aspiration, the arch or ellipse for the female completeness containing this aspiration." "Truth is, in actual experience, that momentary state when in living the union between the male and the female is consummated," whether it be physical or spiritual (P, 460).

This takes us closer to *The Rainbow* itself. In that novel, the great arch, whether it unites nature and culture, flesh and spirit, male and female, recurs throughout the successive generations from the "timeless consummation" of Lincoln Cathedral, "where the thrust from earth met the thrust from earth and the arch was locked on the keystone of ecstasy," to Ursula's vision at the end:

And then, in the blowing clouds, she saw a band of faint iridescence colouring in faint colours a portion of the hill. And forgetting, startled, she looked for the hovering colour and saw a rainbow forming itself. In one place it gleamed fiercely, and, her heart anguished with hope, she sought the shadow of iris where the bow should be. Steadily the colour gathered, mysteriously, from nowhere, it took presence upon itself, there was a faint, vast rainbow. The arc bended and strengthened itself till it arched indomitable, making great architecture of light and colour and the space of heaven, its pedestals luminous in the corruption of new houses on the low hill, its arch the top of heaven.

And the rainbow stood on the earth. She knew that the sordid people who crept hard-scaled and separate on the face of the world's corruption were living still, that the rainbow was arched in their blood and would quiver to life in their spirit, that they would cast off their horny covering of disintegration, that new, clean, naked bodies would issue to a new germination, to a new growth, rising to the light and the wind and the clean rain of heaven. She saw in the rainbow the earth's new architecture, the old, brittle corruption of houses and factories swept away, the world built up in a living fabric of Truth, fitting to the over-arching heaven.

Earlier, Ursula's mother as a child is figured between the arches of her parents:

She looked from one to the other, and she saw them established to her safety, and she was free. She played between the pillar of fire and the pillar of cloud in confidence, having the assurance on her right hand and the assurance on her left. She was no longer called upon to uphold with her childish might the broken end of the arch. Her father and her mother now met to the span of the heavens, and she, the child, was free to play in the space beneath, between. [R, 92]

Both in and beyond time, the Rainbow bridges the gulf between the generations as well as between the sexes; and its fragile unity, ephemeral and recurring, suggests the ideal balance of the generative act for each new generation. The Rainbow, then, is the parental bond which begets and overarches the self.

The novel opens with an account of the Brangwens who "had lived for generations on the Marsh Farm," working in the horizontal fields beneath the church tower of the little country town. The nineteenth-century period is made hazy by the biblical resonance of the prose ("So the Brangwens came and went without fear of necessity. . . . Neither were they thriftless"), and by recapturing the even more remote mythological scheme of existence:

But heaven and earth was teeming around them, and how should this cease? They felt the rush of the sap in spring, they knew the wave which cannot halt, but every year throws forward the seed to begetting, and, falling back, leaves the young-born on the earth. They knew the intercourse between heaven and earth. . . .

On the women was the "drowse of the blood-intimacy, calves sucking and hens running together in droves," but they too wanted more than the complementary ebb and flow of natural cycles. The first individualized Brangwen, however, is Tom, who, having lost his mother at age twenty-three, finds himself soon after in love with a foreign woman living at the vicarage, Lydia Lensky, widow of a Polish doctor and landowner. On an occasion when he gives her and her daughter Anna a ride, he notices the wedding ring on her finger. "It excluded him: it was a closed circle. It bound her life, the wedding ring, it stood for her life in which he could have not part" (R, 34).

Lawrence's working title of *The Rainbow* was *The Wedding Ring*, and he worked on it during the early months with Frieda, another foreign lady with a husband and children. In contrast to the wedding ring, however, the Rainbow is an open form; it unites opposites by being a broken circle. And it was Frieda who suggested the final title. Lawrence, claiming he was not good at titles, was satisfied with the evolution of a symbol, whose complexity owed a great deal to his own struggle to define the violently oppositional Rainbow of his parents' marriage in order to create a new Rainbow of sexual love in his own life.

4

It is true that the tendency of dreams, and of the unconscious fantasy, to employ the sexual symbols bisexually, reveals an archaic trait, for in childhood the difference of the genitals is unknown, and the same genitals are attributed to both sexes.—Freud, The Interpretation of Dreams, *1900*

Apart from the Sphinx, there is perhaps no richer or more complex and enduring symbol than the Phoenix. Its origins also appear to be Egyptian, but it is found in other Mediterranean cultures, was later to be appropriated by the Romans, and was eventually introduced into Christian iconography. The bird is sacred, one of a kind; and being best known for its radiant plumage and fiery death, followed by a renewal from its own ashes, it is connected with solar myths. "The *Benu*, a holy bird even during the period of the Old Kingdom, was represented as sacred to Osiris."[3] Later on, "Benu" is the name given to the morning star, called a rising god, which by reason of its morning and evening appearance served to express periods of renewal. It was then a nocturnal or "hidden sungod." The bird soon came to symbolize Osiris or his soul, and as the language becomes more personalized, the Phoenix becomes a "kind of primaeval soul" and an image of the self risen from the dead." Thus on the basis of early accounts of his great life-span of 500 years or more and his powers to be reborn from his own ashes, he is seized upon in the Christian era as an image of Christ's resurrection, and by extension, that of the individual soul's immortality. The solar radiance turns from the Roman emperor's apotheosis to the saint's halo.

Yet his colors endure. Herodotus has him red and golden; Pliny describes "brilliant golden plumage around the neck, while the rest of the body is of purple color; except the tail, which is azure, with long feathers intermingled of a roseate hue."[4] In Jewish legends he "runs with the sun on his circuit, and he spreads out his wings and catches up the fiery rays of the sun"; he has a "purple color," and, to make the obvious point, is "like the rainbow."[5]

Although the sacred bird is traditionally male in keeping with his solar origin, Lawrence in his first extended treatment brings about a sex change:

The unique phoenix of the desert grew up to maturity and wisdom. Sitting upon her tree, she was the only one of her kind in all creation, supreme, the zenith, the perfect aristocrat. She attained to perfection, eagle-like she rose in her nest and lifted her wings, surpassing the zenith of mortality; so she was translated into the flame of eternity, she became one with the fiery Origin.

It was not for her to sit tight, and assert her own tight ego. She was gone as she came.

In the nest was a little ash, a little flocculent grey dust wavering upon a blue-red, dying coal. The red coal stirred and gathered strength, gradually it grew white with heat, it shot forth sharp gold flames. It was the young phoenix within the nest, with curved beak growing hard and crystal, like a scimitar, and talons hardening into pure jewels. [C, 34]

Otherwise, although his treatment here is traditional, he manages to enlist the bird into the service of his most enduring theme: the necessity for modern man to die out of his "glassy envelope, the insect rind, the tight-shut shell" of culture and to be born again into the great Cosmos (C, 57). The *ego* is a despicable little insect jammed into its tight little shell; the *self*, as Ursula discovered, is "oneness with the infinite."

The infinite is not the everlasting, however, but the ever-changing, ever-recurring cycle of nature. The Phoenix points the way, and Lawrence soon injects his sexual innovations into the archetype:

. . . my blood goes forth in shock after shock of delirious passing-away, in shock after shock entering into consummation, till my soul is slipping its moorings, my mind, my will fuses down, I melt out and am gone into the eternal darkness, the primal creative darkness reigns, and I am not, and at last I am.

Shock after shock of ecstasy and the anguish of ecstasy, death after death of trespass into the unknown, till I fall down into the flame, I lapse into the intolerable flame, a pallid shadow I am transfused into the flux of unendurable darkness, and am gone. No spark nor vestige remains within the supreme dark flow of the flame, I am contributed again to the immortal source. I am with the dark Almighty of the beginning.

Till, new-created, I am thrown forth again on the shore of creation, warm and lustrous, goodly, new born from the darkness out of which all time has issued.

And then, new-born on the knees of darkness, new-issued from the womb of creation, I open my eyes to the light and know the goal, the end, the light which stands over the end of the journey, the everlasting day, the oneness of the spirit. [C, 26]

Thus the light-dark opposition, the dissolution-renewal process, and the human sexual encounter, in which the male dies into the dark flow of the phallic flame, are all brought together again as they were in the rainbow-iris imagery.

The courtship and lovemaking between Will Brangwen and Anna in *The Rainbow* is rendered in a somewhat similar way. He carves for her a strange vital emblem to be used as a butter stamper, "a phoenix, something like an eagle, rising on symmetrical wings, from a circle of very beautiful flickering flames that rose upwards from the rim of the cup." Then when they are with each other in the dairy:

Her breast was near him; his head lifted like an eagle's. She did not move. Suddenly, with an incredibly quick, delicate movement, he put his arms round her and drew her to him. It was quick, cleanly done, like a bird that swoops and sinks close, closer.

He was kissing her throat. She turned and looked at him. Her eyes were dark and flowing with fire. His eyes were hard and bright with a fierce purpose and gladness, like a hawk's. She felt him flying into the dark space of her flames, like a brand, like a gleaming hawk. [R, 112]

It is only their first kiss, but after they are married:

His head felt so strange and blazed. Still he held her close, with trembling arms. His blood seemed very strong, enveloping her.

And at last she began to draw near to him, she nestled to him. His limbs, his body, took fire and beat up in flames. She clung to him, she cleaved to his body. The flames swept him, he held her in sinews of fire. If she would kiss him! He bent his mouth down. And her mouth, soft and moist, received him. He felt his veins would burst with anguish of thankfulness, his heart was mad with gratefulness, he could pour himself out upon her for ever.

When they came to themselves, the night was very dark. Two hours had gone by. They lay still and warm and weak, like the new-born, together. [R, 152−53]

The Phoenix kind of lovemaking expresses a perfect balance of consummation, but throughout, their relationship is a struggle for dominance over the powers of life. As a young artist, Will was "carving, as he had always wanted, the Creation of Eve":

Adam lay asleep as if suffering, and God, a dim, large figure, stooped towards him, stretching forward His unveiled hand; and Eve, a small vivid, naked female shape, was issuing like a flame towards the hand of God, from the torn side of Adam.

Now, Will Brangwen was working at the Eve. She was thin, a keen, unripe thing. With trembling passion, fine as a breath of air, he sent the chisel over her belly, her hard, unripe, small belly. She was a stiff little figure, with sharp lines, in the throes and torture and ecstasy of their creation. [R, 116]

The composite panel remains unfinished and Anna begins to jeer at the Eve. "She is like a marionette. Why is she so small? You've made Adam as big as God, and Eve like a doll."

She draws the inevitable conclusion, along much the same lines that led Lawrence to conclude that certain male writers, like Hardy, were unable to create a positive woman. "'It's impudence to say that Woman was made out of Man's body,' Anna continued, 'when every man is born of woman.'" Will no sooner goes back to work than it comes to him that Anna is pregnant. Later on she dances in shameless exaltation "before her Creator in exemption of man." And when Will accidentally comes upon her he is burned and consumed into obliteration by her dancing. The chapter's title is "Anna Victrix." The Phoenix-Rainbow balance is destroyed, but this is at least in part due to Will's allegiance to an equally ill-balanced, patriarchal church. The struggle continues between them and then within their child, Ursula. Because Lawrence believed that "male" and "female" are opposites, both between the sexes and within one's own sexual being, existence depends on "inter-opposition": "Remove the opposition and there is collapse, a sudden crumbling into universal nothingness" (C, 6). Hence the Rainbow crown affirms the "perfect balance of the fight" in consummation, whereas for one to triumph is for both to perish. Thus through his creative, revisionary laboring over these archetypal symbols, Lawrence has begun transforming the violent battleground of his parents' marriage into "the fight of opposites which is holy" (C, 18).

As a "self-form" (AR) which integrates both masculine and feminine components of the psyche, the Phoenix serves both as a kind of internalized Rainbow and as a test for Lawrence himself. In *Kangaroo*, Lovat Somers (the Lawrencean persona) is tempted to reinstate the "mystery of lordship" by embracing a brand of proto-fascism. On the good ship of their marriage, *The Harriet and Lovat*, he would like her to yield to his mystery and divination and let him raise his flag of a "phoenix rising from a nest of flames in place of that old rose on a field azure." But he is saved from this "masculine posturing" by a "streak of sanity" named Frieda—Harriet, in the novel (PL, 191).

"It's a lovely design!" cries Harriet in an imaginary exchange. "But as a flag it's absurd. Of course, you lonely phoenix, you are the bird and the ashes and the flames all by yourself! . . . I don't exist."

"Yes," he said, "you are the nest."

"I'll watch it!" she cried. "Then you shall sleep on thorns, Mister."

"But consider," he said.

"That's what I am doing," she replied. "Mr. Dionysus and Mr. Hermes and Mr. Thinks-himself-grand. I've got one thing to tell you. Without *me* you'd be nowhere, you'd be nothing, you'd not be *that*," and she snapped her fingers under his nose, a movement he particularly disliked.

"I agree," he replied, "that without the nest the phoenix would be— would be up a tree—would be in the air—would be nowhere, and couldn't find a stable spot to resurrect in. The nest is as the body to the soul: the cup that holds the fire, and in which the ashes fall to make form again. The cup is the container and the sustainer."

"Yes, I've done enough containing and sustaining of you, my gentleman, in the years I've known you. It's almost time you left off wanting so much mothering. You can't love a moment without me."

"I'll admit that the phoenix without a nest is a bird absolutely without a perch, he must dissipate in the air. But————"

"Then I'll make a cushion-cover of your flag, and you can rest on that."

"No, I'm going to haul down the flag of perfect love."

"Oh, are you? And sail without a flag? Just like you, destroy, and nothing to put in its place."

"Yes, I want to put in its place this crowned phoenix rising from the nest in flames. I want to set fire to our bark, *Harriet and Lovat*, and out of the ashes construct the frigate *Hermes*, which name still contains the same reference, her and me, but which has a higher total significance."

She looked at him speechless for some time. Then she merely said:

"You're mad," and left him with his flag in his hands. [K, 175—76]

He is then driven to a series of harsh conclusions:

He had nothing but her, absolutely. And that was why, presumably, he wanted to establish this ascendancy over her, assume this arrogance. And so that he could refute her, deny her, and imagine himself a unique male. He *wanted* to be male and unique, like a freak of a phoenix. And then go prancing off into connection with men like Jack Callcott and Kangaroo, and saving the world. She could *not* stand these world saviours. And she,

she must be safely there, as a nest for him, when he came home with his feathers pecked. That was it. So that he could imagine himself absolutely and arrogantly It, he would turn her into a nest, and sit on her and overlook her, like the one and only phoenix in the desert of the world, gurgling hymns of salvation.

Here the symbol is handled like a shared object; it is consciously tested and toyed with, passed back and forth, altered and adapted and fitted into the current relationship in such a manner as to bring to mind Winnicott's formulations on "transitional phenomena" and "subjective objects," inhabiting an intermediate sphere of experience that allows for an interplay of reality and illusion.[6]

The dialectics of the novel are fairly simple. Somers finds himself fed up with prevailing varieties of Christian Democracy and embarks on a quest for a "new-life-form." In Australia he encounters the clash of diametrical opposites. Willie Struthers is heading up a proletariat movement, and on the opposite end a number of returning army veterans have cast their lot with Benjamin Cooley, who offers a form of benevolent despotism. The allure for Somers is the same as Lawrence's abiding need to establish some kind of strong bond—be it *blutbrüdershaft* with Cooley or being mates with the Aussie vets—which will preserve his singleness against the engulfing powers of woman.

This need, however, pits Harriet against Cooley, the Kangaroo of the title. "And he *was* a kangaroo" (K, 105), but a most ambiguous figure, now like Jehovah with a "pondering, eternal look," and now like a "sheep," a blending of the beautiful and the ugly:

For Kangaroo was really ugly: his pendulous Jewish face, his forward shoulders, his round stomach in its expensively tailored waistcoat and dark grey, striped trousers, his very big thighs. And yet even his body had become beautiful, to Somers—one might love it intensely, every one of its contours, its roundness and downward-drooping heaviness. Almost grotesque, like a Chinese Buddha. And yet not as grotesque. Beautiful, beautiful as some half-tropical, bulging flower from a tree. [K, 112]

His gender is nominally male, but, as a man among men and one who has turned away from women, it is also most ambiguous. The "kangaroo is the king of the beasts," but this one would use his "pouch to carry young Australia in" (K, 116, 118). "I offer myself," he tells Somers, "my heart of wisdom, strange warm cavern where the voice of the oracle steams in from the unknown" (K, 111). His

failure, in Somers's eyes, is the denial of true oppositions. Identifying himself hermaphroditically with the life-principle, he holds
that the only evil lies in resistance to his cause.

In a sense he is a counterfeit phoenix, unwilling to accept dualism and the death-principle, and so he must die from a fatal bullet
in the bowels of his pouch, delivered by his opposite number
Willie Struthers. And Lovat Somers goes back to the composite of
his marriage aboard the good ship *Hermes* (her and me) and affirms by his resistance to the bowellike pull of Cooley's love-of-
humanity doctrines the spinal independence and ambivalence
compressed into his own *Lovat*: Love-hate. Cooley remains fixed
"as odd as any phoenix bird I've heard tell of. You couldn't mate
him to anything in the heavens above or in the earth beneath or in
the waters under the earth. No, there's no female kangaroo of his
species" (K, 102). If the animal symbolizes bisexuality, the character evokes the dreaded Phallic Woman.

In the course of the story, Somers meditates on an alternative to
universal benevolence and revolution, one that may at least make
him lord of his own marriage:

[He] must open the doors of his soul and let in a dark Lord and Master for
himself, the dark god he had sensed outside the door. Let him once truly
submit to the dark majesty, break open his doors to this fearful god who is
master, and enters us from below, the lower doors; let himself once admit
a Master, the unspeakable god: and the rest would happen. [K, 178]

The "dark god he wished to serve" was the god from whom the
"dark, sensual passion of love emanates. . . . He wanted men once
more to refer to the sensual passion of love sacredly to the great
dark God, the ithyphallic, of the first dark religions" (K, 205).

5

*. . . Lucifer is brighter now than tarnished Michael or shabby Gabriel. All things fall in
their turn, now Michael goes down, and whispering Gabriel, and the Son of the Morning will laugh at them all. Yes, I'm all for Lucifer, who is really the Morning Star. The
real principle of Evil is not anti-Christ or anti-Jehovah, but anti-life. I agree with you
in a sense, that I am with the anti-Christ. Only I am not anti-life.—Lawrence,
12 June 1929*

When Lawrence discovers himself in close contact with the "first dark religions," the "unspeakable god" assumes a name. He is called Quetzalcoatl, the Plumed Serpent.

In Hebrew accounts, where phoenixes are not viewed as unique, they are joined with *Chalkidri* in attending the journey of the sun. The *Chalkidri* are translated as "brazen serpents."[7] Thus by day sacred birds wing the sun across the heavens, while by night serpents drag him through the earth. In later Egyptian times the Phoenix became a humanized form of a god with the head of the ruler.[8] Likewise, as Kate in *The Plumed Serpent* vaguely remembers, Quetzalcoatl was a sort of fair-faced bearded god, like the later phoenix, associated with the morning star and traditionally with seasonal winds, fertility, and renewal. As a dying-reviving god he is reputed in one version to have immolated himself by burning, his ashes turning into birds, his heart into the morning star.[9] Like the young Phoenix rising renewed from its nest of flames, man must win "his own creation inch by inch from the nest of cosmic dragons" (PS, 299). That a classical line from Egypt should also connect the newly born worm with the serpent of night and with the primeval waters from which the rising Phoenix must separate, further connects the two myths.[10]

Now adrift in Mexico, Kate Leslie, the widow of an Irish patriot, thinks of the god as having receded from the Aztecs: "Gone back as a peacock streaming into the night, or as a bird of Paradise, its tail gleaming like the wake of a meteor" (PS, 61). "Quetzal," she had read, "is the name of a bird that lives high up in the mists of tropical mountains and has very beautiful tail feathers. . . . Coatl is a serpent." The bisexual composite is divine as well as corrective of the fearful lamia image of woman as "serpent which mesmerizes the fated, helpless bird," and then crushes him in her powerful arms (AR).

It is also something of a reversal. The coatl images—dragon, reptile, lizard, salamander—emphasize aspects of vitality, "cosmic, half-evolved, inert or fiery energy," in turn, whereas the snake is "primarily an ordinary living animal."[11] The coatl energy, be it cosmic, earthly, or human, is "simultaneously creative and destructive," but is mostly associated with the two leading male characters. The quetzal image is found to have no similar "set of synonyms to serve as a structural basis." But regardless—perhaps because one occupies a lower realm, the other a higher—coatl leans more to the instinctual and unconscious, quetzal more to

62

the rational and conscious end of the spectrum. Mexico is more coatl and male; Europe is more quetzal and female. Thus Kate finds in the sex act that the "beak-like Aphrodite of the foam" type of orgasm with its sharp birdlike frictional excitement must yield to the deeper lava flow of the Mexican volcanic vitality. And as she succumbs to the coatl pull of her gravity, she loses the older sense of wonder "when she spread the wings of her own ego, and sent forth her own spirit" (PS, 481). At the end her spent, European individualism is wrapped around by Mexican blood-unity. "You won't let me go!" is the final ambivalent line of the novel. The serpent has snared the bird.

As Quetzalcoatl is also Jesus' dark twin, returning rejuvenated, Christianity is pulled into the cycle of nature. There are to be no further flights out of life. The day of worshipping the sun of the Catholic Church is drawing to a close as the morning star of Quetzalcoatl is drawing near. The catalyst of this ancient worship is the aristocratic Don Ramon and his Indian general, Don Cipriano. With both of them Kate becomes vacillatingly involved, bringing her own brand of love-hate meant to epitomize the tenacity and failure of Western individualism. The two men work out their *blutbrüdershaft* in an idiosyncratic series of rituals, and after Don Ramon rises from the ashes of a wound similar to that suffered by Cooley, the two men set out to revive the virility of the natives; meanwhile Kate, whose need for singleness is compromised by a widow's loneliness and impending middle-age, becomes a reluctant Malintzi, the priestess bride of Cipriano, though even to the last she retains her ambivalence toward this programmatically savage, dionysian cult.

6

No mind can engender until it is divided in two.—Yeats, Autobiography

It may now be fairly evident that the composite symbol is extensive in the topography of Lawrence's work. He not only projects patterns of vital opposition onto nature and reinterprets traditional symbols in myth and art, but he also conceptualizes reality in patterns of opposites, like the "coinciding contraries" of Bruno, Blake, and Joyce.[12] Thus presented, thought processes can be both ritualized onto diurnal and seasonal cycles (light, spring, renewal; darkness, autumn, dissolution) and psychologized into male-female polarities.

Onto history he also casts two great conflicting principles, which he often delineates in confusing, quasi-biblical terms. In the beginning was the Father, the prime mover and great lawgiver of the cosmos. Eventually he was supplanted by the Son, who is the Word. Insofar as these terms coincide roughly with biblical eras, the Son is identified with spiritualized Love, while the Father (Law) can only now be approached through woman as Flesh. And for this task the Son as mere mental consciousness is ill-equipped. Although there is no reconciliation between the eternal opposites of Law and Love, a new era is anticipated, which is to be the coming of the Holy Ghost or Paraclete as Comforter and Reconciler. In the meantime, only certain natural images like roses and "artistic form" itself can reveal the "two principles of Love and Law in a state of conflict yet reconciled" (PS, 477).[13]

Because these polarities can be found in the novels in almost identical form, albeit within a richer and more ambiguous texture, one can conclude that as creative artist and creative thinker Lawrence was essentially in harmony with himself. We follow his advice to trust the tale, not the teller, but often enough it turns out that the tale's tail is tucked in the teller's mouth. And perhaps the best connection between the two is the great composite symbols. So now when we consider them on a more complex and intensely sexual level we have been confirmed of their importance.

7

[Have you observed that] the sexual theories of children are indispensable for the understanding of myth?—Freud to Jung[14]

Traditionally both Quetzalcoatl and the sacred Phoenix have had unusual properties related to fertility and renewal. Quetzalcoatl had a reputation as a miracle worker whose greatest achievement was the creation of man. He thus resembles Jehovah and Prometheus. And the Phoenix is not so much the creation of life as the life process itself. He compresses the act of sexual union along with the act of birth; or simply death and rebirth. And whereas both are male, neither needs a mate for the act of reproduction. This suggests a peculiar mingling of religious purposes and psychological forces.

As the Phoenix reproduces his own kind without female intervention, he recalls other patriarchal myths of Eve's creation from Adam's rib, of Zeus giving birth to Athena from his fertile brow, and of Prometheus making man from mud figures. As a composite (bird, nest, worm) he recalls other mythological composites, chief among whom is the Sphinx. This fascinating creature, who possesses the head of a lion, the body of a woman, and the wings of a large bird, has been understood psychoanalytically as the sexually combined parents in the act of reproduction. The images refer to male, female, and the wings of sexual excitement; hence the answer to its riddle is man, the child as the resolution of this animal configuration. In at least one account the Phoenix is given a Sphinx-like composition: the feet and tail of a lion, the head of a crocodile.[15] Lawrence himself appears impressed by its talons.

There are various reasons for the perception of parental intercourse being rendered in bestial terms. One of these is that children, in pondering the riddles of adult sexuality, often refer to direct observations of animals, which are then superimposed onto humans. This common tendency also coincides with children's fear, confusion, or ignorance about the presence or functon of female genitalia, resulting in such aberrations as the cloacal theory of sexual intercourse, the *à tergo* position. Along with ignorance, castration fears may further prompt the substitution of the anal for the genital, and the common enough sight of the bird perched on the nest out of which babies soon appear would easily confirm anal birth theories. Because of the adherence of olfactory and excremental components to the Phoenix myths,[16] its psychoanalytic import suggests fantasies of anal birth. The Phoenix thus plays a variation on mythological versions of birth along with the Sphinx, Athena's springing from the forehead of Zeus, and the mud-baby process in Genesis that produced Adam. Inasmuch as Primal Scene schema in both classical and idiosyncratic variants virtually pervade Lawrence's imagination, we should not be surprised to find them grounded in the conditions of his childhood and ultimately in his unconscious as distorted memory-fantasy fragments of parental intercourse. Accordingly, behind and through his composite symbolism we can glimpse the conflicting male and female identities at war in his psyche.

8

"Childhood memories" are only consolidated at a later period, usually at the age of puberty; and . . . this involves a complicated process of remodeling, analogous in every way to the process by which a nation constructs legends about its early history.—Freud, "Family Romances," 1909

As we plunge into Lawrence's early years, the reader may be surprised that the author manages to genitalize this myth in the ways quoted above. Indeed, it is remarkable to find that although the woman is the fiery nest of his death and renewal, he is nonetheless giving birth to something in himself. To arrive at the full implications of the self-renewing Phoenix we turn to Lawrence's life where his tendencies to polarize the world of experience are first manifested. His "father was a collier, and only a collier," he writes (N, 7); his mother, who spoke the King's English and read poetry, had cultural aspirations. Her father was an engineer and a "fiercely religious" preacher in the Methodist Church, and her grandfather had been a well-known hymn writer (PL, 9). Lawrence's own father read nothing but the newspaper, and while the class differences of the parents have perhaps been exaggerated by Lawrence, in point of fact it *was* his father who went into the dimly lit mines at the age of seven, and it *was* his mother who took a strong hand in the children's enlightenment. In the house they spoke proper English, in the street the father's Nottingham dialect. But the household was polarized along more than social and religious lines. The father was fond of animals and encouraged the children to have pets; yet when they brought home a dog or a rabbit, the mother objected to having the messy things around. The father would come home covered with coal dust, but the children were clean and fastidious in their dress. "My father was a working man," runs a later poem. "My mother was a superior soul. . . ."

We children were the in-betweens
little non-descripts were we. . . .
  [CP, 490]

But apparently they did not remain in-betweens for long. In the tug of war of family loyalties, the mother quickly won them over to her camp, though not without much later regret on their part. "I can remember my father as a handsome man of medium height with black wavy hair, dark brown beard and moustache," writes the younger sister. "I wonder if there would have been quite so much misery in our childhood if mother had just been a little more tolerant" (N, 10). Lawrence, who early on shared the mother's intolerance and sense of superiority, would devote much of his later literary efforts to rehabilitating the common male to uncommon rank. But in the short run even his father seems to have succumbed to the mother's superiority, vowing after her death that he would never again marry: "I've had one good woman—the finest woman in the world, and I don't want another." But her victories did not come cheap.

That Lawrence sided with his mother, even identified with her at profound levels of his personality, need not exclude his strong feelings of ambivalence. The manifest signs of his identification are easy to read. He was a "scrupulously clean, neat, and tidy child"; would never "tolerate dirty or vulgar stories"; often preferred girls' company to that of boys, and was teased for being a "mardarse" (sissy). Along with his mother's puritanism, he also identified with her contempt for things "common" and considered himself a naturally "superior" person. It was his mother's "one desire to see him become a great writer," according to Jessie Chambers; and he was able to place his first novel in her hands during her final illness. Unfortunately it was too late for her to respond, which is perhaps just as well, for earlier she had seen a draft and expressed shock at one of the mildly sexual passages: "To think that *my* son...." In fact the *way* he became a writer, as well as the *kind* of writer he became, best illustrate his problematic maternal identifications.

An odd detail—one of those illogical pieces of biography that doesn't want to fit into the evolving design—will open up this line of inquiry. In the summer of 1923 Lawrence had left Mexico, where he had begun *The Plumed Serpent*, and accompanied Frieda as far as New York. Instead of returning to England with her, significantly to visit her children, he about-faces and heads west. After stops in Buffalo and Los Angeles, he is on a train bound for Mexico with his Danish friend. Lonely, obviously restless, he is also fatigued from all his traveling and writing (Frieda will later say during his grave illness the following year in Oaxaca, that writing the Mexican novel took too much out of him).

There then appears in Moore's biography an odd little detail: "But with all the hazards and fatigue of travel, Lawrence worked on a novel during that trip" (PL, 375). Not resting? One reads on. "He was rewriting a manuscript recently sent to him by the nurse he and Frieda had met in Australia." He had offered to help her recast the work, and "their names could appear as collaborators or they could invent a pseudonym." Granted "she had a gift for writing," but why should he thus devote his precious time? It hardly makes sense for a major writer—especially one who sensed that his time was running out. When the book did come out as *The Boy in the Bush*, it turned out to be little more than an adventure story, with the "rough background of the Australian frontier, which Miss Skinner supplied, touched up with Lawrencean gusto" (PL, 375). It slowly dawns on one that what carried Lawrence along on this dubious enterprise was the opportunity for collaboration.

It may be recalled that work on the Australian novel occurred during a separation from Frieda, one which, for awhile at least, Lawrence believed would be permanent. But in the early years of their marriage Lawrence had completed *Sons and Lovers* and the two novels, *The Rainbow* and *Women in Love*, which grew out of the work in progress called *The Sisters*. This was perhaps an apt designation for the collaboration, for Frieda, who is often linked with such fictional heroines as Ursula or Kate Leslie, took an active part in their production. "I lived and suffered" *Sons and Lovers*, she claimed, "and wrote bits of it" when asked how his mother might have felt in certain situations—an excellent example of how the creative process can go hand in hand with the emotional process of restoration following mourning (NI, 56). Indeed, Frieda seems to have midwifed the later work on the novel as Jessie Chambers had midwifed its earlier stages.

Before Frieda there had been Helen Corke. In 1908 at the fatal age of twenty-three—fatal because it was the age at which his older brother William died—Lawrence left home to become a teacher in the London suburb of Croyden. Early the next year he met Helen Corke, a colleague. She had just recently undergone a disturbing experience. Her music teacher, after a few days holiday with her on the Isle of Wight, had returned to his wife and family and committed suicide. Lawrence persuaded her to show him her diary, and soon both were embarked on writing different fictionalized accounts of the "theme"—his to be called *The Trespasser*, hers to be called *Neutral Ground*. She recalled that he was to show her "his work as it grows; nothing shall stand with which

I am not in agreement. It will be a finished study, based on my fertile suggestions" (CR, 7). He also showed her his other writing, and "they enjoyed long and intimate literary discussions" (MW, 69). Her resistance to his sexual advances is presented in many of his poems. Once when she showed him her poem, "Fantasy," he reworked it into his own, "Coldness in Love." "I always feel," he explained, that "when you give me an idea, how much better I could work it out myself" (PL, 102).

Lawrence's competitive collaborations with Helen Corke soon came to end, but he had only been on loan, as it were, bound by a prior arrangement with his earliest and chief secret sharer, Jessie Chambers. All his poetry belonged to her, he insisted, and it was she who sent off his first poems to be published (in the *English Review*) and made possible his meeting with Ford Maddox Hueffer. Her role in criticizing the early manuscripts of *Sons and Lovers* and forcing Lawrence to be more true to reality is justly celebrated. More than anyone else, she came closest to being his muse. If only they had been able to discover a way of dealing with "that," as Lawrence awkwardly referred to his sexual needs in a conversation with her. As it was, he claims that had it not been for her he would have destroyed all his early poems (P, 252). He was not so confident or brave in allowing his early writing to fall in the hands of men. Once he sent a sampling to G. K. Chesterton and received a note back from his wife with the material unread. "I've tried and been turned down, and I shall try no more," he lamented to Jessie, who continued to try for him until success came.

Before then, it had been her nearby family farm that had provided him with breathing space away from his intense family conflicts, and where he felt first accepted as a person. It was also there that he and Jessica initiated the creative process by poring over literature and nurturing each other from its resources; and there that he realized his first incentive to write a joint endeavor which he specified as "I its creator, you its nurse."[17] Thus, his partnerships with women could affirm a similarity of interests while allowing him to assume an ostensibly male role, if still a pre-oedipal one in its affiliation with the maternal function.

Lawrence also shared the creation of his first novel, *The White Peacock* (and its various drafts, *Laetitia*, and *Nethermere*), with Helen Corke, Jessie Chambers, Blanche Jennings (a woman who worked for the postal service), Alice Dax (her married, feminist

friend), and with his mother ("he and his mother criticized it together, and he rewrote parts of it until it satisfied them" [N, 72]).
His mother's family name of Beardsall is borrowed for the characters, who are drawn very close to the Eastwood originals.

The collaborations with Blanche Jennings and Alice Dax turn
up more surprises. Unlike the others, neither of these provincial
women was apparently very literary, yet Lawrence waited on their
reactions with bated breath as if they were the ultimate arbiters in
literary craft. Their qualifications must have resided primarily in
their gender. To Blanche Jennings he revealed one set of motives
when he wrote: "Because you are nearly a stranger, and one may
always scatter the seeds of one's secret soul out to a stranger,
hoping to find there fertile soil to replace exhausted home earth,
to which we will not, even cannot confide what is precious to us,"
he will come to her with "that sore, that sickness of mine which
is called *Laetitia*" (CL, 8). Alice Dax's pregnancy heightens Lawrence's play of fantasy. He refers to the unborn child as his "pretty
sister Phyllis" and envisions Alice reading his *Laetitia* in bed. The
unborn child and the unpublished book come to be seen as equals
and rivals. "I do not expect Mrs. Dax to give me back my tiresome
girl *Laetitia* until my sweet sister Phyllis? has had a fortnight to
oust me" (CL, 8). But what clinches the connection is that Lawrence's working title approximates the name of his younger sister,
Ada Lettice. If their book is their baby, then their partnership can
be seen as corrective, a replication in the creative sphere of the
procreative Primal Scene.

After much coy complaining to Blanche Jennings about Alice
Dax's failure to appreciate his books, he refers to Miss Jennings's
apparent desire to pass the book on to a friend: "It seems to me my
little girl's circle of feminine acquaintances is soon to be quite
large; she has not a male friend, poor child" (CL, 19). The book, it
seems, is fated to repeat Lawrence's own childhood. After such extensive midwifery it is not too surprising that upon publication,
one contemporary critic assumed it to be written in the "feminine
hand."

A few years later Lawrence will insist that "man is not a creator"
(SY, 36); "fatherhood's a myth" (WB, 290); "only woman can create,
properly speaking." And so "there is no getting of a vision . . . before we get our souls fertilized by the *female*," for "the only re-
sourcing of art, revivifying it, is to make it more the joint work of

man and woman" (CL, 291, 198). Just as in the Primal Scene, the creation of art requires two complementary partners; and the author's continuing collaborations with women confirm their part in "authorizing" his creative fantasies.

These conclusions must remain tentative for the present. We will be satisfied by having established that important to Lawrence's creativity is a peculiar but profound kind of feminine identification related to childbearing. Such identifications stemming from very early processes are easily obscured by later and more visible oedipal roles; and then the earlier material—which may have established in large part so individual a way of living and relating to the world-at-large—is never brought to light. By the same token, a Jungian analysis of the composite symbols would reveal archetypal vistas, and invite speculations on the composition of, say, the mandala of the self. Our own interest, however, centers on the more elusive questions of how the creative writer becomes.

10

Every man as long as he remains alive is in himself a multitude of conflicting men.—ST

And women, one might want to add. But of equal interest to Lawrence's feminine identifications is his struggle to implement his masculinity. In an early letter to Blanche Jennings, he expresses a remarkable freedom to move within the range of the sexes, as though as artist he was neither one nor the other:

Various folk vibrate to various frequencies, tones, whatever you like. Now a woman's soul of emotion is not so organised, so distinctly divided and active in part as a man's. Set a woman's soul vibrating in response to your own, and it is her whole soul which trembles with a strong, soft note of uncertain quality. But a man will respond, if he be a friend, to the very chord you strike, with clear and satisfying timbre, responding with a part, not the whole, of his soul. [CL, 22]

An opportunity thus arises for establishing deeper correspondences among Lawrence's sexually composite symbols, his dualistic mode of consciousness, and his divided sexual identity.

The term *bisexuality* implies constitutional roots, a condition Freud held to be innate; but it may also be stimulated by defensive identifications with both parents, prematurely provoked by violent scenes such as portrayed in *Sons and Lovers*. Lawrence, a shy, teased, sniffly lad, came out of himself and first gave vent to his creative impulses when as an adolescent he began to visit the Haggs' farm (Miriam's family): "It was really a new life began in me there." "He became almost one of the family," recalls Miriam's real-life original, Jessie Chambers. What is surprising are his choices of roles. He appeared to be equally satisfied haymaking with the men ("work goes like fun when Bert's there," said the father) as with cooking and cleaning house with the women ("I should like to be next to Bert in heaven," said the mother). A similar dualism is played out during the early war years when he is haymaking and carousing with the Cornwall farmhand, John Thomas, while living with Frieda. Subsequently, during his first winter in Taos with his two young Danish painter friends, Lawrence finds himself contentedly chopping firewood and horseback-riding as well as baking their bread. Moreover, emotional ties with the two Danes were established by sharing in creative work. One was to paint Lawrence's portrait; the other was to illustrate his books. It was through this appeal that the young men cast their lot temporarily with the Lawrences. On a later visit it was Dorothy Brett who accompanied the Lawrences, and although her collaboration was confined to typing his manuscripts and to working on an occasional painting together, she was fitted into the virginal Miriam-role against which Frieda, herself cast in the sensual role, at length bridled and insisted that either the other two should have an affair or Brett should go. (Brett went.)

These recurring patterns suggest that Lawrence struggled to align his mental pictures of reality with his external relationships, while enacting in a sublimated fashion a sort of bisexuality—for his earliest identifications appear to include both parents as well as their highly conflicted relationship. The question of how his early environment began shaping his inner reality can now be addressed.

As a never-too-hale infant and toddler, Lawrence shared close quarters with parents who were making love along with doing battle. It was during this period of his sister's conception and shortly thereafter that primal identifications with both parents likely took place. Róheim once remarked that the Primal Scene is so overwhelming that the child's only recourse is to internalize this strange compilation of love, power, and authority.[18] Similarly, Winnicott states that if the parents quarrel in front of the child at a time when he is occupied by other concerns, such an experience—beyond his power to deal with—is handled by identification. This "internalized bad relationship" may result in depression, fatigue, or physical illness; the child may even behave as if possessed by the quarreling parents and act "compulsively aggressive, nasty, unreasonable, deluded."[19] In "The Drive to Become Both Sexes," Lawrence Kubie makes it clear that he is not describing a basic instinctual drive, but instead one that grows "out of early preconscious and guiltless identifications and misidentifications, rivalries, envies, hostilities, and loves."[20] These multiple identifications are not the kind which make for happy androgyny. On the contrary, the result is a deep "inner schism in the personality," in which "everything becomes split."

This earliest period is elided from *Sons and Lovers*, which begins in the second family residence, The Bottoms, and continues until the family moved again (Lawrence was going on seven) to the Walker Street house on the brow of a hill. In front was a "huge old ash tree." After the children had gone to bed they could hear their mother by herself sewing below.

Having such a great space in front of the house gave the children a feeling of night, of vastness, and of terror. This terror came in from the shrieking of the tree and the anguish of the home discord. Often Paul would wake up, after he had been asleep a long time, aware of thuds downstairs. Instantly he was wide awake. Then he heard the booming shouts of his father, come home nearly drunk, then the sharp replies of his mother, then the bang, bang of his father's fist on the table, and the nasty snarling shout as the man's voice got higher. And then the whole was drowned in a piercing medley of shrieks and cries from the great, windswept ash-tree. The children lay silent in suspense, waiting for a lull in the wind to hear what their father was doing. He might hit their mother again. There was a feeling of horror, a kind of bristling in the darkness, and a sense of blood. [SL, 59 – 60]

In the poem, "Discord in Childhood," the ash tree's "terrible whips" are sexually differentiated between the "slender lash / Whistling she-delirious rage" and the "male thong booming and bruising" until the two voices are drowned "in a silence of blood."

Such troubling and ambiguous impressions of the parents together would ordinarily suggest a screen memory overlaying an earlier Primal Scene sequence—which remains feasible—but here the memory traces of parental violence are not likely to be solely the product of overexcited distortions by the children. In the repression of the erotic element from memory, it appears that sexual activity must be expressed through violence. Clearly, the stamp of traumatic identification is pressed into the next poem, "Cherry Robbers," which presents a strangely poised moment between a youth and a girl (similar to a scene between Paul and Miriam in *Sons and Lovers*) with the ash tree turned into a cherry tree: " . . . like jewels red / In the hair of an Eastern girl / Hang strings of crimson cherries, as if had bled / Blood-drops beneath each curl." Beneath the tree are three dead birds, "Stained with red dye." Nearby, a girl with "Cherries hung round her ears / Offers me her scarlet fruit: I will see / If she has any tears." Or so he boasts; but more likely the taboo against virginity will hold, the vaunted cruelty merely underscoring the oedipal impasse.

For Lawrence, the dilemma is not simply the Sphinx's riddle of adult sexuality as it had been for Oedipus and Freud. To fulfill what emerged as a mission in his prose—namely, to set the sex relation straight between men and women—he must reconcile or assimilate the warring images of the carnal parents which have become indelibly stamped into the very structure of his psyche. In reality he could no more right the wrongs of his parents' marriage than he could undo their traumatic impact. But they could enter his creative womb and reappear in his imagination where they would be represented indirectly, in mythic or symbolic forms, especially in the great composites which presently hold our attention. And then through the give-and-take of his relationship with Frieda et al., the archetypal symbols could be further modified and meliorated.

The record of these processes is discernible in Lawrence's recourse to composite symbolism. We can now conclude that they stand both for the sexually combined or quarreling parents, and also for his own bisexual formations. From a psychological standpoint the two entities appear to be reciprocal. From a creative standpoint, the same symbols which bind up and help to contain or make more manageable the artist's early conflicts also serve to organize the art.

Thus the Rainbow is the objectified balance of sexual consummation, corresponding subjectively with the iris as both witnessing eye and foetal flower; but also as being "arched in their blood"—both "battlefield" and "meeting-ground"—the Rainbow is a transfiguration of the parents' "carnal, bloody" marriage.

What I see
when I look at the rainbow
is one foot in the lap of a woman
and one in the loins of a man.

The feet of the arch
That the Lord God rested the worlds on.

And wide, wide apart,
with nothing but desire between them.
    [CP, 818 — 19]

The Phoenix, as rainbow bird of sexual dying and creative self-renewal, becomes poignantly humanized in the last work of fiction, *The Man Who Died*. The Plumed Serpent is the fierce and fertile joining of heaven and earth. Modulating in different keys and tonalities, these great composites spring from a common matrix and convey essentially the same thought-complex. The Phoenix may also represent for Lawrence not only the consuming flames of sexual passion, but also birth fantasies related to defensive identificatory needs of the critical second year of his life, when his mother was preoccupied with another pregnancy. It is at this juncture of threatened maternal loss—amid a flood of mental images and primary-love ties—that symbol-formation begins and with it the dawning of creative process. For the symbol achieves its distinctive unity through diversity, by a "throwing-together" as its etymology tells us, of strange and perhaps discordant elements. Ultimately, the biparental relationship, as threatening as it is indispensable to the child, can only be reconstituted internally and then it must be mastered by symbolic displacement through the creative process.

As an artist, Lawrence discovered in primitive art, occult writings, and modern anthropology a "universal mystic language" which "consisted in symbols and ideographs" and which confirmed his sense of a myth of primordial unity. And although generally hostile toward psychoanalysis, he suggests in the same 1917 passage that "the whole of psychometry and psycho-analysis depends on the understanding of symbols (SY). The more inclusive psychoanalytic method of reconstruction employed in this section has examined the mutability of symbols as they reveal instinctual patterns, the internalized parents, and emerging self-forms. Symbols blend the unconscious and the conscious into new wholes. Their hidden components notwithstanding, symbols are, due to their communicative powers, clearly adaptive. They condense and convey multivalent meanings, designate boundaries, and clarify relationships; but they do not exhaust the creative enterprise. To do full justice to the scope and depth of Lawrence's creative struggles we will next accompany him on his profoundly subjective descent into the origins of the self as a reconstituted body.

4

Body

*The mind can assert anything, and pretend it has proved it. My beliefs I test on my
body, on my intuitional consciousness, and when I get a response there, then I
accept.*—P, 575

*My great religion is a belief in the blood, the flesh, as being wiser than the intellect.
We can go wrong in our minds. But what our blood feels and believes and says, is
always true.*—CL, 180

I was born bronchial—born in chagrin, too.—CL, 994

1 The Real Body in Creativity

Recalling that the Family Romance serves to restore and regulate
a vulnerable self-esteem which has been damaged through a felt
injury, we can now state the corollary: that creative processes are
initiated as self-remaking.[1] A brief digression may serve to set the
scene. How seriously ought metaphors about the body—or *cor-
pus*—of an author's work be taken? How do such expressions get
started? In a parody of the Mass, James Joyce's alter ego refers
to his art as the "soul's bodiment."[2] And it does seem that the
author's self enters his work in a very real sense—not literally, of
course, but perhaps more than metaphorically.

Many creations of the human mind have been closely modeled
on the human body. Plato's *Republic* is based on a tripartite division of the psyche which is structured after a hierarchical human
anatomy. At the lowest level, corresponding to stomach, bowels,
and genitals (the appetitive), are the artisans, tradesmen, and
laborers; at the heart and lungs are the "spirited" guardians; and
at the head is the philosopher-king. Dante's *Inferno* is an inversion
of Platonic Man, structured to resemble a gigantic human form,
with the head plunged furthest from the divinely radiant sun. In
King Lear there is "only one overpowering and dominating con-
tinuous image": that "of a human body in anguished movement,
lugged, wrenched, beaten, pierced, stung, scoured, dislocated,

flayed, gashed, scalded, tortured and finally broken on the rack."[3] Swift's distorted body imagery in *Gulliver's Travels* has been studied by Phyllis Greenacre.[4] And Joyce's *Ulysses*, in which a human organ is assigned to each section, has been described as a "portrayal of an archetypal man who would never appear and yet whose body would slowly materialize as the book progressed, linguafied as it were into life."[5] Lawrence himself wrote that a novel, "after all this coming into being, has a definite organic form, just as a man has when he is grown" (CL, 330). The fact that Lawrence often referred to novels-in-progress by the names of those characters he had projected himself into—Laetitia for the *White Peacock*, Paul Morel for *Sons and Lovers*—suggests that his work grew as a sort of transplanted self. He first referred to *Lady Chatterley's Lover* as "he," then later as "she," and thought it to be as "beautiful and tender and frail as the naked self is" (CL, 972 – 73).

Thus the body enters works of the mind in ways that may be structural (or diagrammatic), thematic, and metaphorical. There is also, perhaps underlying all of these, the narcissistic mode of perception: the essentially anthropocentric viewpoint of the primitive as well as of the classical and medieval world, right down to Freud's jarring assaults on human narcissism.[6] Freud's accounts begin in the seventeenth century with Copernicus et al., and culminate in the nineteenth and twentieth centuries with himself and Darwin. Yet there is something perennial and persistent in man's locating himself in the center. "As human beings," Michael Polanyi has written, "we must inevitably see the universe from a centre lying within ourselves."[7] Scientists, too, appear to be returning to this ancient view along a different and seemingly more empirical route when they emphasize the singularity of human evolution.[8] (The complementary primary-love or object-relations mode would be to represent prehistory in consecutive matriarchal and patriarchal phases.)

The narcissistic mode (see figs. 1 and 2), based on correspondences between the microcosm and the macrocosm, depends on a two-fold operation which entails (1) the body's being represented in the mind, and (2) the larger geography of the environment's being comprehended by the smaller geography of the body. "All imaginative thought attempts to bridge the gap between man and what is outside him," Leonard Barkin has recently written. "One method of bridging this gap," he continues, "is to see

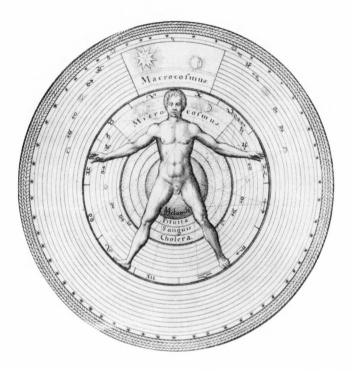

I "I try to keep the *middle* of me harmonious to the *middle* of the universe" (CL, 967 [2/27]).

these two points of reference as fundamentally similar."[9] In the ancient and enduring mode of the occult, man is a "small copy of the great world," the "epitome of the universe."[10] Or, he is "a little world made cunningly," in the sonnet of Elizabethan poet John Donne. Such formulations or schema for relating self and world highlight the difficulty in distinguishing between early representations of the self and others: *I am the world*; but the world gets inside by being introjected, because originally for the infant the mother is the cosmic object. *I am the world because I have taken the cosmic object inside*. The microcosmic self first begins to define itself in terms of a macrocosmic other.

In prescientific thought, to which Lawrence was deeply attracted, correspondences go with influences, like to like. Law-

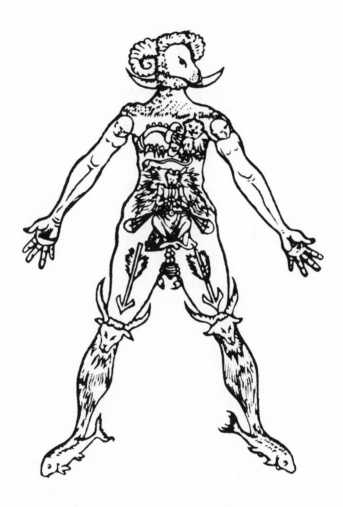

2   "... the clue is in the microcosm, in the human body itself, I believe, and the Zodiac is only used from the table of the Zodiacal Man, and the Man in the Zodiac has his clue in the man of flesh and blood. ... The subtle thing is the relation between the microcosm and the macrocosm. Get that relation—the Zodiac man to me ..." (6/18/23). Zodiak man reproduced from a manuscript in Vienna (National-bibliothek Cod. 11182). It represents in its extremest form the astrological doctrine of the relation between the signs of the Zodiac and the parts of the human body.

rence referred to the way a place "attracts its own human element," and to how a particular "race drifts inevitably to its own psychic geographical pole" (SY, 20). A geography of the psyche—or a psychologizing of geography—may sound strange, but I can think of no better term than "psychic geography" to describe Lawrence's peculiar anatomic mode of perceiving the world. Like the term Family Romance, it seems to yoke contradictory conditions of being and relating. Similarly Eissler's description of a phase of Goethe's creative work as a "constructive disease" may also suit Lawrence. Perhaps such formulations should be referred to as "bridge concepts."[11]

Psychoanalysis reveals a possible genetic basis for the micro / macrocosm position. "Early in its formative process, every concept and its symbolic representatives develop two points of reference, one internal with reference to the boundaries of the body, and one external," according to Lawrence Kubie.[12] This "dual anchorage" forms the basis for acquiring knowledge, and serves as a "bridge between the inner and outer world." And here Kubie makes a crucial point: "The infant experiences his psychic needs as changes in his vague sensory percepts of the parts, the products, and the requirements of his own body." Thus, (1) the "first learning concerns itself entirely with bodily things"; (2) "all expanding knowledge of the non-bodily world must relate itself automatically to that which has already been experienced in the bodily world"; and (3) conceptualizations of the body and the outer world beyond it so interact that each can be "used to represent the other."

Of course Freud had already written that the ego may be regarded as a "mental projection of the surface of the body"—a surface which, he notes, we know from sight as well as from touch.[13] Because these operations stem at least from as early as birth, they necessarily entail distortions. The ego is a distorted representation of the body, just as it is the distorted precipitate of abandoned object cathexes (e.g., Lawrence's internalization of the parental relation).

By analogy with Locke's *tabula rasa*, Lawrence made a living table of body-imagery to read the total self and the dynamic geography of the surrounding world (see table 1). By this means he interpreted for himself—and often for us—the inner significance of the cultures which were perceived as springing from one bodily

Table 1   D. H. Lawrence's "Pollyanalytics"*

I. *Brain*: Seat of ideal consciousness, and moon of reflective love, which has its root in the *idea*
—terminal instrument of dynamic consciousness
—source of the incest motive; knowing is the dead end of an organic process: "To know is to lose. . . . to die" (FU, 108)

II. *Body*: Four-fold psychic activity as dynamic consciousness (also primary, primal, pristine, and the "pure unconscious")
—Correspondence and opposition, both vertically and horizontally among all centers: health as residing in their proper balance

Sympathetic nerve centers	*Voluntary nerve centers*
object-relations	self-realization and realization of
female mode	otherness
	male mode
Cardiac Plexus (heart's mind)	*Thoracic Ganglion* (shoulders)
(modern civilization)	

Objective centers (2d stage: object internalized
and established in environment includes oedipal.)

active respiratory (productive and creative)	passionate discrimination of the object as the other; others are
devotional, ministering	interesting, seat of the imagination,
object-centered love: *you are you*	curiosity
affect of blissful transfusion with	affect of intensity
the beloved derivative: tenderness	aspiration
symbol: sun as light	bull—symbol—animals of prey
Solar Plexus (abdomen)	*Lumbar Ganglion* (spine)
(Egyptians, Etruscans, American Indians)	

Subjective centers (1st stage of separation: pre-object or cosmic object.)

Sexual-alimentary (procreative)	eliminative, urinary, assertiveness,
Processes: imbibing, nurturing	rage, defiance
Basic instincts of love derivative:	hate
sensuality blood-tie (and blood-	
consciousness)	
State of interdependency	strivings toward autonomy
navel-breast-mouth-nipple-hand	kicking
Symbol: lotus flower	symbol: horse, serpent, curled
dark or lower sun, source of energy	cosmic powers at the base of the spine: Kundalini

Primary object-love and primary narcissism:
I am I, one with the universe—I am I, other than all the universe.

*In *Psychoanalysis and the Unconscious* and *Fantasia of the Unconscious*, D. H. Lawrence zone or another. Thus Northern Europe and White America—often modern industrial society in general—correspond to the uppermost centers and circuits of nervous, mechanical energy. Associated with the cardiac plexus was the "intense powerful nodality of that great heart of the world," which was London before the Great War and which "during the war . . . for me broke" (P, 100 – 106). This sundering at the emotional center of his life, which was seen as closely connected with the preceding loss of his mother (that culture's direct embodiment and voice), initiates a series of quests for more profound and lasting connections. If the heart is rent, the solar plexus may yet be sound, and with it the races of healthy ruddy-skinned peoples, often placed in a semi-mythical country called "Egypt." More immediately accessible were the "pristine, unbroken" American Southwest (JF, 110) and Mexico, "the sort of solar plexus of North America" (P, 105). Thus does Lawrence move toward the "lower centres" by means of dual anchorage or psychic geography.

2   The Body in the Mind of the Analyst

But we are maimed, crippled, contorted and sick
When it comes to our emotional selves. [CP, 833]

Lichtenberg has elaborated on three component groups of self-images derived from the body: (1) those of the overall body image; (2) separated-self images; and (3) those of the "grandiose" self.

Throughout the entirety of infantile life, feelings originating within the body unit and on the body surface contribute first and foremost to one grouping of self-images, that of an over-all body image—the body self. Some of these experiences, especially those connected with the body surface and with external perceptions vis-à-vis the care-taking mother, lead gradually to the establishing of body boundaries. These, then contribute to a second grouping of self-images, those of the self as separated from a discretely perceived object. Finally, there are experiences in which body parts are sources of greatly heightened sensations. It is these experiences that lend themselves to the idealization and contribute to a third grouping of self-images—those of the "grandiose" self. In this third cluster of self-images, the self, rather than being felt as differentiated from the object, is experienced as sharing with the object feelings and capabilities of grandiosity and omnipotence.[14]

The "blending and balancing" of these component groupings develops toward a cohesive self and corresponds remarkably well to aspects of the creative self of the artist being considered. Thus:

1.	The over-all body image	$\tilde{=}$	Lawrence's "pollyanalytics," quasi-mystical system of psychology based on the anatomical model of the body (Table 1).
2.	Self-separation images	$\tilde{=}$	The Phoenix process of object-fusion, loss, and rebirth
3.	"Grandiose self" and "idealized parents"[15]	$\tilde{=}$	The Family Romance, which allows full elaboration of these needs through fantasy.

Each of these correspondences has already been mentioned, but the first requires elaboration. Almost contemporaneously with Lawrence's pollyanalytic theories, Freud was writing in *The Ego and the Id* that the "body itself, and above all its surface, is a place from which both external and internal perceptions may spring." Neither these kinds of perceptions nor other bodily sensations found a systematic outlet in Lawrence's early writings. It is very likely that they did not become conscious at all until 1912, when he began his readings in Oriental philosophy and the occult. Chief among these were the Vedas, the Upanishads, Bhagavadgita, Madame Blavatsky's theosophical work, *Isis Unveiled* (1877), and James M. Pryse's *The Apocalypse Unsealed* (1910). References to this body of material begin to appear in Lawrence in 1915 and continue to the end of his life, as in his own *Apocalypse* (1929), though they receive fullest treatment in his two essays, "Psychoanalysis and the Unconscious" (1919) and "Fantasia of the Unconscious" (1921 – 22).

3   The Occult Body in Creativity

. . . so much one has fought and struggled, and shed so much blood and made so many scars and disfigured oneself. But all the time there is the unscarred and beautiful in me, even an unscarred and beautiful body.—CL, 242

Lawrence had been moved by classical Greek sculpture to express these thoughts in 1913, but that "pure" mode of "eternal stillness

84

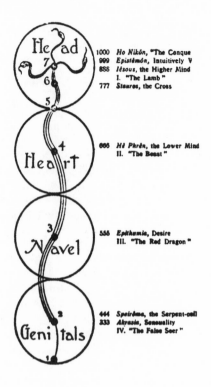

1000 *Ho Nikôn*, "The Conque
999 *Epistḗmón*, Intuitively V
888 *Iēsous*, the Higher Mind
I. "The Lamb"
777 *Stauros*, the Cross

666 *Hē Phrēn*, the Lower Mind
II. "The Beast"

555 *Epithumia*, Desire
III. "The Red Dragon"

444 *Speirēma*, the Serpent-coil
333 *Akrasia*, Sensuality
IV. "The False Seer"

3   From James M. Pryse, *The Apocalypse Unsealed* (1910)

that lies under all movement" would not be his. In 1939 William York Tindall first charted how in 1915, Lawrence was influenced by the peculiar mingling of occult doctrines with anthropological studies (notably *The Golden Bough*).[16] Most revealing of these borrowings is Lawrence's adoption of *Kundalini*. This "electrical life-force" is symbolized by the serpent, which flows along the spine from the "chakra (ganglia, centres) of the loins, through those of the navel and the heart, into that of the head," and through the pineal center of the Third Eye.[17] Lawrence adopted only four of the seven chakras, changed the flow of *Kundalini* from upward to outward, and put it to the uses of polarity, according to Tindall (see figs. 3 and 4).

The implications of these shifts will become clear as we pro-

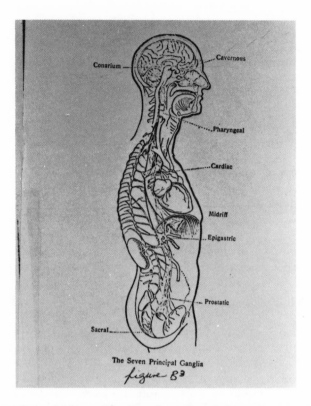

The Seven Principal Ganglia

4   From James M. Pryse, *The Apocalypse Unsealed* (1910)

ceed, but it should be emphasized here that occultism and recent
anthropological rediscoveries of the mythical substratum of humanity served to provide Lawrence with objective correlatives,
approximate as they may have been, for what must have been
hitherto undifferentiated and perplexing bodily sensations, affective states, and inchoate mental processes. "Now I am convinced
of what I believed when I was about twenty," he wrote while reading Frazer, "that there is a blood consciousness which exists in us
independently of the ordinary mental consciousness" (CL, 393).
This discovery might be compared to Freud's discovery of "psy-
chical reality" twenty years earlier. One can begin to appreciate
Lawrence's need to safeguard his realization from the incursions
of psychoanalysis, even if it meant attacking, distorting, and push-

ing his own system to extremes, especially when one takes into account its intimate sources. For this "blood knowledge comes either through the mother ['to the embryo in the womb'] or through the sex ['a transmission, I don't know of what, between her blood and mine, in the act of connection']" (CL, 394). But at least after reading Frazer, he could feel that he was not merely being hysterical and imagining things that could never be.

As it comes to be represented in the mind, the body also comes to represent parts of the mental apparatus. The anatomical system Lawrence devised not only became a way of assimilating the body into consciousness but also of structuring drives, affects, needs, and above all of representing intrapsychic anomalies, lapses, and conflicts (see Table 1). Although intended as an act of corrective self-reconstitution, this sectioning the body and playing-off one part against the other means nothing less than that the organism was felt to be cleft and riddled with inner division. Here Balint's concept of the basic fault nicely corresponds to the series of fault lines in Lawrence's psychic geography. Consciously, Lawrence may have believed he was "only trying to stammer out the first terms of a forgotten knowledge." Although this is true, it is not the whole truth, for he was also articulating the body as a highly individualized field of conflict. He knew "that there is war in all the members of man," reports his sometime collaborator on the *Apocalypse*, Frederick Carter, and "he appreciated that in this knowledge lay the whole history of mystical research."[18] He evidently hoped that the anatomical mode would provide a conflict resolution by somehow realizing the "unscarred and beautiful body" he sought in himself. But what he more explicitly seeks is a balancing of forces and polarities between lower and upper centers, between sympathetic and voluntary modes, and among all their crisscrossing diagonals. Once achieved, the person may then seek out a correspondingly balanced other.

Others, in fact, have been present all along, for not only does Lawrence's commentary ingeniously outline a development of the self, but it also includes a structuring of influences from object-relations. The pollyanalytic shape of a body is cruciform, and this sign of opposition may bear the imprint of early object-relations as they form opposing identifications, perhaps later to be manifested as a bisexual disposition. In any case the crucifixion is one of Edelheit's primal scene schema.[19] And in his poem, "The Cross,"

Lawrence declares that on the cross of division into sex, "the human consciousness was crucified."

The composition of this construction may now be considered in sharper detail. What Lawrence calls "pristine consciousness" (also "primal," "primary," "pure unconscious," and "blood consciousness") resides beneath the navel in the solar plexus; this center attempts to "heal the new wound [of birth], to re-establish the old oneness" with the maternal organism, and so "directs the little mouth which, blind and anticipatory, seeks the breast." Although its state of being is like the primary narcissism of psychoanalysis—"I am I, the vital centre of all things"—it also demonstrates primary love in its need to reconnect with the newly separated object: "The child is drawn to the mother again."

Balancing this pull of the sympathetic center is the "blind almost mechanistic effort on the part of the new organism to extricate itself from cohesion with the circumambient universe." This resistance rises from the great voluntary nerve center at the base of the spine: the "little back has amazing power once it stiffens itself" and "kicks away, into independence" (PU, 23 – 24). "Hence, a duality, now, in primal consciousness in the infant," and with it the beginnings of a sense of self.

The "diaphragm really divides the human body, psychically as well as organically," between the lower centers and the ones directly above. Here are located a more developed sense of self and object, and Lawrence takes pains to designate the upper centers as *objective*. The cardiac plexus continues the operations of its lower complement; only now there is greater object regard, based on the perception, "You are you." The ministering, devotional sort of love that rises from love of mother (et al.) as a definite person is balanced by the thoracic region, which induces an "objective realization" and a "passionate discrimination" of the beloved object, i.e., comparison with others. Thus, "consciousness develops on successive planes." On each is the "dual polarity, positive and negative, of the sympathetic and voluntary nerve centers" (PU, 34).

Removed from this dynamic system is the "seat of ideal consciousness" in the brain. It is the "terminal instrument" which "transmutes what is a creative flux into a certain fixed cipher" (PU, 46), and invites idealizing about the "human spirit." Against this solipsistic "self-aware-of-itself" is pitched radical self-awareness and "vital sanity" (P2, 76). But it is at the extreme remove from the body that Lawrence locates the source of incest motive in a virtual inversion of psychoanalytic instinct theory. The incest motive is an *idea*, a "logical deduction of the human reason which is introduced into the affective, passional sphere, where it now proceeds to serve as a principle for action" (PU, 11). It is sex-in-the-head that disposes the boy to share his mother's bed. Culture, not nature, is to be blamed. Paradise can be regained. But although Lawrence has actually painted Adam heaving the apple at Jehovah, the venerable gentleman does not vanish—nor does mental consciousness, nor, presumably, the incest motive. In his Freudian revisions, Lawrence has evidently confused the instinctually rooted drive with the socially imposed prohibition against it—the wish for the taboo.

Although a strict psychoanalytic reading of these passages would conclude that the anatomical model has been twisted to serve defensive needs, a close reading of the total text might take us even further to conclude that the whole history of parent-child relations may be read therein. Not that one would want to prove this, of course. But it may be sufficient if we now view the pollyanalytic system as a complex yet believably coherent group of body images wherein a history of early development—part fact, part fantasy—may be studied. Initially it is really neither the occult connections nor the psychoanalytic inversions that are arresting about Lawrence's organicism, so much as its being so tortuous a system for anyone to come to terms with, as well as in its own way so highly conceptualized. And Lawrence himself, when he had paused long enough to contemplate his as yet uncompleted "eightfold polarity" within a "fourfold circuit," had to acknowledge the compounding of difficulties in achieving balance, both within the person and between persons. "It may be that between two individuals, even mother and child, the polarity may be established only *fourfold*, a dual circuit." One of the spontaneous circuits may never be established. "This means for the child, a certain deficiency in development, a psychic inadequacy" (PU, 44). Included in the chakras or nerve centers which Lawrence does not treat are those of the Higher Mind and the genitals: "In public it would hardly be allowed us to hint at them" (FU, 49). And it is not for several years, not until *Lady Chatterley's Lover*, that he attempts to open the body's seven seals or ganglia, which now is believed to have occurred in the novel's seven key sexual encounters and to involve the man as much as the woman.[20]

Remarkable indeed is the absence of any phallic development in the system. It is as if part of the body surface had been scomotized (i.e., blanked out). No less remarkable is the virtual absence of the father in the developmental scheme. His belated entry in the essays and the rather contrived business of fitting him in only underscore the dyadic makeup of the whole operation (FU, 70). The father is real for Lawrence as is the phallus in the later works, but his absence is as marked in molding the topography of the body as are the genitals. The "fucking with a warm heart" which greets the reader in the later work is discreetly veiled in the occult jargon of the former work: "From the hypogastric plexus and the sacral ganglion . . . the dark force of manhood and wo-manhood sparkle" (FU, 213). Lawrence evidently had to overcome an enormous resistance which went beyond shyness: "When I was a very young man I was enraged with a woman, if I was re-minded of her sexual actuality. I only wanted to be aware of her personality, her mind and spirit" (P2, 568).

The deemphasis of anatomical sexual distinctions complicates the bodily self's struggle to differentiate itself from the original object, and instead of phallic-vagina awareness, there is for a long time a persistent blurring in the blood-consciousness insight, "A transmission, I don't know of what, between her blood and mine, in the act of connection" (CL, 394). Consequently the lower cen-ters, the solar-plexus bond, and the mystical assertive power of the *Kundalini* coiled at the base of the spine, are summoned forth from the genie's lamp of occult doctrine to clarify and resolve matters. At best, one feels, these multiple and conflicting identi-fications struggle toward a kind of half-concealed bisexuality—or perhaps a scant ways beyond. But that, of course, is only on an individual level; on a creative level, the story is far different.

4   The Injured Body and the Healing of Self

She said as well to me: "Why are you ashamed?
That little bit of your chest that shows between
the gap of your shirt, why cover it up?
Why shouldn't your legs and your good strong thighs
be rough and hairy?—I'm glad they are like that.
You are shy, you silly, you silly shy thing."—CP, 254

The hallmark of the pollyanalytic system is a perceptual modality which, in emphasizing the primacy of the self over the otherness of the object, may be designated as narcissistic. This mode perceives other objects in terms of self, and that includes the bodily self as already described. Traditionally in psychoanalytic thought this may mean, as we have seen, that the infant assumes mother has a penis. But I am wondering if here the opposite might also attain: mother's "castration" is internalized and the genitals are scomotized—or so Lawrence's topographical texts seem to imply, and so his choice of words suggests when in his youth "some part of the natural sympathy" for a woman's "sexual actuality" had to be "shut away, cut off," a "mutilation in the relationship all the time" (P2, 568). In any case it is possible that a narcissistic attachment to the total body-image along with a magnification and a mystification of its parts, orifices, and functions serve to compensate for, or balance off, significant deficiencies in incorporated masculinity.

What Niederland (1967) finds most engaging about creative individuals are (1) "the presence of a permanent and usually severe injury to infantile narcissism"; (2) the accompanying "rich and florid fantasy life"; and (3) the "circumstances and effects of the unresolved narcissistic injury." Niederland's work encompasses both the clinic and the field of psychobiography. The crucial "narcissistic injury could be traced to feelings of incompleteness derived from early physical frailty or disability, [or] protracted illness in childhood." Thus what emerges is not the physical problem as such, nor the inevitable blows to narcissism which everyone suffers, but a peculiar interrelatedness and a "choice" to represent the one in terms of the other. Although Niederland's first presentations drew much adverse criticism, especially against creativity's becoming too closely associated with anomalous factors, nonetheless, the accumulation of his work over the years grows increasingly persuasive. Clearly, he has tapped into something significant if not altogether universal.

These formulations pertain to Lawrence's early life in light of the following: (1) in his first weeks he nearly died of bronchial pneumonia; (2) as a result of his own frailty and continuing disposition to illness, and out of her own needs, his mother formed an intensely emotional bond with him and, as he grew older, jealously resented his taking an interest in a rival; (3) before he was "hatched out" from the symbiotic union, his mother became pregnant. The sequelae are: a heightened awareness of, and conflict over, the body image; an intense and protracted involvement with the mother, resulting in profound identifications not only with her values and prejudices, manners and tastes, but also with maternal functions; a series of humiliations from peers who teased him as a youth and called him "Mardarse," literally, soft-assed, slang for a sissy, treatment that fostered his resorting to the company of females; and the whole sequence was capped by a humiliating rejection in 1915 during a physical examination for induction into the Army (recounted in *Kangaroo*). The overall result is a reactive sense of innate superiority and a pattern of oscillating periods of illness and creativity—entailing physical loss and renewal—that contributes to the Phoenix sense of self. Frieda's provocative lead that "often he was ill when his consciousness tried to penetrate into deeper strata" (NI, 68) will be taken up later.

Lawrence's actual body, as opposed to its mental representations, was tall, but frail and thin; height aside, it resembled the body type of his mother, who would be typically described as a delicate little vivacious woman (in *Sons and Lovers*: "Paul would be built like his mother, slightly and rather small"). Lawrence's distressing disposition to illness along with his amazing recuperative powers may account at least in part for his component representations of the invalid Clifford Chatterley, fumbling at writing and at the nurse's breast in turn, and the flamelike vitality of the lean gamekeeper, himself prone to pneumonia. The little flamelike bantams who appear so consistently in Lawrence's fiction (Count Dionys in "The Ladybird," Don Cipriano in *The Plumed Serpent*, the Gypsy in *The Virgin and the Gypsy*) along with Lawrence's preoccupation with ruddy-skinned primitives (such as the Egyptians, the Etruscans, and the American Indians), attest both to his Phoenix-like needs to be reborn out of an earlier self (a self diseased, or female-dominated and enclosed) and to a concern with color imagery. "For me," he told Jessica Chambers in his youth, "a brown skin is the only beautiful one" (PE, 111).

The brown or red-skinned males are solar, in touch both with the cosmic sun and the dark, inner sun of the solar plexus (EP, 35). To this blood-consciousness is opposed the cerebral consciousness of white civilization, which is lunar, frictional, and feminine. It is depicted as the "white peacock" that would like to be the

rainbow-hued phoenix. In many stories this brittle, reflected consciousness is shattered like the shell of a "mollusc" (as in "The
Blind Man"). White is an unmanly color, and not only women are
white.[21] Lawrence's own naked flesh was observed by his Danish
friend at an outdoor bathing spot in New Mexico as "ivory whiteness like sculpture." It was so white partly, one must assume,
because it was most often covered, but more probably because
Lawrence was shy about his body and may well have formed
images of it as deficient, due to its propensity to illness, its being
treated as an object of ridicule, and its affinities with his mother's
delicate body-type. Here also lies one clue to his protest against
the overemphasis in modern life on the visual mode of perception,
and his preference for a "democracy of touch." In modern painting, the "optical vision, a sort of flashy photography of eye," is
contrasted with the whole imagination representing "substantial
bodies" (P, 559 − 60). His are to be "organically alive and whole"
(CL, 1067).

And yet in a 1928 painting, "Dance Sketch" (fig. 5), which embodies his central ideas, there is also a distinct deficiency in one of
the figures. The painting is certainly "organically alive" in its sense
of spontaneous rhythm, but it is not "whole," for in order to capture the motion of the male dancer Lawrence has pared his leg
down to a mere stick, thinned out and all but vanished from sight.
This seems to be more than technique. None of the other limbs
suggest such rapid movement, and one's sense of distortion is enhanced by the fact that the far leg is larger and more whole than
the near one. Although it alone is affected, appearing as a withered
limb or grafted-on animal's hind leg, the phallus is rendered in
a remarkably complete manner, a dark center ruddy with blood.
Leading the dance is a ghostly goat, the spirit of Pan, and his
spindly limbs are no doubt drawn consciously to account for
the male's anomalous hindquarters. The brown-skinned male
may represent blood-consciousness; the white-skinned female
mental-consciousness; but she is placed in front of the "damaged"
limb, partly shielding it from our view. In addition, it is her features
only that we see, contributing to the possibility that in effect only
one figure is represented, the androgynous or bisexual self with its
dual consciousness.

As understood in the object-relations approach, creativity is
modeled on early object-loss (i.e., when the mother is still in the

5   *Dance Sketch.* c. 1928. Oil (inscribed Lorenzo) 17 × 15 in. Collection of
Saki Karavas, Esq.

process of being perceived as a whole person), followed by the
struggle to recover the lost relation by reparation and by recovery
on an internal or symbolic level. But Niederland's emphasis on
"an unconscious remaking of the body ego" includes narcissistic
injury or emotional losses to the self (or any of its bodily represented parts) as equally strong creative drives. Moreover, at the
early level from which creativity originates, the differentiation between self and object is not all that sharp, and *object loss may be
experienced as self-loss* (Niederland would say "body-loss"). Thus
what may be involved in this creative process is not so much ego-
regressive, in Ernst Kris's classic formulation, as *ego-reconstitu-
tive.*[22] Lawrence's emphasis on the lower centers as the solution

to modern dilemmas may indeed bear the traces of a regressive process to the pretraumatic period, but the result is a radically new version of the self.[23]

Reconstituting the ego through the recreation of the body image, especially along male lines, may tell us much about the motive behind Lawrence's creative drives. We may also be able to recognize several of the levels these drives operated on. It seems to me that clearly underpinning the need for sexual and social regeneration is the deeper struggle to correct a deficient, in his words too "mentalized" body-image (CL, 981). In this connection we might consider another observation by his Danish friend, who noted that during one of their outings Lawrence mounted on a tall sorrel, towering over the others "like a general."[24] And on their riding parties he always insisted on taking the lead. The horse, so important in Lawrence's imagination, may assist in completing the body image; in his works the horse is consistently a mark of masculinity and vital energy. In *St. Mawr*, the horse of the title fuses its name with its author's in a verbal equivalent to the way the Welsh groom "seems to sink himself in the horse" in a centaur manner. Even the white-loined gamekeeper, Mellors, had been with the cavalry in India.

For self-awareness to become masculine, the body image must include the hitherto elided male genitalia; this corrective process entails disengagement from the mother, renunciation of bisexual superiority, and a quest for a suitable feminine replacement as an erotic love-object. In this he was assisted in no small way by his involvement in the occult, for it was there that he found a means of representing a new stage of development. Though female in Hindu thought, the latent *Kundalini*—or slumbering serpent of mystical energy coiled up at the base of the spine and necessarily associated with the bowels—is referred to by Lawrence's mentor Pryse as synonymous with the paraklete, a "regenerative force," which in Christian tradition is the Holy Spirit, or dove.[25] In Lawrence's earlier treatment (e.g., "The Study of Hardy," 1915), this mysterious being is the unknown Comforter or Reconciler between flesh and spirit, male and female. But in his later writings (e.g., the letters of 1928) "blood consciousness" is clearly identified with the "phallic reality" of *Lady Chatterley's Lover*. Thus a vaguely mystical state of consciousness gradually becomes specified and rooted in the male organism, as the "serpent, with a crushed head, learned to brood along his spine" and discovered his brand of strange sapience.

The chief barrier to a fuller implementation of this process is illustrated in the pollyanalytic system itself and in a painting shortly to be considered. A further look at table 1 discloses an interesting cluster in the upper centers where the devoted love for the mother as a real object is rooted in the area of the heart and lungs. "The nerves that vibrate most intensely in spiritual unisons are the sympathetic ganglia of the breast, of the throat, and the hind brain," Lawrence wrote apropos of Poe (ST, 75 – 80). "Drive this vibration over-intensely, and you weaken the sympathetic tissues of the chest—the lungs—or of the throat, or of the lower brain, and the tubercles are given a ripe field." In the modern period, Lawrence feels that the two lower, sensual centers have been subordinated and suppressed. "We have so unduly insisted on and exaggerated the upper spiritual or selfless mode—the living in the other person—that we have caused already a dangerous overbalance in the natural psyche." Carried too far, the "nerves begin to break, to bleed, as it were, and a form of death sets in."

In his forty-fifth year, after several years of protracted illness, Lawrence (not Poe) died of tuberculosis. Although first formally diagnosed for him five years earlier in Mexico City, it was in all likelihood only the last phase of a chronic condition. To say that the lungs formed the battleground for his intense feelings of love and hate for his mother is but a portion of the truth. "I do believe the root of all my sickness is a sort of rage," he wrote in a 1929 letter. The *root* of the rage he does not attribute to his mother, however, but to Europe, the cultural tradition which she articulated, often in its "ideal"—i.e., decaying, puritanical forms—and inculcated in her children. But as early as 1913, he had placed the blame closer to home, on England:

I am one of those fools who take my living damnably hard. And I have a good old English habit of shutting my rages of trouble well inside my belly, so that they play havoc with my innards. If we had any sense we should lift our hands to heaven and shriek, and tear our hair and our garments, when things hurt like mad. Instead of which, we behave with decent restraint, and smile, and crock our lungs. [CL, 225]

Niederland found among his patients that the afflicted or damaged part of the body, which had brought on the narcissistic

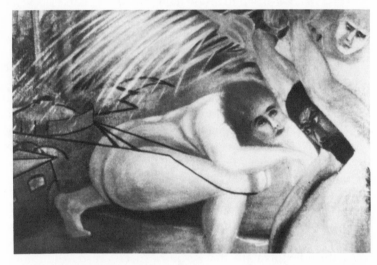

6   "I'm just finishing a nice big canvas, Eve dodging back into Paradise,
    between Adam and the Angel at the gate, who are having a fight about
    it—and leaving the world in flames in the far corner behind her"
    (2/9/27). *Flight back into Paradise.* 1927. Oil (inscribed Lorenzo)
    58 × 39 in. Collection of Saki Karavas, Esq.

wound, had been *hypercathected.* The painting in Figure 6 represents a peculiar Lawrencean scene with a man and a woman, re-
sembling himself and Frieda. The woman (Eve) is bent over and
anxiously trying to escape from the shackles of modern industrial
civilization; the man (Adam) is frantically struggling to disarm the
angel with the flaming sword and thereby to allow Eve's reen-
trance to Paradise. While they battle, Eve slips past, but her bent
posture suggests an imbalance in the spinal ganglia, both lower
and higher, and it seems that her sympathetic centers are running
away with her. The man's anatomy is no less distorted in his enormous chest cavity. Mammary in its swelling, a source of muscular
strength, and oddly tumescent, it renders him peculiarly androgynous. This swollen center is also the direction of the woman's
flight. There may also be a suggestion in this aspect of the composition of the child's tubercular power over the mother, for by falling ill he regresses and regains the threatened or lost object.
Certainly enough ambiguity resides in these figures to speculate

about a reversal, with the female as the helpless, afflicted child, the other figure as the all-powerful mother with the life-sustaining breast. "Have a real stock-taking of my manly breast" opens a stanza in the remarkable cycle of poems celebrating Lawrence's discovery of sexual love with Frieda. But in another place he is chided for covering "that little bit of your chest" (CP, 254). It is worth comparing these images with the second (1927) and third (1928) versions of *Lady Chatterley's Lover*. It is "the white torso of the man" bathing that strikes Connie as "so beautiful" in the 1927 version, whereas in 1928, it is "the pure, delicate white loins." In the former this vision touches her "soul," in the latter her "womb." In the former he had been "maimed" from previous sexual contacts, and "balked and humiliated in his wife"; in the latter he "had a wound from old contacts." A wound can heal, but being "damaged" or "maimed" is more problematic. Some of this healing seems to occur through the process of creative revision and gender specificity: as the body image improves so does the prose.

In any case the ambiguity appears to touch on questions of bisexuality and the blurring of self and other, while the hypercathected chest provides a locus for the grandiose self as merged with the idealized parent. More interesting, the *intensity* of the cardiac plexus circuit may well be the affective transformation of early instinctual processes and responses involving both normal nursing and the more anxious care a mother summons to restore a sick child. The word itself comes from the Latin past participle *intensus*, meaning "stretched out," to which one could add, *toward an object*. To balance the counterdepressive, stretching-out tendency of the cardiac plexus is the passionate urge to objectify, and along with it the faculty of imagination. Here also then is the felt anatomical locus of Lawrencean creativity. It is balanced against both the mother-attraction and the tendency to illness; it strives to restore the object internally and eventually to re-externalize it. Within this context are the terms *inspire*, "to inhale, to impart life," and *aspire*, to "yearn towards the heaven of air and light," a "yearning constant and unfailing" (FU, 79). "Nobody," Lawrence wrote as his mother was dying, "can come into my very self again and breathe me like an atmosphere" (CL, 70). Yet he will soon breathe new life into created forms.

This remarkable interpenetration may be construed as the primary-love complement to the narcissistic mode of perception.

It forms the basis for future interplay with objects in the immediate environment, just as the narcissistic or anatomic mode serves to assign meaning to the larger zones of the environment. Thus Taos Pueblo is like a "dark ganglion spinning invisible threads of consciousness" out of its "old nodality," while in the mountain ranch nearby, Lawrence interacts with a tall pine tree. "With a powerful will of its own it thrusts green hands and huge limbs at the light above, and sends huge legs and gripping toes down, down between the earth and rocks, to the earth's middle." This quasi-human entity "vibrates its presence into my soul," Lawrence writes. "The piny sweetness is rousing and defiant, like turpentine, the noise of the needles is keen with aeons of sharpness. . . . I have become conscious of the tree, and of its interpenetration into my life." And perhaps through this "vast force of resistance" as its "shivers of energy cross [his] living Plasm," he will achieve a balance between it and the sympathetic pull of the Taos Indian Pueblo below (P, 22 – 31; 100 – 106).

The medium for this natural rapport, obtainable between the centered man and his surroundings, must be organic, and it is in this light that Lawrence's narcissistic mode proves most promising. It proposes a natural state in which "the many doors of receptivity in oneself" are opened and the living organism responds to other life-forms through similarity and interpenetration. It accepts the otherness of objects, while rendering them at least in part as self-objects: the tree is figured forth as being both non-human and strangely humanlike. This medium, incidentally, differs from typical Romantic modes of sympathetic identification or ecstatic fusion ("no real truth is ecstasy"; CL, 300), nor is it transcendent and unlimited. Rather it is an enlivening series of correspondences and spontaneous recognitions of parallels and oppositions.

It also appears to have had its less adaptive side. From a developmental perspective, the child's relative physical frailty and the father's minimal participation increased and prolonged interaction with mother. Their mutual availability and interpenetrating emotional needs would retard the separation process, weaken the mother's becoming for her child an internalized shield against instinctual striving, and so impair formation of ego boundaries. The ego's emergence seems to coincide with the picture one conjures of the diseased part of the body itself—the lungs and their delicate membrane which could become inflamed by the "nerves," that is, by emotional stress. Illness might alleviate such conflict by fostering regression to an earlier physical state in which the body was cared for by the mother. Healing becomes a recovery of bodily integrity, and on at least two occasions the creative process accompanies this process of self-reconstitution. During the "sick year" following his mother's death, Lawrence struggled with an autobiographical novel he referred to as *Paul Morel*, but without much progress, until Frieda's arrival on the scene catalyzed it into *Sons and Lovers*. Twelve years later, following the breakup of the mostly nonsexual *ménage à trois* with Dorothy Brett, and another period of grave illness in Mexico, he returned to Taos and wrote his biblical play *David* (1925). Once again the creative process stems from a reconstitution of self for *David* Herbert Lawrence.

5   The Taboo against Naming

*. . . my lungs are crocky, but I'm not consumptive—the type, as they say. I am not really afraid of consumption, I don't know why—I don't think I shall ever die of that."—*CL, 225

During these protracted periods of illness, when the outer world is eclipsed, and to a certain extent the self along with it, Lawrence appears to be reliving the experience of his mother's death—itself perhaps only the climax to a series of disturbing emotional events dating from the infantile period. For it was her relationship which had bound him to the world of objects: "From the death of my mother, the world began to dissolve around me, beautiful, iridescent, but passing away substanceless. Till I almost passed away myself, and was very ill. . . . Then slowly the world came back: or I myself returned: but to another world" (CP, 851). Both as a child and early adolescent, when Lawrence was ill his mother would come to his bed ("Paul loved to sleep with his mother" [SL, 67]). During "convalescence everything was wonderful" (SL, 67); the world being perceived afresh, as Paul describes snowflakes clinging for a moment like swallows on his windowpane, is the world being created anew.

But the real physical organism could comply with these self-reconstituting endeavors for only so long before endangering its own vital systems. Sooner or later the body's ability to resist foreign substances would be weakened, the frayed capillaries along the walls of the lungs eventually would give way, and hemorrhaging would spread until it had become massive. When his mother's death was imminent he described a champagne glass about to be crushed by a hand: "That's how my heart feels . . . [a] crush of misery . . . concentrated in my chest" (CL, 70). And in the "sick year" following, his chest nearly yielded to the crushing pressure felt by that death.

If prior to her death Lawrence's illness had come to mean the retention or recovery of the mother in a profoundly enveloping union, then after her death, falling ill would assume a far more lethal, ambivalent attraction. Illness may no longer be able to reproduce the lost love-object, but it may recreate a sense of the lost object-relation. And although both during the war years and again toward the end of his life Lawrence wrote of a peculiar sense of being "in the tomb" (CL, 309, 993), the wish itself—whether seen as an instance of the hypothetical death instinct or as part of an urge to be reunited with a lost love-object—was on the whole to be repressed. Along with his in-the-tomb feelings are the "glassy envelope, the insect rind, the tight-shut shell of the cabbage, the withered walls of the womb"—sensations which precede or resist the bruising process of self-renewal (P2, 394). The self is "oneness with the infinite," whereas the ego is solipsistic and "stuffed full of clichés that intervene like a complete screen between us and life" (P, 582). The active concentration is always on the resurrected god (or self). It is clear, however, that the reborn self must undergo the life-shattering process of separation, portrayed most searingly in the late poem "Ship of Death":

Now it is autumn and the falling fruit
and the long journey towards oblivion.

The apples falling like great drops of dew
to bruise themselves an exit from themselves.

And it is time to go, to bid farewell
to one's own self, and find an exit
from the fallen self.

Lawrence never forgets that life itself is a Phoenix process where opposites intersect and renewal becomes cyclical. It seems to be the harsh lesson carved into his lungs by his illness, for even up to the last he dreamed of renewal. And what must have sustained him, when he was coughing up blood through the night and too weak for more than a few steps during the day, was an enduring creative romance. In another late poem, in which the journey out of life is imminent, the poet comes to the gate of the naked white moon, "great glorious lady" and "nearest heavenly mansion," and prays that she "will give me back my lost limbs / and my white fearless breast / and set me again on moon-remembering feet / a healed, whole man, O Moon!" And in this extreme utterance, the source of the Rananim-utopia urge for a new "holy centre: whole, heal, hale," is implicitly identified in the moon-mother's power.

Death may not have been denied, but the lengths taken by Lawrence to deny the nature and extent of his illness, to avoid doctors and medical care until they were forced on him, and even to eschew the very word, "tuberculosis,"[26] while substituting such euphemisms as "my poor bronchials" and "chests" or "flu and the grippe," may all be pieces of a pattern.[27] Other pieces may be his resistance to psychoanalysis, his opposition to science *in toto*— especially scientific method and evolution—and his sometimes ill-placed trust in the body's ability to heal itself. "I am tired of being always defeated by bad health," he wrote several weeks before his death (CL, 1235). "But the body has a strange will of its own, and nurses its own chagrin" (recall the caption at the head of this chapter: "I was born bronchial—born in chagrin, too"). "The thing to do is to take one's hands entirely off the body, and let it live of itself, have its own will," he wrote on the same day. "It is by the body we live and we have forced it too much." In addition, a commitment to an occult version of the body could only conflict with modern medicine. The late poems, "The Scientific Doctor" and "Healing," present these disparities:

When I went to the scientific doctor
I realized what a lust there was in him to wreak his so-called science
    on me
and reduce me to the level of a thing.
So I said: Good Morning! and left him.

And

I am not a mechanism, an assembly of various sections.
And it is not because the mechanism is working wrongly, that I am ill.
I am ill because of wounds to the soul, to the deep emotional self
and the wounds to the soul take a long, long time. . . .

Granting some validity to these avoidance tendencies and to their strategic importance in the art, they could still be overdetermined by a deeply private element, which, like the disease, remained unspoken. The missing piece of the pattern then becomes the missing meaning of the illness. There are sufficient grounds for connecting the dangerous yet protected illness with wishes for reunion with the early mother—lost through a chain of separations and death, but never in the core of the self quite relinquished, the candle-flame of the son's life burning itself up on the mother's grave (CP, 115). Implicit is the ultimate merging of wax and earth. The taboo against naming the illness resembles implicitly the taboo against a forbidden union: the *thought* of incest is then repressed by repressing the *word* tuberculosis—at least so one could infer. In that case the continual minting of illness and creativity could in part be the coinage used to bargain with the powers of life and death. The epigrammatic, "To know is to lose," as the highly condensed thought behind the pollyanalytic system of dark knowledge and deeper repression, can be completed as follows: To know one's love to be incestuous is to lose that love. Therefore, in terms of profound emotional attachment, "To know is to die" (FU, 108).

If the drive toward regeneration, which has here been reconstructed as the motive force of creativity, seems to encompass something more archaic, one can only concur that rebirth and renewal cannot be genuinely sought without first having welcomed death. Thus in the above-quoted caption, Lawrence affirms the reality of "consumption" by denying its personal reference ("I don't think I shall ever die of *that*"); but having introduced the idea, he can then reveal to himself that he is "not really afraid" of it, yet not "know why." His conscious mind seems baffled at what may be an unconscious position. But we have now entered the id's realm where one can only speculate and take note of the few dim pointers and signs one passes on the way to its darkest chambers.

6   Individual Stages As Creative Stages

Now she was gone abroad into the night, and he was with her still. They were to-
gether. But yet there was his body, his chest, that leaned against the stile, his hands
on the wooden bar. They seemed something. Where was he?—one tiny upright speck
of flesh, less than an ear of wheat lost in the field. He could not bear it.—SL, 420

Risen from the dead, he had realized at last that the body, too, has its little life, and
beyond that, the greater life.—MD, 177

The direction of the three major creative periods reflect these
processes in numerous ways, which here can only be noted
schematically:

1. *(1912 – 1917) Separation-individuation. Sons and Lovers* and
The Rainbow depict the treacherous coming of age within traditional family groups; the one of a male, Paul Morel, the other of
a female, Ursula Brangwen. *Women in Love* explores amid a gen-
eralized condition of corruption and decay the possibilities of
freer human relationships, stated as "a mutual union in separateness." For the first time *Kundalini* figures in the love-making
scenes between Birkin and Ursula and thereby marks the beginning of a quest for a source of energy "deeper than the phallic," yet
one not derived from the *Magna Mater*. As Lawrence comes to
realize that what interests him is not "the drift toward death" but
"the physic-nonhuman, in humanity," the body becomes more
the central issue. Yet it is usually hidden in the veils of occult
mystification, with the woman pouring over the "strange fountains" of the man's body, and its occasionally perverse functions
being obliquely rendered as "bestial." Interestingly, in the can-
celed prologue to this novel, Birkin's secret of a "passionate and
sudden spasmodic affinity for men" is felt to be the "'ultimate
mark of my own deficiency.'"

2. *(1917 – 1925) Phallic ascendancy in the leadership novels.*
Kangaroo, Aaron's Rod, and *The Plumed Serpent* continue the
above-noted explorations in the direction of the dark gods; the
writing is phallocentric and is either ambivalent toward, or biased
against, the feminine, who is seen as having usurped prerogatives
of the male in modern society. Phallic issues emerge as a kind of
phallicism, often in a hostile, cruel, autocratic context, either as
a sort of weapon or else cloaked in mysticism. This is also the

American period, and the theme running through many of these works is that of the woman of culture who rides away and either dies or suffers her mental consciousness being overwhelmed by emissaries of the lower centers. These creations may be seen as both recapitulating the loss-experience of the mother who rode away to death, and as the son's disengaging himself from her dominating, nonadaptive images (the earlier-noted female-devouring / male-predator axis), while preserving other more beneficial, life-generating maternal images. Overtly, he becomes antifeminist.

3. *(1926 – 1930) The quest for tenderness and sensuality.* Lady *Chatterley's Lover* and *The Man Who Died* struggle to integrate phallic reality in a context of sensuality, tenderness, and concern. The phallus, as Peter Balbert notes, is set free from political power-drives and is given over to spontaneity; it now becomes "the Comforter, the reconciler, the agent of rebirth" and "the bridge to the future."[28] In the former work as Lawrence returns his vision to the same "country of my heart" as *Sons and Lovers*, Mellors speaks the lowly dialect of Morel; yet the gamekeeper is a world traveler and theorist of sex, and it is evident that some attempt at coming to terms with the discredited father is in the making. Clear and at times lushly vivid descriptions of the lovers' respective genitals emphasize the need for self-object differentiation along gender lines and for a balancing of respective functions, powers, and parts. The phallus is greatly fussed over, but Connie's orifices are also celebrated. At times, organs do get in the way of the organic, but the making of the novel itself may have functioned as the re-generating of a missing bodily part—thus its designation as a "tender and phallic novel" (CL, 1225). The phallus dies so that his phallic novel might live. Addressing this paradox, Mark Spilka notes the overlooked importance of chastity ("the peace that comes of fucking"), but also of the need for separateness and absti-nence as a valid alternate when, as Lawrence noted, many women and men are "happiest when they abstain and stay sexually apart, quite clean: and at the same time, *when they understand and real-ize sex more fully.*"[29] This fuller realization of sex is conducted less by the phallus than by the phallic imagination.

That the emergence of the phallus into creative work is other than either a literal or symbolic reality is hinted at by the terms Lawrence associates with it. The "book *isn't* improper but it is phallic"; it is "good and sunwards" but verbally "shocking. . . . Says shit! and fuck! in so many syllables"; yet it is "too pure and un-diluted" for the "vulgar public"; it maintains the truly moral and religious position" and is neither pornographic nor impure ex-cept to the puritan, to whom "all things are impure"; finally its phallic reality is depicted as the old insouciance, basic conscious-ness, vital impulse, freedom and common sense (CL, 1030 – 49). Thus it is conceivable that what Lawrence belatedly internalized is the paternal phallus, rejected as impure by the all too pure and puritanical mother, and conditioned by super-ego features suggested by the moral and religious summoning of sanctions. Connie's fussing over its size subtly suggests that it is somewhat oversized and ill-fitting by reason of its paternal derivation. An overdetermined concept, image, and ideal, the phallus is por-trayed as a "column of blood" and "bridge to the future." It also concentrates narcissistic libido in order to realize a new ego-ideal—or to revitalize an ancient cultural one (see fig. 1). And even in this "nice and tender" phallic phase, sadistic residues persist along with the castrated mental consciousness of crippled Clif-ford Chatterley, left behind by the genital lovers—but not left out of the reader's consciousness.

In *The Man Who Died*, the Phoenix motif of death and resurrec-tion is recast in a form at once human and mythic. The Man who died has died away from his former life, one filled with self-importance, the grandiosity of his mission, and the craving for worshipful spiritual love (see fig. 7). He returns to life without a mother and without a will, his face still "dead-white" with a "black beard growing on it as if in death," and "wide-open black sombre eyes." Having rejected the "higher" love of Mary Magda-lene, he embarks on an uncertain quest, taking with him only a peasant's orange and black gamecock which had called him back to life at dawn. This surging object of animal energy (literally to be given away, i.e., returned to nature) is metaphorically inter-nalized by the man as a way of completing his deficient body im-age: it becomes his cock and his inner sun of solar consciousness. As his own solar center is rejuvenated, he takes a step toward be-coming Osiris, the Egyptian solar deity. At the temple of Isis his flesh wounds are bathed and dressed in a significant acknowledg-ment of male dependency and renunciation of pseudoautonomy: "Suddenly she put her breast against the wound in his left side, and her arms around him, folding over the wound in his right side,

7 "I did paint a bit of my 'Resurrection' picture—I got him as impersonal as a queer animal" (CL, 976 [5/27]). "I finished my 'Resurrection' picture, and like it. It's Jesus stepping up, rather grey in the face, from the tomb, with his old ma helping him from behind, and Mary Magdalen easing him toward her bosom in front" (CL, 981 [5/27]). *Resurrection.* 1927. Oil (inscribed on reverse: 'Resurrection' D.H.L. 1927) 37 × 37 in. Collection of Humanities Research Center, University of Texas at Austin. Reprinted by permission of Laurence Pollinger, Ltd. and the Estate of Mrs. Frieda Lawrence Ravagli.

and she pressed him to her in a power and living warmth. . . ." The final resurrection is a sexual pun during the love-act between Osiris and Isis: "I am risen!" Following which, he touches her "white-gold breasts" and "her deep, interfolded warmth . . . living and penetrable. . . ."

Thus does interpenetration achieve its final stage. For phallic reality to enter these works in a new way, it must have also entered Lawrence's creative consciousness in a new way. Perhaps self and world are no longer perceived so markedly through the feminine apparatus of the possessive and puritanical mother (sitting "in the throne of my eyes," as one early poem to her puts it), but more in the way things are or might be. The emphasis may be on the object and society's regeneration through Connie Chatterley's awakening to life, or on the self and the resurrection of the body through the ministrations of the priestess of Isis. But it is preeminently a process of regeneration throughout, from beginning to end.

7 Placing the Occult Body in the Body of Art

Intense I would put down as the keynote to his temperament . . . —George Neville's Memoir, *p. 64*

Niederland speaks of his sampling as having "feelings of being different from others" and of frequently favoring "birth and rebirth fantasies." "Giving birth to oneself as a spiritual being" in the "imperishable solar body" is the explicit promise of occultism, although Lawrence turned it upside down even as he appropriated it. His preferred resurrection is into the flesh, and the preferred heavenly body is lunar and feminine. How true this is of Lawrence is felt only as one comes to recognize how deeply embedded in his imagination was the Phoenix image and how all its variants (including regeneration of self, object, and, quite possibly, phallus) flowed through his works, until it became less an emblem of dualism than a self-form.

The hypercathexis of the whole body fostered an idealization of the healthy male body along with its secondary sex characteristics, and an excessive trust in its capacities for validating experience (the body doesn't lie), while necessarily impeding other modes of reality testing.

The astrological or zodiacal body (see fig. 2) replaces the deficient body-image with an elaborate series of micro/macrocosmic connections centering the individual and enhancing his participation in the operations of the universe. What had been unconscious, now, in a changed form, enters the preconscious and conscious. Occultism androgynously preserves both concealed feminine identifications (represented as chakras or diffuse orifice-like centers), and also permits secret homosexual wishes, aimed partially at perversely incorporating a suitably masculine body-self. The hypercathexis of certain bodily zones, notably the cardiac and anal-spinal, presumably impedes phallic-genital development. When the latter belatedly appear to advance—or begin to show up in the writing—perhaps a new self-cathexis is on the way to being established ("tender and phallic"); following this, the lungs finally give way, and the ultimate fusion with the nonorganic takes place.

The rich body of source material in the occult renders it an important resource for the artist. Between the primary-process drives of infancy and the maturity of perfected art, it occupies an intermediate zone corresponding to latency. Although its inherent ambiguity suggests that it may be used as readily in the service of the "illness" as in the art, it can often serve a healing and corrective function, both in the area of self and of object-relations. Preeminent is its representability. By connecting his intense bond with his mother to the cardiac region, Lawrence seems to have circumscribed the otherwise overwhelming import of her loss and thereby to have staved off a more severe break with reality; by discovering in the occult new centers of the self (solar plexus, *Kundalini*), he turns back toward reality. Other great artists, including Strindberg, Yeats, Joyce, Hesse, and Eliot, have at one time or another and in varying ways incorporated occult material into their own. By this means an otherwise impossible synthesis may take place.

This favoring of the occult even among the more orthodox artists underscores its importance in reconciling oppositions in early relationships or in mediating between grandiosity and injury within the self. For the occult legitimates secret correspondences and meanings amid blatant incongruities and differences. The occult both supports the artist's peripheral vision—i.e., his tendency to see around or beyond the obvious—and facilitates the creative urge to turn the appearance of natural objects into palimpsests of hidden order.[30] In perceiving the purple dawn of occultism in our noonday sun, the artist restores a rainbow sense of life to the often flat or washed-out shades of mundane living. The occult thereby becomes the *means* through which artists may find their way back to reality, but it is not their *destination*. Art is more than sublimation.[31]

It is also more than self-presentation: "Not a turning loose of emotion, but an escape from emotion . . . not the expression of personality, but an escape from personality," so writes T. S. Eliot, adding: "But, of course, only those who have personality and emotions know what it means to want to escape from these things."[32]

And of whom could this be more true than Eliot's own bête noire, D. H. Lawrence? Rather than "personality," the artist, Eliot tells us, strives to express a "particular medium." But only in the final stage is this a bona fide cultural medium; in its earlier phases it may owe more than a little to the occult. Depending on whether one begins with the prevailing culture or with the self, the occult can be read as either a step toward or away from narcissistic concerns. The extent to which Lawrence developed certain primitive narcissistic modalities may be a measure of the distance between art and pathology; on the other hand it may have been no further than anyone ever moves from his own body. It is clear, though, that his creative correspondences took him far beyond self-cathexis and into the realm of object-relations both with others and with the cosmos, and in this respect his narcissistic modalities were transformed and transcended.

Two instances may be cited by way of conclusion. In 1917 Freud spoke of three profound assaults on the "general narcissism, the self-love of humanity." These are the *cosmological* (Copernicus, Newton), which dislodged man from his cherished illusion of being at the center of the universe; the *biological* (Darwin), which abolished man's privileged status as a special creation apart from the rest of the animal kingdom; and the *psychological* (Freud), which severely limited the power of the ego to rule its own house. These larger issues intersect at many points with the deeply felt injuries to the self that we have been able to discern in Lawrence, although what his reading-public encounters are more likely the precisely rendered cultural conflicts and the healing balm of creative vision arising from the intersections. Lawrence is most challenging in his no-less-than-heroic attempts to recenter man in the cosmos by means of recovering vital organic correspondences between macrocosm and microcosm. At his best he mitigates those cosmological and biological fissures and alienations—of which we are aware today—with a new sense of urgency brought on by energy and environmental crises. The psychological realm remains more problematic; the jury, let us say, is still deliberating various aspects of the question.

Certainly, the sense of one's self as rooted in the body is a value both in mental health and in Lawrence. And it is here that his second achievement may be noted. The system of values and dogmas which Lawrence inherited largely through his mother has been succinctly summed up by Northrop Frye as a "mythological universe" which "retained a close analogy with the body":

God was associated with the sky and the brain, devils with the organs of excretion below. Any rising movement, attempting to leave the demonic world behind, would have to determine what and how much would have to be symbolically excreted. Because of the close anatomical connection of the genital and excretory systems, and even more because of society's constant fear of Eros, sexual love, even the physical body itself, was among the things that had to be left behind.[33]

Although lip service is paid to the doctrine of bodily resurrection, "in Dante the journey to paradise is made by a soul floating out of [his] body." It was Lawrence, more than any other modern writer, who struggled to keep Eros on earth and embedded in life; the success of this struggle, which came only late in his career, also consumed his life. To Frieda, "he tried, with his fierce and responsible love for his fellowmen, to free them of the stale old past, and take the load of all the centuries of dead thought and feeling on himself" (NI, viii).

This feat paradoxically required that he hold the sense of his own death constantly in abeyance while affirming the "polarity of the dynamic conscious, from the very start of life": "From our bodies comes the issue of corruption" toward dissolution "as well as the flow of sex toward creation" (P, 676). In the next chapter we will examine how this dual awareness first found its creative channels through the unlikely area of play.

5

Play

... the third part of the life of a human being, a part that we cannot ignore, is an intermediate area of experiencing, to which inner reality and external life both contribute.—D. W. Winnicott[1]

But he had a genius for inventing games.... —Ada Lawrence, on her brother

While the creative process draws on the wishes that flow through fantasy, it also binds up fantasy, memory, and desire into symbol and form; it remakes the self and early environment by taking the body as paradigmatic, and, as we shall see, retraces and revises origins. But creative processes are not so intensely subjective as to disregard objective poles of experience in a real environment. The completed work of art is neither one nor the other, neither so subjective as a daydream nor so objective as a rainbow. Neither belonging purely to mind nor to nature, art uniquely represents both. This "intermediate area of experiencing" which concerns Winnicott encompasses culture and all its productions, systems, and accomplishments, which we invest with relative values; but it begins more humbly in the emerging spaces which first appear between the weaning mother and her child. The blankets, toys, dolls, and games that populate this world are called "self-objects," because they preexist and are the first in a series of the individual's not-me possessions. Transitional objects and phenomena are neither within the infant nor part of the mother, and so they are objective; but because they are "created" by the child—by being invested with such enormous affect as to assume a wishful significance all their own—they are also subjective. Consequently, they inhabit a separate third area of shared experience. In the evolving sequence of the present study, the child who is engaged in creating a sense of himself and of the primary figures in his immediate world, finds his efforts facilitated by recourse to a separate world—one that is neither purely a fantasy nor one that is beholden to others—where he can enjoy mastery, assimilate and integrate emotions, and consolidate early identifications.

Works of art in particular inherit transitional attributes, balancing reality and illusion in ever new ways, for the sphere of art is in many respects a continuation of play, as indeed is culture in the light of Johan Huizinga's *Homo Ludens*. In play, energies are released and also structured—psychic energy accompanies physical energy and is bound or transformed in its passage from the id- to the ego-system. New discoveries, new resources, new capacities within the self are continually occurring. Only thereafter will these energies become available for creative and cultural ends, and so *how* this process comes about may tell us a great deal about *what* will be its results. Fantasy has often been viewed as the internal continuation of play, and the artist's adaptive play with images is equivalent to the kind of transitional fantasy which bridges the gaps between primary attachments and those "collective alternates" comprising his creative romance with the world.

A play episode in *Sons and Lovers* illustrates and extends these general notions. Whether the event actually occurred outside the work cannot be decided, but what can be shown is its decisive influence on the author's creative development (for which reason I would lean toward its historical basis).[2] The episode is indeed pivotal for concentrating earlier experiences and for shaping, coloring, and toning future creative material.

The novel, as we well know, provides a wealth of emotional material and psychological motives upon which critics have never been reluctant to seize. We are familiar with the intense tie to the mother spelled out by the title. We quickly grasp that Paul Morel views his father principally as violent / violator. Before he was born, the older brother has his year's growth of "crescent-shaped curls" cropped like a sheep by Morel. Paul's earliest memories are branded with parental warfare; we recall that Morel hurls a drawer at his wife making a gash over her brow with blood spilling onto her infant. Interspersed with these violent episodes were periods of "peace and tenderness" between the parents, the fruits of which would be a new family member. In their upstairs bedroom Paul and the other child would listen to the "booming shouts of his father, come home nearly drunk, then the sharp replies of his mother"; and as their violence mounts it mingles with the wind-swept ash-tree "near the window, until at last there would be a silence," which they feared might be a "silence of blood."

Lawrence is direct about Paul's feelings: he "hated his father." But another episode around this time hints at more complex responses. So far Paul has been described as trotting after his mother "like her shadow," and at three or four as having fits of depression, "crying on the sofa." At this time he would make a switch to his older sister Annie, notably "living her share of the game, having as yet no part of his own." It is in this context of his not yet possessing a self-determining ego and so not yet completely hatched out of the symbiotic nest that a minor event of major implications occurs:

She had a big doll of which she was fearfully proud, though not so fond. So she laid the doll on the sofa, and covered it with an antimacassar, to sleep. Then she forgot it. Meantime Paul must practice jumping off the sofa arm. So he jumped crash into the face of the hidden doll. Annie rushed up, uttered a loud wail, and sat down to weep a dirge. Paul remained quite still.

"You couldn't tell it was there, mother; you couldn't tell it was there," he repeated over and over. So long as Annie wept for the doll he sat helpless with misery. Her grief wore itself out. She forgave her brother—he was so much upset. But a day or two afterwards she was shocked.

"Let's make a sacrifice of Arabella," he said. "Let's burn her."

She was horrified, yet rather fascinated. She wanted to see what the boy would do. He made an altar of bricks, pulled some of the shavings out of Arabella's body, put the waxen fragments into the hollow face, poured on a little paraffin, and set the whole thing alight. He watched with wicked satisfaction the drops of wax melt off the broken forehead of Arabella, and drop like sweat into the flame. So long as the stupid big doll burned he rejoiced in silence. At the end he poked among the embers with a stick, fished out the arms and legs, all blackened, and smashed them under stones.

"That's the sacrifice of Missis Arabella," he said. "An' I'm glad there's nothing left of her."

Which disturbed Annie inwardly, although she could say nothing. He seemed to hate the doll so intensely, because he had broken it. [Pp. 57 − 58]

Contained therein appear to be all the condensations, visualizations, and symbols of a dream, yet it is a piece of a certain kind of reality which blends illusion or fantasy with actuality, and occurs within the sphere of children's play (specified by Winnicott as transitional and so including the doll as transitional object). The question becomes, what do dolls represent in children's play, when living qualities are not yet clearly distinguished from non-living (as Freud notes in "The 'Uncanny'")? A related question is whether Paul jumped accidentally or purposely on the "face of the hidden doll." The effect of his action in either case is the simultaneous discovery and destruction of something. It is also the first step of creativity within the transitional sphere brought about by making an imprint on a preexisting part of his environment. What is discovered hidden beneath the sofa-wrap may evoke what he has recently discovered in among the covers of the parents' bed where he once had exclusive claim—namely a younger sibling, whom he would not mind trouncing. At least an analogy presents itself.

But the facts that the new arrival is male in the novel (though female in Lawrence's life) and that Paul refers to the doll as "Missis" Arabella, suggests that it may stand not only for the baby but also for the mother who bore it. Perhaps he would like to trounce her as well. Certainly, Paul's responses imply that the doll is a hated object he would be better off without. He is very upset so long as Annie wails and his mother may scold him, but instead of undoing the damage or undertaking steps toward reparation—as recognitions of guilt—he behaves in a surprisingly deliberate and even creative way. He appropriates the damaged object and, making Annie his fellow-conspirator, sets out to burn it in "wicked satisfaction." Does he hate it, as Annie senses, because he had broken it? Or did he break and burn it because of his hatred? The latter seems more probable. The doll must be an overdetermined object, representing revenge against a mother or sibling. But a great deal more is involved.

Upon closer examination we can see that in the process of one doll's destruction, another "doll," namely Paul, hitherto the will-less follower and passive object in the family comes alive and begins consciously to act. Perhaps as Paul takes over the doll and decides its fate, it becomes a "bad" self-representation that needs to be destroyed. Even though the action may be a narcissistic triumph for Paul—if viewed by its conservative aim to reestablish an earlier state of affairs, in the household—it is from this point on that Paul ceases to be only a shadow-self. Hitherto, his behavior and feelings—tagging along, moodiness—had been tied to mother and sister, but his smashing the doll serves to make Annie the grief-stricken one. And during the burning, Paul experiences new clusters of feelings—hatred, wicked satisfaction, rejoicing, gladness—which help establish a new sense of self, an inner quickening, to reappear as the flame image.

Years later, for example, under the pressure of Paul's overheated adolescent love, Miriam "lay as if she had given herself up to sacrifice," and "he had to sacrifice her" (pp. 289 – 90). But Miriam is not the only living figure to be treated like a doll. At the end of the novel, when the mother languishes with terminal cancer, it is the same sibling-pair, Paul and Annie, who laced her milk with morphia and "laughed together like two conspiring children" as they prepare the mother for sacrifice.[3] The immolation of Missis Arabella makes matricide feasible, and the question of whether the doll was alive to the children extends to the guilt of the young adults—which indeed seems minimal. When Missis Arabella burns she looks "stupid" and sweats; before Mrs. Morel dies, the prescribed morphia has "wasted" her body to "a fragment of ash." The inanimate assumes qualities of life; the living assumes the shape of death.

Moreover, Lawrence's biographer Harry T. Moore states that "the question remains: Did Lawrence kill his mother?" Lawrence is quoted as telling a friend who was troubled by the euthanasia episode, "You see, *I* did it—I gave her the overdose of morphia and set her free."[4] Presumably, he is speaking *proprio persona*, and by "free" he may imply the need to free himself from her as well as her from her pain. Yet when such an act by Paul Morel is regarded as out of character, it may be that his cruel childish glee at the violent annihilation of the doll is being overlooked.

A more inclusive interpretation of the doll-episode and its bearing on creativity may now be attempted. Paul's jumping on the doll, willed or not, resulted in an act of physical violence. As such it resembles in a childish way the other acts of violence—also unintentionally cruel—that Morel previously carried out against his children: shearing the infant brother's curls; impulsively hurling the drawer which resulted in blood spilling onto the infant. Morel's violent interaction with his wife when they are alone, and the periodic appearance of new arrivals, suggest an association of male/female violence leading to babies, with dolls appearing and breaking. In other words, what is being suggested is more than violent Primal Scene reenactments frequent in children's play, for in

Paul's pouncing on the doll, allying with a female in its final destruction, and in his sense of triumph, there may also be intimations of primitive, acted-out identifications with the sexual father.
True, those with his mother may follow when he animates his own
doll-children in the sphere of art, but it may be this tenuous yet
real link with the masculine image that enables him to smash the
protracted symbiotic bond with mother—first symbolically in
play, later in actuality with morphia. Killing in the child's mind
may be misconstrued as a means of immediate control or domina-
tion, not as a final, irrevocable act; and for Lawrence, perhaps a
kind of freeing, an exercise of power or retaliation in kind, in either
case bound up with play.

Lawrence's mother did not encourage either his needs for identification with his father or indeed any positive feelings for him
("All the children, but particularly Paul, were peculiarly *against*
their father, along with their mother"). Such feelings may have
contributed to the ambivalence he felt toward her, making her
demise less intolerable if not consciously desirable. Moreover,
play allows dualistic, even contradictory, states of mind regarding
hate/love, alive/not-alive to be enacted with no immediate cause
for reconciliation.[5] Play can result in mastery, but may also promote and preserve irreconcilable ideas or identifications with
both parents.

In the novel it is assumed that only the father is hated, and
Paul's repeated prayer was, "Let my father die." Only, he added,
"Let him not be killed at pit." The short story, "Odour of Chrysanthemums," in which an irresponsible miner dies in the pit and is
carried home to a family almost identical to the Morel-Lawrences,
may be seen as the fulfillment of Paul's uneasy prayer. In this
family too, amid all the quarreling, there is the riddle of sexuality:
"The children had come for some mysterious reason, out of both
of them." The miner was not crushed, as his widow feared, but
was trapped and smothered instantaneously, with the result that
he is finally composed in a state of peace. As his still warm body is
undressed and washed by his mother and his widow, he "appears
a man of handsome body, and his face showed no traces of drink.
He was blond, full-fleshed, with fine limbs. But he was dead."

Or was he? The simple medical fact is undermined by his sudden emotional power over the others. Sympathy grows as the
reader sees him less as the bad husband through the wife's eyes,

than as the good son through the mother's: "White as milk he is, clear as a twelve-month baby, bless him, the darling!" And his widow now comes alive to feelings for him that she had never before allowed: "She had denied what he was—she saw it now." Yet he is no more (and no less!) alive than a doll that children dress and undress and bathe. In each revision Lawrence made of the story, the father gains in sympathy.[6] But he had to be killed before he could be accepted, destroyed before he could be recovered.

The Captain's Doll further explores the ambiguities of living/non-living. And Clifford Chatterley exercising his will from his wheelchair is strangely both alive and not-alive after having been "shipped home smashed" from the war. If not yet fully clear, there does seem to be a connection between Paul's coming alive within himself by investing an inanimate object with great meaning, and Lawrence's development in the more extensive transitional sphere of art, which continues to pose reality against illusion. Several examples will reinforce this connection, for a remarkable extension of the paradigmatic doll episode can be widely traced through Lawrence's predilection for expressing death—either as a literal fact or as a subjective state—by using the verbs *break* (including *smash, crash*) or *burn* (italics added below).

1. Morel, after wounding his wife with the drawer: "He watched, fascinated . . . then his manhood *broke*"; " . . . he insisted to himself it was her fault. And so he *broke* himself." Earlier, the mother had "felt as if the navel string that had connected its [Paul's] frail body with hers had not been *broken*." In death, she regains a maidenly repose and "lay like a girl asleep and dreaming of her love." Yet Paul feels everything has gone "smash," and "he felt he should *smash*." The doll image also exerts a recurrent latent pressure on events. When Paul's adolescent love for Clara Dawes, for example, provokes a clash with her husband, Paul is beaten up, "flung away, helpless," and kicked into unconsciousness, as if he had become the doll. On one level he may be continuing his identification with the violent father who pays by being broken. But the son has healing resources unavailable to the parent. Following his roughing up, Paul succumbs to bronchitis and must be nursed back to health, i.e., restored to life by his mother from his lifeless doll-state. But what may be compulsive-repetitions for Paul, become creative strategies for his author.

2. In *The Rainbow*, Will Brangwen watches his wife's exultant

fertility dance "as if he were at the stake. He felt he was being *burned* alive." Their child is Ursula, and when she comes of age her early sexual experiences take this turn:"He kissed her, and she quivered as if she were being destroyed, shattered. The lighted vessel vibrated and *broke* in her soul. . . ." In a subsequent episode it is her lover's turn: "Her mouth sought his in a hard, rending, ever-increasing kiss, till his body was powerless in her grip, his heart melted in fear," and thereafter "he knew he could never touch her again. His will was *broken*. . . ."

3. In *Women in Love*, Gerald Crich gradually isolated himself from his party in the Alps as Gudrun takes on another lover; he "wandered unconsciously, till he slipped and fell down, and as he fell something *broke* in his soul, and immediately he went to sleep."

4. The American stories: "It had *broken* something in her" (referring to the emotional strain—brought on by the fierce climate and wilderness in nineteenth-century New Mexico—affecting the New England woman in *St. Mawr*).

The heroine's spirit in "The Princess" was "hard and flawless as a diamond. But he [the Mexican Romero] could *shatter* her." And in "some peculiar way, he had got hold of her, some unrealized part of her which she never wished to realize. Racked with a *burning*, tearing anguish, she felt that the thread of being would *break*, and she would die." Her name is Dollie, and she is born with the "wide amazed blue eyes" of a doll. A "quick, dainty little thing," she "never really grew up" and became a woman. She remains Lawrence's most doll-like character. Moreover, she is the doll-child of a doll-father: "His very flesh, when you touched it, did not seem quite the flesh of a real man." With his "wide-open blue eye" he "seemed sometimes to be looking at nothing." Outwardly he was "charming, courteous, perfectly gracious. . . . But absent." His wife withstood three years of marriage to him, "and then it *broke* her." Although Mrs. Morel was not a doll-mother in the way Dollie's father was, Paul may have found himself to be a doll-child, possessed and molded by his mother. In any case as a female counterpart to Paul, Dollie is unable to smash out of her shell and ends up like her father, "a little mad."

In "The Woman Who Rode Away," the woman sleeping out on the desert senses a "great *crash* at the centre of herself, which was the *crash* of her death." This premonition prepares for her "obliteration" in the awesome climax of her sacrifice by the Indian tribe to the savage gods.

5. The English stories: In "Odour of Chrysanthemums," the men bearing the miner's body knock over a vase of chrysanthemums, and as the widow "picked up the *broken* vase and the flowers," the reader is made aware of the death of the marriage.

In "England, My England," Egbert drifted into the Great War to find a shell that passed unnoticed in the rapidity of action . . . finally *crashed* a noise and a darkness a moment's *flaming* agony and horror." In the "extremity of dissolution" these thoughts pass through his mind: "To *break* the core and the unit of life, and to lapse out on the great darkness. Only that. To *break* the clue, and mingle and commingle with the one darkness. . . ."

In "Tickets Please," after John Thomas has been clawed and trounced for leading on the tramway girls, he finally consents to choose one. It is Annie, the instigator whose love had turned to wild hatred. And as he "rose slowly, a ragged, dazed creature," Annie remains still: "Something was *broken* in her."

At the end of "The Blind Man," Bertie "could not bear it that he had been touched by the blind man, his insane reserve *broken* in. He was like a mollusc whose shell is *broken*." ("Bertie" may refer both to Bertrand Russell and to Lawrence himself: a composite reality.)[7]

In "The Prussian Officer," the orderly wrestles with and strangles the captain until his "nostrils gradually filled with blood." The orderly stood and looked at it in silence. It was a pity *it* was *broken*."[8] The orderly wanders in a daze, "*burning* with dry heat." Night falls, and the next morning "his brain *flamed* with the sole horror of thirstiness." Soon he grows self-detached, as though his functions were dismembered parts. After he too dies and is found, the "bodies of the two men lay together . . . the one white and slender . . . the other looking as if every moment it must rouse to life again. . . ."

6. In *Aaron's Rod*, Aaron Lilly expresses his breakdown in the following words: "But I did myself in when I went with another woman. I felt myself go—as if the bile *broke* inside me, and I was sick." Though a minor work, it is interesting in light of the previous story, because here the broken male is stripped naked and gradu-

ally restored to life by an oil rubdown conducted by his friend until "the spark had come back in his eyes, and the faint trace of a smile, faintly luminous, into the face."

7.   Finally, in *The Fox*, the situation of two females and one male in a destroying role is recapitulated, only here, instead of a sister and her doll, it is two lesbians. In order to separate the women, Henry accidentally (?) fells a tree, smashing the weaker— only here it is neither quite an accident nor quite a legal murder. And his victory almost destroys the other girl as well. She shudders, and then "with a little *crash* came the tears and the blind agony of sightless weeping. She sank down on the grass...."

Each of these examples is of course different; sometimes images of darkness, dark powers, or healing also cluster around the destructive act. But even though genders switch, functions vary, and the gravity of injury fluctuates, they still stem from the same nucleus. We may be able to see now that these recurring verbs are figurative—implicit metaphors; that the often latent term of comparison or identification is the doll; and that the special mode of experiencing through play might have something to do with the developing mind's formation of the metaphoric capacity. For it is through the changes wrought by play on the child's doll that Lawrence's central symbol first comes into being. Inevitably, we are led to the unifying symbol of the Phoenix, who bursts into flame over its nest, succumbs to the darkness of ashes, and breaks from his shell anew. The archetype of the Phoenix is a complex solar representation of fertility, which Lawrence appropriates both as an expression of sexual union and as a figure of the reborn self.

And so it is not surprising that his last two works most vividly emerge from the broken wills and smashed bodies, the immolations and the dissolving darkness, of his early and middle periods. In the one work a man "woke cold and numb," inside a dark cave. He stirred and "slowly crept from the cell of rock, with the caution of the bitterly wounded." He is "The Man Who Died" and yet did not die on the cross ("They took me down too soon"); he "died" out of his striving, messianic self only to find himself resurrected into the body. As Osiris, he makes his way to the priestess Isis-in-search, who takes his naked body and heals the wounds he had inflicted on himself (heals him as the dead miner's wife has been unable to do). In the other work, it is the woman's body that "was going meaningless . . . so much insignificant substance. It made her feel immensely depressed and hopeless . . . old at twenty-seven, with no gleam and sparkle in the flesh." Connie Chatterley felt "forlorn and unused," the sight of two brown pheasant hens over their brown eggs almost "broke" her heart. Her revivication begins with the first lovemaking in the dark of the gamekeeper's hut in which she is undressed, lies in a deathlike sleep, and gradually begins awakening as he spends himself in the act of sex. He will later tell her there's no escaping life. "So if I've got to be broken open again, I have." The self-alien, breaking-apart process is gradually replaced by a self-healing breaking-open process that can be assimilated to a new state of consciousness.

These more inwardly alive and sexually mature figures act within an ambience of rebirth, pastoral or mythic settings, and rescue motifs; yet they end problematically with the woman pregnant and the man in temporary separation. The distance is great from children's playful aggression with dolls, to healing symbol-formation where life/death/rebirth are joined, and further to intricate narrative forms where characters break in their wills or bodies, flame inwardly, or are consumed in their spirits, finally—in certain instances—to be reborn in organic wholeness. But the distance also expands beyond play to emotional involvement with the sexual/violent parents.

The doll-breaking/burning episode (whether or not it literally occurred) is an important milestone in the creative process, when presumed early emotions and inevitable conflicts first undergo a degree of representation and mastery. It also reveals Paul for the first time acting in a deliberate—hence, human—manner, and it is in this respect that the Phoenix symbolizes Lawrencean creativity. For the actively chosen burning of the doll (the old Phoenix) results in the emergence of an assertive self (the new Phoenix). The burning itself seems to have been internalized to stand for that sense of nuclear self Lawrence characteristically imaged as a flame. "So the body of man is begotten and born in an ecstacy of delight and suffering," he writes in *The Crown*. "It is a flame kindled between the opposing confluent elements of the air. It is the battle-ground and marriage-bed of the two invisible hosts. It flames up to its full strength . . ." (also, CL, 180). The sexual flaming and the suffering doll further seem to suggest primal-scene fantasies.

Paradoxically, Paul appears to come alive by destroying and replacing the all-important parent or parents, but only in their capacity as a "bad" object or relationship. The doll assumes the affect of badness, from the child's perception of the parent—the mother who betrays, possesses, restrains; the father who hurts, etc.—and so the badness is also within the child. Or we could say the dollness is within the child, for what is a doll but that which is possessed by another? The shell of dollness must be smashed before the child can hatch out into separateness, an act that entails smashing the possessor of the doll, that is, she who controls it—the maternal female. But because the parent cannot be destroyed literally, it is only when an intermediate space appears that a suitable representative can be found or created. The doll is a subjective object, a preexisting entity, but also "created" as a character, perhaps the artist-to-be's first impulse toward characterization in its blend of imagination and reality. The created doll performs a role, while the power of the doll to externalize negative feelings allows the primary-love relationship with the good mother to thrive unharmed.

The play episode "works" because the child is able to transfer feelings, to displace negative self-images, and to invest an inanimate object with emotional significance. As suggested, the intermediate sphere of play balances the fantasy/illusion of inner reality and the objective/actuality of outer reality. Play appropriates the spaces between the receding presence of the all-gratifying mother and child's projected, magical wishes; in these spaces, objects inherit some of that original magic. These possessions or transitional objects are neither under the child's total magical control nor beyond control, as the mother becomes during weaning. Since the "task of reality-acceptance is never completed," no one is "free from the strain of relating inner and outer reality." And since this third area of experience is shared throughout such cultural spheres as art and religion, play, rather than the dream, may be the proper matrix of art. Other species may dream and other species may play, but human beings alone have that protracted childhood called "neoteny," and human beings alone create art.

Thus it may be said that Winnicott did for play what Freud did for dreams. Each took his respective phenomena seriously in a radically new way and thereby made them available for future study. Each opened what had been sealed off or confined to limited interest. Johan Huizinga had already made play important in the larger sphere of culture; Winnicott established its underlying importance in the sphere of individual development. But he also enabled us to encounter culture with a fresh vision: It is not that he connects culture with play, but that he links both with illusion. Whenever there is space for differences in meanings, one allows subjective elements in willy-nilly, and with them, necessarily, illusion. And so we invest our cultural (security) objects with our own "realities" and yank or tug them away from the "illusions" of others. In supporting a normally healthy role for illusion in culture, Winnicott has also directed the psychoanalytic study of creativity and creative artists away from pathology toward variations on normal development or conflict resolution.

More particularly, there is something unusual in the balances between living / nonliving, real / illusory, cruelty / compassion, and loss / recovery that needs to be clarified in Lawrence's evolution as an imaginative writer. A clue appears in his famous statement about not being interested in the stable ego or in personal feelings, but in the physical, nonhuman element in humanity.[9] Many episodes in his most experimental works, like *The Rainbow* and *Women in Love*, seem to exist in a realm other than either naturalism or hallucinatory dream states.[10] They promote a heightened sense of reality which is yet not symbolic, parabolic, or allegorical. Anne Brangwen's exultant pregnancy dance before Will, the rhythmic heaping of the grain sheaves by the boy and girl, Ursula's lovemaking sequences with Anton Skrebensky, the wild horses that surround and threaten her later—all appear in *The Rainbow*. In *Women in Love*, almost every significant action seems lit from within by a peculiar radiance—but especially, Birkin's stoning the moon in the pool, Gudrun's dancing before the cattle, the interlocked couple dredged up from the lake, Gerald's rearing his horse before the locomotive, and several of the mystical (or mystifying) scenes of sexual congress. Ambiguity abounds, but of a very distinctive order to say the least. If before, one had to question one's senses about living and nonliving, in these scenes one has to revise radically one's sense of the real and unreal as depths and surfaces fuse and intermingle. "Away from the style of *Sons and Lovers*," writes Paul Delaney, the later novels "move toward a more rhapsodic and incantatory mode, which dissolves the outlines of individual characters."[11] At times the effect is truly incandescent.

These scenes, certain persisting motifs in depicting sexuality within an ambience of violence/mysticism, the noted verbal linkage, Lawrence's repeated tendency to seek a woman's partnership in the creative enterprise, and perhaps the creative faculty itself, may thrive on the emotional energies first unleashed toward the inanimate objects of play.

"What is created is not an entirely new environment but a *transformation* of that which already exists," writes Arnold Modell in a paper connecting paleolithic cave art with transitional objects.[12] "This suggests that an essential element of creativity is an *acceptance* of that which is outside the self." For Lawrence, the doll preexists, and because it is not especially mother (or sister), he can re-create it. What then ensues is a transformation. Using the infant's blanket, Marian Tolpin shows how the mother's soothing function is displaced onto the blanket the infant uses to soothe himself. This allows him gradually to learn to soothe himself and eventually to internalize the process referred to as "transmuting internalization."[13] "From the soft, furry, smelly, pliable, warm, concretely available blanket the psyche acquires inner regulatory functions which eventually enable the child to *calm and soothe* himself with 'the normal workings of the mind.'" Such an ability to adapt transitional objects inclines Tolpin to designate them among René Spitz's "psychic organizers."[14] The blanket preexists, but the child, having "emerged sufficiently from the symbiotic state to begin to perceive his mother as the chief instrument of his well-being and of his relief from stress," *creates* the "illusion for himself that the blanket soothes." Thus the area of transitional objects and phenomena can justly be considered not only as providing psychic organizers, but also as the earliest organizers of that psychic activity which becomes creativity. Tolpin speaks of the blanket-soothing operation as a special kind of transitional mental structure; our investigation of Lawrence's doll episode specifies it as a mental structure especially well adapted for creativity.

Through this structure, the young artist-to-be must have first sensed the power of projecting his inner world onto a recognizably real one as his emotional energies were first being visibly organized in children's play activities. His fantasies, memories, and real experiences could now undergo the first molding process of creativity. Eventually, he will discover the intermediate sphere of art where many diffuse and contradictory elements gather to form his distinctive vision of reality.

In helping to structure the young artist's inchoate unconscious material—primitive emotional states, early drives, and identification conflicts—play is as important in the creative process as it is in the developmental one. The adaptive functions of play presume preexisting conflicts (to which we will return in the next chapter). These were only touched on here as ambivalent feelings, or more clearly as polar male and female identifications stemming in part from the polarized parents. The parents' unresolved conflicts are transmitted to the child and are first manifested through the medium of play, which in turn becomes the first medium of the creative process.

The doll is the most clear-cut example of the early transitional phenomena in play evolving into the more advanced forms of culture and art. But Lawrence probably treated as transitional phenomena many of the actual places, the birds, beasts, fruit, and flowers of his natural world—all preexistent and first encountered in play—thus investing them with a richly expressive potential. Entering the wider sphere of culture, he aligned himself with a preexisting literary tradition as well as with occult systems and archetypal symbols, all available to be reworked and remolded until they fit into his own creation, as Missis Arabella (who may have been named by Lawrence after a character in Hardy's fiction) once did.

The doll episode provides the first external piece of evidence, assuming it has some biographical reference, of turning away from the possessive mother and toward the destructive father. It also illustrates an aggressive projective tendency carried out on the environment that extends both in the directions of Lawrence's later life and into the creative-restorative process (see chap. 7). Just as psychoanalysis unfolds the psychological birth of the individual, Lawrence's art encompasses both the psychological birth and the psychological death of the self. In two of his best stories, "The Women Who Rode Away" and "England, My England," the central characters undergo a psychological death which precedes, and is more important than, their literal biological one. Through a period of play when alive/not-alive were not sharply distinguished, Lawrence may have first freed up death for creative ends. The episode with Missis Arabella was like creating a potent fiction: a doll could be destroyed with impunity, yet real people would be affected by it. Death was neither real nor unreal; only the game being played was real. Believe strongly enough in the game and one might get away with murder. But for the artist to sustain the magic of play later on in his art, something else was required: a dual consciousness, and a split—for Lawrence also felt the breaking he visited on his fictional dolls.

Finally, an appreciation of the medium of play as a unique sphere of shared experience enables us to grasp how characters may be both his (the author's) and ours (the readers'); and how they may, in Lawrence's case, also burn.

6

Origins

I think the only re-sourcing of art, revivifying it, is to make it the joint work of man and woman. . . . Because the source of all life and knowledge is in man and woman, and the source of all living is in the interchange and the meeting and mingling of these two: man-life and woman-life . . . —CL, 280

But one sheds one's sicknesses in books—repeats and presents again one's emotions, to be master of them.—CL, 234

D. H. Lawrence grew up in three successive residences, each of which may focus a succeeding stage of origins in his creative work. Each has something to contribute to his childhood's total Primal Scene that is the source of his art's re-sourcing. Specifically though, the sites correspond approximately to birth, the dyadic phase, and the oedipal phase. Although Lawrence seems to have been engaged in reworking or re-sourcing his origins whenever he wrote a serious or sustained piece, three works in particular reveal him concentrating on questions of beginnings by drawing on places of origins. Highlighting also his periods of literary development, these are *Sons and Lovers* (early), *St. Mawr* (middle), and *Lady Chatterley's Lover* (late). Each covers extensive emotional territory and so marks a stage in his progressive awareness of human sexual relations.

This is a study in threes, an exploration into how these groupings of mind, place, and creative work can be interrelated, and what they can further tell us about the sources of art as a re-sourcing of origins.

1

Even after allowances have been made for distortions in the Jessie Chambers (Miriam) episodes, *Sons and Lovers* is usually understood as an intensely autobiographical work; but one significant change worked on the sources has so far gone unnoticed. Refer to Table 2 to distinguish the sequence of family residences, and you will see that the first Lawrence-family home is excluded from the novel. Although this may be in keeping with economy and unity,

Table 2

LOCATION/SETTING

1877 – 87. Victoria Street House	1887 – 91. The Breach ("Bottoms" in SL)	1891 – 1902. Walker Street House
Row house in Eastwood, with a little shop in the front room.	In lowlands north of town where miners' tenements were erected; Lawrences' an end house with "an extra strip of garden." For this Mrs. Morel "enjoyed a kind of aristocracy among the other women" (SL, 2).	"On the brow of the hill, commanding a view of the valley. . . . In front of the house was a huge old ashtree" (SL, 59).

TIME/HISTORY

Birthplace of three older children, and DHL, 9/11/85 ". . . I was born in the little corner shop . . ." (P, 134).	DHL: 17 months to 6 years. Birthplace of Paul Morel and younger brother Arthur (Ada Lettice Lawrence born 6/6/87).	Through early adolescence. Triadic phase: a "big house" for "mother and all the people we like together" (PE, 49).

PSYCHOLOGICAL CORRESPONDENCE

Area of the Self. Primary Creativity: mythic image of tribe living breast to breast with cosmos (A, 159).	Dyadic phase, including early loss and sense of the Basic Fault: it is "our being cut off that is our ailment (CL, 993). Origins revised to clear the way for the artist's creative romance with the world; onset of the oedipal (necessarily overlaps the others).	Climax of the oedipal period and the revival of its drives outside the family during adolescence. "We have loved each other almost with a husband and wife love" (CL, 69).

Lawrence *in effect* may have "repressed" in his fiction the scene of his biological origins. But whatever his motives, the shift involved more than artistic strategy. Before Lawrence had generated a fictional self to be born in the second home, his mother was kicked out of the first residence by her drunken husband. That this actually happened is attested to by Jessie Chambers: "'He hates his father,' she [Mrs. Lawrence] said. 'I know why he hates his father. It happened before he was born. One night he put me out of the house. He's bound to hate his father'" (PE, 138).

That this account is given—irrationally—by the mother as the son's reason for hating his father, suggests that she was pregnant then. Indeed she was pregnant in the novel, and gives birth to Paul in the following chapter. But in real life Mrs. Lawrence would have been put out of the first house *which had no garden*, and that remarkable passage, perhaps the first to bear the stamp of her son's genius—wherein she walks through her garden and mingles with the moonlight and the flowers, "trembling in every limb while the child boiled within her" and lapsing into a kind of delirious ecstasy—*could not have occurred*. It had to be created—but not from thin air or pure imagination—because the alteration permits her to undergo something on the order of a second impregnation, or pollination, by means of purely natural elements:

She became aware of something about her. With an effort she aroused herself to see what it was that penetrated her consciousness. The tall white lilies were reeling in the moonlight, and the air was charged with their perfume, as with a presence. Mrs. Morel gasped slightly in fear. She touched the big, pallid, flowers on their petals, then shivered. They seemed to be stretched in the moonlight. She put her hand into one white bin: the gold scarcely showed on her fingers by moonlight. She bent down to look at the binful of yellow pollen; but it only appeared dusky. Then she drank a deep draught of the scent. It almost made her dizzy.

Mrs. Morel leaned on the garden gate, looking out, and she lost herself awhile. She did not know what she thought. Except for a slight feeling of sickness, and her consciousness in the child, herself melted out like scent into the shiny, pale air. After a time the child too, melted with her in the mixing-pot of moonlight, and she rested with the hills and lilies and houses, all swum together in a kind of swoon.

When she came to herself, she was tired for sleep. Languidly she looked about her. [SL, 24]

"We have been great lovers," Lawrence wrote in a letter shortly before his mother died and well before he had met Frieda or been introduced through her to the theories of Freud (CL, 68). But in further specifying the bond between him and his mother, he refers to it as a "fusion of soul." This sense of oneness is borne out in his first novel in which the lead character is Cyril Beardsall, the family name of Mrs. Lawrence, rendering Cyril the virginal son of the virginal mother. It also prefigures the son's "immaculate conception" in *Sons and Lovers*, which does not quite deny paternity, but does go far to minimize the father's vital role in begetting the child; and true to the mother's script, he writes, "I was born hating my father," adding somewhat cryptically, "he was very bad before I was born."[1] "Bad" to sleep with mother? Or "bad" to put her out of the house? If the "good" mother prefers the child over the "bad" father, who shall be summoned to protect it from the "good" mother? Surely not the "bad" father?

No simple answers emerge. Lawrence's life seemed pitched between two areas of conflicted needs, aptly stated as "atonement with the ghost of his mother" and as honorable "conciliation with [his] father."[2] It is a rebounding dilemma which finally can only be resolved creatively by transforming it into conscious utterance as "*the* problem of today": the "relations between men and women," demanding either the "establishment of a new relation, or the readjustment of the old one" (CL, 200).

By affirming the mother's virginal purity and by downgrading the father's sexual role, Lawrence thus delivers his oedipal lines in the family script, but he makes little headway in implementing his own "life work of sticking up for the love between man and woman" or in bringing his creative energies into a new alignment with reality (CL, 172). Indeed the oedipal triumph of *Sons and Lovers* was more than a little offset by the narrowly averted "drift toward death" of its main character (CL, 161).

In Lawrence's middle, so-called wander years when he is absorbed in defining a new basis for the sexes, his travels intersect most intensely in the area of Taos, New Mexico, where he composes *St. Mawr* and where, by transposing his origins onto strange soil, he transforms them into a new vision of sexuality beyond the wasteland of his society's and of his own past. The two events—one private, the other public—which led to this restless questing and its artistic culmination were the death of his mother and the outbreak of the war less than four years later. Along with the self, the cosmos must also be rebuilt. It would be accomplished in part through re-sourcing.

2

The quest for new centers, new gods, and new beginnings (variously symbolized by the solar plexus, Egypt, or Rananim) concentrates on the still-intact lower centers and on the mystical *Kundalini* energy coiled at the base of the spine. America is perceived as offering "something pristine, unbroken, unbreakable"; and in the fierce volcanic terrain of Mexico, with its surviving altars of blood sacrifice, Lawrence senses a "sort of solar plexus" of the continent (P, 105). In a mythical sense it does become, as Cowan has shown, a quest to the "solar plexus of the cosmos, the navel of the world" where "'an unlocking and release again of the flow of life into the body of the world'" can occur.[3]

Fire and blood are the matching elements that direct the quest in *St. Mawr*. As horse, St. Mawr is an apocalyptic figure, announcing the end of Western Industrialism. But with his hot breath drawn from another world and his emblematic redness like a "bonfire in the dark," he is also a courier for the characters into the primitive world of centaurs and goat-gods, an emissary from the long-forgotten land of archetypal unity, and a symbolic link with the living cosmos. And so he manages to throw the effete Rico, Lou Witt's husband, and to inspire her to rescue both him and herself from an enervated culture waiting for the "sting-a-ling-a-ling" of death. They travel to the new world, and after the horse is returned to a suitable natural setting, Lou presses on with her quest for the Pan-mystery. But as her quest is westward and solar, it is also downward and into the solar plexus.

In New Mexico the wild flowers hang like "fierce red stars . . . as if the earth's fire-centre had blown out some sparks" (SM, 140). And after purchasing a decrepit goat-ranch (*Las Chivas*), she says, "I've got to live for something that matters, way, way down in me. And I think sex would matter, to my very soul, if it were really sacred" (SM, 157).

The place is holy not only because it is in rapport with the center, but also because it offers the potential for a new beginning. And it is remarkable how closely it is structured on that other place where the author's origins first underwent a critical revision—"the country of my heart" as he would later think back on it (CL, 952). But to recognize the carefully drawn resemblances, we must read the text more closely and at crucial points interject pertinent biographical details.

There is, for example, an unexpected roadblock put into the narrative before Lou's quest can be fully rendered: the reader must wait while the history of the ranch's former owner is recorded.[4] She is the nameless "New England wife" of the trader who had taken the property off the hands of a schoolmaster but was himself gradually defeated by a "curious disintegration working all the time, a sort of malevolent breath, like a stupefying irritant gas, coming out of the unfathomed mountain" (SM, 144). The trader having dropped out of the account, it is now the wife who attempts to domesticate the property. With her "tense, fierce soul and her egoistic passion for service," she imposes her New England will on the ranch (SM, 147). She encloses the cabins with a white fence and cultivates a little kitchen garden. Her puritan spirit thrills to the grandeur of the country, the "pale blue crests of mountains looking over the horizon, as if peering in from another world altogether." The "pure . . . *absolute* beauty" fed her ideal of "paradise on earth" (SM, 146, 153).

But, as increasingly becomes apparent, such an order might be created by a deity who would "stop at the navel and leave the rest to the devil" (CP, 418). For closing in on her was the "seething cauldron of lower life": the "underlying rat-dirt, the everlasting tussle of the wild life, with the tangle and the bones strewing. . . . Most mysterious but worst of all, the animosity of the place: the crude, half-created spirit of place" (SM, 152). This is indeed the other half, that which has been denied by her spiritualized belief in ideal beauty. It is all the lower elements which intervene on the path toward the center, a malevolent "pre-sexual world," in which a "passionless, non-phallic column of a pine-tree" was a "bristling, almost demonish guardian." It is the Pan-domain: "A world before and after the God of Love" (SM, 151).

It locks her out and bit by bit defeats her: "It had broken something in her . . . she hid from herself her own corpse, the corpse of her New England belief in a world ultimately all for love" (SM, 153). She finally abandons the ranch for the valley, and when war makes hired help scarce, she gives it up entirely. Thus her stay at the ranch roughly coincides with the period when Lawrence was growing up; and the woman's fenced-in garden evokes the family's second home in the Breach, where the original puritan mother had presided over her household by a "sort of divine right of motherhood," based on, in Jessie Chambers's not altogether unbiased view, "her unassailable belief in her own rightness" (PE, 138). The "mother of my generation," Lawrence wrote, "felt herself the higher moral being. . . . So she proceeded to mould a generation" (P, 818). And yet, she too was defeated before her time.

As a distant yet uncannily faithful re-creation of the English midlands, the New Mexican wilderness qualifies as a "sacred place" and locus for a new beginning. Mrs. Morel's immersion in elemental beauty, especially during the evening of ecstatic fusion in her garden in which she touches the "binful of yellow pollen" in the tall, reeling lilies and drinks deeply of their perfume, is sufficiently evoked by the New England woman to be counterbalanced and completed in *St. Mawr*'s wild landscape, by that "tangle of long drops of pure fire-red, hanging from slim invisible stalks of smoke colour" (SM, 150). Such imagery is evocative not only of a new blood center, but also peculiarly of feminine bleeding (hymeneal or menstrual), a supremely vital function at the center of life glossed over and denied by the sublimating lily-white will as it seeks only ideal forms of beauty. Like Lou herself, who is both sexually experienced and one of the eternal virgins, these flowers are the "purest, most perfect vermillion scarlet" (SM, 150); like the New England woman, they are nameless; and like the ghost mother they stand on "slim invisible stalks"—both present and absent. The lesson on a deeply private level for Lawrence seems to be that if flowers can bleed and still retain their appeal so perhaps can the virginal mother. "My love is like a red, red rose only when she's *not* like a pure, pure, lily," comments the mature Lawrence elsewhere (P, 181). Juxtaposing *purest* with *scarlet* is in addition his way of commenting on a classic American work very much on his mind at the time: he would redeem Hawthorne's heroine from her scarlet shame by affirming her sexual nature, something her maker, ambivalent puritan that he was, would not do. As Lawrence sees it, the sin in *The Scarlet Letter* arose from Hawthorne's attempt "to idealize the blood" (ST, 116)—a tendency Lawrence also had to overcome.[5] He does so in part by re-sourcing American classics.

In effect, the New England woman's "moth-still ghost-centred mariposa lily with its inner moth-dust of yellow" conjures up the straining moonlit lilies and ricocheting moth in Mrs. Morel's garden (SM, 151). The deathlike stillness may be a reminder that the original is only a ghostly presence in her son's creative mind. Other biographical details are similarly reworked. The Lawrence children loved animals and made pets out of mice and a stray pup, neither of which the exacting mother—in her aversion to dirt—suffered willingly. In this version there are "pack-rats with their bushy tails and big ears" menacing the New Englander, and the "grey ratlike spirit of the inner mountains . . . attacking her from behind" (SM, 149). The smell of goats that "came up like some uncanny acid fire," and that "sort of malevolent breath, like a stupefying irritant gas," suggest the miners' pits in Eastwood (SM, 143 – 44). More precisely, this suggests the atmosphere of the vulgar father, sooty and evil-smelling, who is disgraced by the pious mother—as Pan is made over by the Christians into a beastly demon and condemned to a "hell-fire and brimstone" underworld (P, 23). "His nature was purely sensuous," Lawrence writes of his father through the filter of Morel, "and she strove to make him moral, religious . . . to force him to face things . . . it drove him out of his mind" (SL, 14).

"The world is a wonderful place," says Mrs. Morel to Paul, in the earlier novel, "and wonderfully beautiful." "And so's the pit," he said. "Look how it heaps together, like something alive almost—a big creature that you don't know" (SL, 123). And at the end of *St. Mawr*, Lou awaits "something big, bigger than men, bigger than people, bigger than religion" (SM, 158). It is of course the Pan-presence, not Mrs. Morel's perfume essence. But as the second version of origins is a sort of corrective "re-sourcing" of the first, it searches for the male component missing from the sexual equation.

Michael Kirkham has shown that Mrs. Morel's "sense of loneliness in an alien world and her fear of sensuality are closely connected feelings"; these are transmitted to the children and Paul in particular as a "fear of the world outside the family," resulting in a revulsion toward male sensuality and a "hatred of the industrial world."[6] But the male world of the pit from which Paul is cut off remains appealing—"these men are passionate enough, sensuous, dark" (CL, 404 – 5)—and gives rise to a quest for its equivalent, whereas the mother's higher world becomes downgraded to a

fenced-in mental consciousness unable to contain life. Psychologically, Lawrence's American quest is for maleness, the old
Adam in the pristine wilderness of an unfallen world figured in
American literary classics. But it presumes the end of the child's
romance with the Virgin-mother in her world. Thus his American
stories repeatedly depict the fate of a woman who rides away to
her own destruction. Lou Witt also rides away, but not so much to
her destruction as toward sexual reintegration.

The unnamed New England woman may be interpreted as the
mother's ghost who haunts the American quest for renewal, but
who also sets in motion the conditions for the creative process as
a critical reworking of past emotional experience. This, I believe, is
L. D. Clark's point when he speaks of Lawrence's "determination
to live the unlived life of his mother."[7] Taken literally, however,
this would turn Lawrence into a functional homosexual, which
was not the case. But if we can see that Lawrence's brand of
reliving was more a "re-sourcing" or "revivifying," both critical
and creative, and that it extended to both his parents' lives, then
we can find ourselves on firmer ground. As Clark notes, the
mother's death seems to be played out over and over in the American stories through "an imaginative female projection"—*but*, it
should be added, on the woman-who-rides-away theme of loss/
separation. Both the mastery of loss and a need for separation appear to be underlying motives in these works. Like the New England woman, the cultured heroines are all *broken*, either by the
wilderness itself or by its aboriginal and modern embodiments.

All, that is, except Lou Witt. She will have another go at it. The
place is, after all, more real to her than anything else; inexplicably,
it also "soothes" her and "holds" her up. She believes—vainly, according to most critics—that the spirit of the place needs and
wants her, and to it her "sex is deep and sacred, deeper than I am,
with a deep nature aware deep down of my sex" (SM, 158, 159).
This awareness issues from her original vision of St. Mawr whose
"mysterious fire . . . split some rock in her," opening her to the new
(SM, 14).

Perhaps, just as Lawrence could not conceive of man apart from
natural surroundings, he could not conceive of nature apart from
man. To reconcile the fierce dualism of the wilderness, Lou's setting down stakes may imply that she is coming between the upper
and lower regions. With her self-knowledge and sense of the sa-

credness of her sex, perhaps she will alter the inhuman and vaguely perverse natural forces all around her. Her regression may be progression, a prelude to a "new beginning"—shucking off the "stiff old thing to let the new bud come through." It will be a breaking *out* rather than a breaking *down*.

Clearly the goat ranch is tied in with the goat god. The Pan-spirit is the "hidden mystery—the hidden cause . . . a great God" (SM, 54). It flashes in the modern darkness like the bonfire of St. Mawr, or it turns up during social exchanges like the face of a debased coin, a mere pancake imprinted with the "twinkling goaty look" of the Dean. But once the horse who "drew his hot breaths in another world" appears, the casual comedy changes and dissolves. By looking with the third or pineal eye of the mystics, Lou begins to see Pan in St. Mawr, and when he "dumps" her husband, the animal has begun to carry the story off into that other world of centaurs and goat gods, of myths and archetypes. Psychologically, Pan is the creative spirit that animates the Family Romance. But he is also the archetype that carries the reader beyond the social types, into an uncreated world where "the germs of the known and unknown" can fuse into new living forms (P, 259).

By connecting the "sacred place" with dirtlike underlife, Lawrence matches Yeats's antiideal treatment of sex that acknowledges, "Love has pitched its mansion in / The place of excrement." Thus the center is dual and paradoxical, containing the "highest and the lowest, the holy and the diabolical."[8] It is like the "core of chaos" itself, which is "quintessentially chaotic and fierce with incongruities" (P, 2). But accepting this dualism may lead to a new beginning, for now those delicate, moonlit lilies, joining the sunlit wild flowers, have been rooted in elemental matter.

What is back of it then? What else is hidden within that dualistic center? Answers lay in the post—St. Mawr sections of the narrative, which, by traveling back in time to chronicle the New England woman's previous occupancy of the goat ranch, also manage to present Lou's immediate challenges. From her doorway, the woman could see the "vast, eagle-like wheeling of daylight" lighting the "great fawn-colored circle of desert" and the "strange bluish hummocks of mountains." This was to her absolute beauty. But she lived amidst another "underlying" world of "rat-dirt" and ill formed pack rats and "pithed" Mexicans, "bones of dead cattle, goats with little horns," the "smell of goats . . . like some uncanny acid fire," and "sexless, rigid pinecones, fallen from the indifferent non-phallic" columns of the pine trees. This "presexual world" forms the "seething cauldron of lower life," where matter and energy, life and nonlife intersect and new forms may be generated. Prior to the archetypal realm, it is not even quite a world of objects or forms so much as one of elements or substances. Yet these partial representations—shapes, smells, colors which precede the representation of a whole object—nurture symbolic and creative processes, "the germs of the known and unknown" which stem from those earliest ties of primary love and meet to form new wholes (P, 259). Meanwhile, Lawrence seems to be saying that the primal elements of being keep one in touch with the Pan-mystery, while also disposing one to accept the later emergence of sexuality out of the "latent fire of the vast landscape" and its "great weight of dirt-like inertia."

Although Lou's character may concentrate the creative process in this reading and personify the quest for renewal, she is also an admirably self-determined literary creation in her own right. Like Vivie in Shaw's *Mrs. Warren's Profession*, she rejects all aspects of her culture by rejecting a series of suitors. After a decisive scene with her mother, she awaits a future, the course of which is turned over to the reader, for whom the characters have been surrogates. For it is really the reader's quest—his or her need for renewal— that Lawrence has been charting. Accordingly Lou represents a shift in consciousness which is still incomplete. She is also a return to the "positive woman," "becoming individual, self-responsible, taking her own initiative" (CL, 273). But unlike Ursula's nightmarish encounter with stampeding stallions, Lou's version of St. Mawr's primitive vigor is more promising. And what is significant here is Lou's rejection of all available men on her quest for a new center. This refusal to accept any male—much less to submit to one—makes her Lawrence's first viable heroine since he turned against feminism during the war years.[9] If not a declared radical feminist, Lou is every bit as uncompromising and turns into a more encompassing cultural radical.

St. Mawr was written between drafts of the more blatantly sexist *The Plumed Serpent*, the last work to treat the male mystic as its dominant theme. Accordingly *St. Mawr* registers changes within Lawrence's emotional and creative development. His essay at around the same time, "On Human Destiny" (P2, 623–29), is also a clearing-away of many cherished Lawrencean beliefs—some of which were only perhaps provisionally entertained, or were misattributed (much like the popular belief in Freud's alleged pansexualism), and then frozen into a cultural stereotype. What Lawrence clearly affirms is that man is a thinking animal; has always—even as a savage—been grinding up his few ideas; was never spontaneous as animals or birds; and that emotion is as useless without thought as thought is without emotion. There is no reversion to primitivism: the great human adventure is into consciousness. Still, one must burst the narrow "pot-bound" confinements of modern consciousness, and "struggle down to the heart of things, where the everlasting flame is, and kindle ourselves another beam of light"—which is pretty much the path of imagination in *St. Mawr*. The paradoxical state of nature at the world's center also exists at the center of man and woman.

Lou will live on for the mysterious Pan-force to produce her male complement, "the mystic new man" (SM, 140). Meanwhile, she endures as one of the "eternal Virgins, serving the eternal fire." With her virginity thus restored—or at least reaffirmed—she is the chaste mother reborn, but no longer imposing her will to conquer or deny, and deeply aware of how sex, if it wasn't the "cheap, modern brand," would matter to her very soul "if it was really sacred." The Pan-spirit which she awaits may someday arise from the pits of the "inner mountains" whose "grim and invidious" gods are both "huger and lower than man" (SM, 153). Just so, the "demonish" father once emotionally excluded from the Lawrence household bides his reentry through the door of imagination. But for this to transpire, a last new beginning and third revision of origins must be created, and the locale must be shifted back again to native soil.

3

"Curiously, I like England again, now I am up in my own regions," Lawrence wrote in 1926, shortly before starting to write *Lady Chatterley's Lover* (CL, 933). "It braces me up," he continues, "and there seems a queer, odd sort of potentiality in the people. One feels in them some odd, unaccustomed sort of plasm twinkling and nascent." Also on his mind was some final incarnation of his utopian dreams: "We need to come forth and meet in the essential physical self," he wrote a disciple, "on some third holy ground" (CL, 941). But in a little more than three years he would be dead, and the only holy ground he would reach alive would have to be created from the three versions of his last novel.

The theme of female-exclusion running through the re-sourcing sequences serves to render the woman available for creative alternatives. In the first sequence, Mrs. Morel was locked out of her house by her drunken husband, only to merge lyrically with nature and her unborn infant. In the second scene St. Mawr summons Lou Witt away from a moribund England and a desultory marriage, while her New England predecessor finds herself driven out of the wilderness by its seething, unrelenting cauldron of lower life. In the third sequence Connie Chatterley is biologically excluded from a true marriage by her husband's disability and emotionally excluded from the sterile conversations and industrial power-plays in Wragby Hall. She too is a woman who rides—or rather drifts—away in a listless, near lifeless state.

She is also a fully sexual woman whose sexuality is largely unrecognized until in her deathlike drift she stumbles into the territory of the obscure gamekeeper, who speaks the country dialect of Morel (and Mr. Lawrence), but who has traveled about the world, known horses, reads, and articulates his opinions quite as fluently, thank you, as Morel's gifted son. Seen with the third eye, Mellors is a verson of Lou's "new mystic man." When Connie does actually observe him bathing in his backyard, "naked to the hips, his velveteen breeches slipping down over his slender loins," she receives the "shock of vision in her womb, and she knew it; it lay inside her" (LCL, 76). This pregnant vision evokes the "peculiar fusion of soul" mentioned earlier (CL, 69). By the end of the novel Connie too will be with child, but instead of the "bloody, carnal fight" of the Morel (Lawrence) marriage, it will be through an integral emotional process with her lover, one which embraces tenderness and sensuality, concern and commitment.

Around Connie the natural world has begun to renew itself, but its human portions remain dormant and bound by their culturally defined selves. Following a March day when the young pines are swaying with curious elastic life and the daffodils with their "faint, tarry scent" are turning "golden, in a burst of sun that was warm on her hands and lap," Connie follows a narrow track to the "secret little clearing" and "hut made of rustic poles," where the man is at work with the pheasants (LCL, 100). Watching him from the doorway, she drifts off "in a dream, utterly unaware of time and of particular circumstances." This recalls, if only briefly, Mrs. Morel's swooning away amid her flowers, but instead of a mystical reconception, Connie soon comes to herself and arranges to return to the place again, an arrangement not at all to the man's liking. They quarrel, and she thinks desperately when she returns in the rain a few days later, "perhaps this was one of the unravished places." But no, it cannot be: the gamekeeper returns and they again quarrel, over keys. Since he too would lock her out he is like the father, ill-tempered and bullying at times; but since he would also rescue her he is like the son, tender and empathic. Neither father nor son, Mellors is another Lawrencean fusion of opposites into something new—a private man with the "courage of his tenderness," as Connie sees him.

In time, the place becomes something special for Connie, every bit as much as the spirit of place took on sacred resonances for Lou in her quest. But here we are keeping within a more human, if still pastoral, framework. Gradually the lovers-to-be acquire histories and distinct personalities, with mixed pasts, rooting them in a world of time and experience. As the hens hatch their chicks Connie becomes more and more drawn to the little clearing, both refuge and reminder of her own sterility. But the keeper has come to accept her intrusions on his own barren privacy.

Here it should be noted that these scenes are glosses on two early texts, and function to correct or complete them. Each had involved a beginning: one of masculinity, the other of adolescent love. The first text presents Lawrence's first masculine character, the gamekeeper Annable in *The White Peacock*, who is the stoic survivor of an ill-fated love affair and precursor to Mellors, a similarly disillusioned survivor of an unhappy marriage. In the early novel, the Lawrencean alter-ego, Cyril, is so attracted to the older man, drawn both from real life as well as from the novels of Cooper, that some sort of perverse relationship is averted only, so one may infer, by removing its threat through removing the man in a trumped-up fatal fall. In the present text Annable is revived, after the fall so to speak, and assimilated as a self-projection, rather than held out as a masculine ideal and ambiguous love-object. And instead of the effeminate Cyril Beardsall seeking him out, it is a fully realized woman.

The second early text concerned one of several abortive episodes of first love in *Sons and Lovers*. Paul comes upon Miriam
kneeling shyly in front of a hen coop, eager to feed a hen, but fearful of getting pecked. He encourages her, and the fowl pecks some
corn from her hand:

> She gave a little cry—fear, and pain because of fear—rather pathetic. But
> she had done it, and she did it again.
> "There, you see," said the boy. "It doesn't hurt, does it?"
> "No," she laughed, trembling.
> Then she rose and went indoors. [SL, 127 – 28]

Thus, the first "masculine" male and a highly suggestive but in-
conclusive scene of adolescent attraction are revived and woven
into the present episodes. One afternoon Connie "arrived at the
clearing, flushed, and semi-conscious" (LCL, 134). Touching the
chicks triggers off her long held-back tears. As she cries "blindly,"
the keeper's "heart melted suddenly, like a drop of fire," and he
begins gently stroking her. The "blind instinctive caress" of "her
crouching loins" awakens more fully the fire that had begun dart-
ing at the back of his loins. Whereupon he bids her enter the hut
and lie down. She is "in a sort of dream" as he starts making
love to her, and "in a sort of sleep" at the end. In the celebrated
later scenes of love-making, the flowers the couple intertwine with
their pubic hair will have been plucked from the same garden and
landscape as the one in which Mrs. Morel walked and dreamed,
but they will be adapted, shall we say, to very different kinds of
conception.

Two aspects of Lawrence's re-sourcing lay claim to serious attention, or perhaps because re-sourcing refers primarily to the
self, this should be called revivifying since it refers to another.
Upon moving to Wragby, Connie experiences the "sulphur, iron,
coal, or acid" of the mines as though "she was living underground" (LCL, 12). And while Tommy Dukes entertains the sterile
world of Wragby with apocalyptic prophecies of civilization "going down the bottomless pit," and the only "bridge across the
chasm [being] the phallus," Connie is thinking with horror of the
"peculiar loathsome whiteness" of the neighboring tombstones
and "the time not far off when she would be buried there" (LCL,
85). And indeed she may as well be literally dead, for her life is a
"kind of painful dream" in which she drifts like "tobacco smoke"

and feels like she is going "blank." She too has begun lapsing away from life, as we've seen, only to be caught up by Mellors. In her weepy, swoonlike state, he draws her into the dark hut and bids her "lie there." Now she is as most nearly entombed as possible for someone still breathing. Her deathlike stillness in this scene (often construed as the author's antifeminism due to the male's apparent indifference to woman's sexual needs) must precede her revivifying. In the dark she is buried, in the dark her identity is blurred, in the dark the mother lies buried. Mellors enters the "peace on earth" of Connie's "soft, quiescent body"; the "activity, the orgasm, was his" (LCL, 136). Lie still, mother, whispers the son. "Now is the time between Good Friday and Easter," writes the author: "We're absolutely in the tomb" (CL, 993). Lie still, pleads the son and artist, and for once allow me the potency of returning you to life, allow me to repay the gift of life and all the debts accrued therefrom. Do not impose your will or strive for your own "satisfaction," but give way to me in this, and when your womb quickens in response to my thrusting you will be reborn in a new flesh like the phoenix. You are dead and I am one with you: "I melt out and am gone into the eternal darkness, the primeval darkness reigns, and I am not, and at last I am" (C, 26). And when at last the son is born into his phallic self, Connie is born out of the mother's tomb: "She was gone, she was not, and she was born: a woman" (LCL, 208). Then the genital love of man and woman flows in mutuality, and the "doors [are] freely opened into the dark chambers of horrors of 'sex'" which is "no chamber of horrors really" (CL, 1158).

The orgasm may be his, but the awakening is hers: this sequence addresses the novel's ultimate revivifying strategy. As he "lay softly panting against her breast . . . in mysterious stillness," she begins thinking and wondering, "Why? Why was this necessary?" (LCL, 137). Initially this activity is in the "tormented modern-woman's brain," but it continues as she later ponders how "men were very kind to the *person* she was, but rather cruel to the female. . . . not kind to her womb" (LCL, 143). Except for the keeper. The next day as she goes to the woods "she could almost feel it [the stirrings of nature] in her body." And as her lower centers start to revive, an oscillating rhythm of attraction/repulsion begins. Once, "she lay still, feeling his motion within her. . . . That thrust of the buttocks, surely it was a little ridiculous"; though on another occasion, "there awoke in her strange thrills rippling inside her" (LCL, 148, 157).

This is Lawrence's "tender and phallic novel" (CL, 1046); its prose really does follow the phallus as it enters Connie and her various centers respond. And we follow along also, our sympathetic or resistant centers likewise responding and awakening. Revivifying the reader as part of society's regeneration is the novel's aim, and it is by this means that the goal is to be accomplished. Do we find the experience liberating? Some have and still do. Do we find it vexing? Many have and still do. Yet in responding we find ourselves coming alive to it and to ourselves in various ways. For "it is the way our sympathy flows and recoils that really determines our lives. And here lies the vast importance of the novel, properly handled. It can inform and lead into new places the flow of our sympathetic consciousness . . . can reveal the most secret places of life . . . the *passional* secret places" (LCL, 117). In the novel's analogy with love-making lies another secret link between father and son, for the novelist taking his craft into the most secret places of life is like the secret labors of miners who, in Lawrence's mind's eye, enjoyed a hidden life of passionate male intimacy deep underground. Mellors again fuses these separate vocations, when as a passionate miner/lover he "smelt out the heaviest ore" of Connie's "body into purity" (LCL, 297). In so doing he made a "different woman of her," the meaning of which can be read psychologically as he relinquished his role of son and assumed an adult male's part, modeled on father but deflected from father's wife.

The three re-sourcings that have now been examined coincide if only approximately with the three Lawrence homes and with the developing areas of mind: the birth of the self, the dyadic, and the triadic. In the first of these residences, Lawrence was conceived, delivered, fell ill, weaned, and began to toddle. But like our earliest experiences and memories, the veil of amnesia descends over this two-year period. Although life in his first home is "repressed" from direct presentation in the writings, it may be felt indirectly in Lawrence's imaginative re-creation, not of his own prehistory, but of mankind's: "An ancient tribal unison in which the individual was barely separated out, then the tribe lived breast to breast, as it were, with the cosmos, in naked contact" (A, 159 – 60). This is a world before the "melting of the glaciers and the world flood" (FU, 55), often represented either as a mythical "Egypt," land of the Phoenix, an emblem of the primary creation of oneself, or as the utopian ideal and Rananim.

The second house with its kitchen garden serves as the setting for the Family Romance to unfold out of the mother/son dual unity. In this fantasy, reality is reversed and it is the father who is locked out. What is re-created through the intimacy with mother is the necessary second birth, a mythic-mystical birth of the artist to ensure his creative romance with the world.

The Walker Street house, the third residence, was perched on a hill, and, being associated in the minds of the Lawrence children with parental violence, would also coincide with their attempts to consolidate earlier memories and fears, along with their desires to effect a change for the better. In his youth Lawrence told Jessie Chambers that someday he would like to be able to afford from his literary earnings a lovely "big house" for "mother and all the people we like together" (PE, 49). The Walker Street house may have been replaced by Wragby Hall, and the associated rescue fantasy may have bridged early conflicts and later struggles toward genital primacy.

The flower imagery—a key perceptual mode through which the three origin versions have been rendered—accentuates the psychological material and carries it to a deeper level. Fittingly, Mrs. Morel in her garden is surrounded by "white phlox" and "white lilies," which attest to her virginity and, as it were, her immaculate re-conception. Yet the mother's sexuality cannot be completely ignored, and during the ensuing quarrel with her husband when she is struck with a drawer, her blood is shed and drips upon her child. Depending on how much one wants to make of such an episode, an association can be drawn between hymeneal bleeding and sexual intercourse (rendered here obliquely in its violent Primal Scene form). What is more readily documented is the absence of, or aversion to, virginal women throughout Lawrence. His gypsy may sleep with the virgin, but he honors the taboo and leaves her *virga intacta* the next morning. His heroes are not for deflowering.

As seen in Lawrence's attitude toward his *Pansies*, his interest in flowers takes him to their roots, to their source in the "black of the corrosive humus" (CP, 418). The desert wild flowers in *St. Mawr* rise from this new lower center in a "tangle of long drops of pure fire-red, hanging from slim invisible stalks of smoke-colour . . . the purest most perfect vermillion scarlet" (SM, 150). Here the purity remains, but it has become separated from the puritanical; it has also turned red, as Lou Witt's virginity somehow survives through the burst hymen; and so the implication may be that if flowers can bleed and remain pure, so can woman. In *Lady Chatterley's* celebrated scenes of lyric sexuality, the seasoned lovers bedeck their genitals with milky forget-me-nots, pink campion-buds, creeping jenny, hyacinth, and bluebells in a series of measured gestures which may be read as re-flowering the total garden of the self.

Flowers point to a subjective, Family-Romance reworking of the objective act of begetting, specified as the Primal Scene. In this revision may lie a basis in *Sons and Lovers* for the child's idealized ancestry in his being named after the biblical Paul. There is a mythic aspect also in the (virgin) mother's fusing with the natural world and taking upon herself the life forming in her womb—as Demeter begets the new season, Dionysus, her divine son. Despite this loop into subjectivity, however, the main thrust of *Sons and Lovers* is in the objective mode of experience closely observed and studied, albeit with lyrical interludes. The point may even be made that the split in Paul's emotional life is objectified in his split relationship with the spiritual Miriam and the sensual Clara. The emotional details of Mrs. Morel's married life are similarly concretely divided: Mrs. Lawrence conceived and gave birth to her famous son on the high ground of Eastwood, but Mrs. Morel "descended" to the Bottoms "on the downward path" during the seventh month of her pregnancy. The sexual act of conception which brought about this lowered condition is offset by a mystical act of reconception which brings about the revised condition proper to a virgin birth.

In effect, it is the total Primal Scene of the parents' marriage, with all its loves, hatreds, and revenge scenarios, through which Lawrence must work his way if he is to differentiate himself from one of the nondescript "in-betweens" (CP, 490), and realize his ambitions as artist and "priest of love." It is the source of his art's re-sourcing. The poem, "Demon Justice" (CP, 562), is interesting in this respect. Demon justice "puts salt on the tails of the goody good / For the sins of omission," such as:

not even a hint. . . .
that you and I
were both begotten
when our parents felt spry
beneath the cotton.

The progression of the three revisions of origins would be as follows. In *Sons and Lovers*, the virgin mother is idealized and projected as sole parent in a symbiosis or dual unity with her son. In
this area of primary creativity, origins are most subjectively determined. Through Lou in *St. Mawr*, the woman is reproduced as
a whole person—combining sexual and idealized components.
This corresponds to the hatching-out of the child in the dyadic
phase. Specifically it marks the transition of woman from a maternal to a genital figure; but the male and his sexuality are not
included. The "bad" father has been transformed into a potent
Pan-presence, but not yet into a person.

All the same, we can infer that Lawrence's response to his own
emotional crisis is inseparable from his response to the larger
cultural malaise: to begin again and generate new life-forms, not
according to societal dicta but to organic energies. To set the
sex relation straight, as he aspires to, he must first relocate and
then re-form woman. The male is still a mystery. But in *Lady
Chatterley's Lover*, adult sexual relations are represented both
through compromise identifications with the working-class father
and recovering the original object of desire by re-creating her
more fully on a genital plane. With these lovers, who have had
childhood attachments and past lovers, we are clearly exploring
the triadic sphere. The creative progression runs from the pole
of subjectivity to the pole of objectivity, from wishful fantasy to
reality-observance, from the asexual Family Romance to the acceptance of adult sexuality.

A degree of mastery over pre-oedipal and oedipal conflicts is
implicit in the acceptance of Connie's pregnancy, while on a less
literal plane the work itself, through a fertile interplay of male/
female motifs, aims to generate new life within the reader and affect a wider circle of renewal. Such may be the general purpose of
art if not always of the artist. Whatever the complex motives behind the re-sourcing process, it clearly succeeds in breaking down
and freeing up the rich and often terrifying area of early life before

adult structures are imposed. As in play, the imagination finds its own life by accepting certain preexisting givens about origins, and, by blending into them subjective needs along with objective perceptions, a new vision of sexual relationships can eventually be realized and shared.

7

Projection

I would like to know the stars again as the Chaldeans knew them, two thousands years before Christ. I would like to be able to put my ego into the sun, and my personality into the moon, and my character into the planets, and live the life of the heavens, as the early Chaldeans did.—P, 298

Nowadays clever people study sun spots through giant telescopes, and your man-made little stars zoom around the earth as if they were late on a job. You have even landed on the moon and left a few plastic bags of urine there and a few chewing-gum wrappers. But I think the Indians knew the sun and the moon much better in those long-forgotten days, were much closer to them.—Lame Deer, Seeker of Visions, p. 188

1 From Symbols to Elements and Back Again

If the psychological modality of "working-through" was best suited to focus the creative re-sourcing of the last chapter, then the fact that the modality of the present chapter is a primitive defense-mechanism called "projection" warns us of dangers ahead. Projection removes subjectively dangerous impulses, desires, wishes—be they libidinal or aggressive—by one's experiencing them as emanating from the outside. For Lawrence the writer, projection is not so readily bound up in fantasy as it is, for example, by a demonic version of the Family Romance: projection is the antithesis of primary love. But our immediate encounter with projection in Lawrence's writings is as sheer elemental energy, epitomized by the sun. To get a sense of how this otherwise maladaptive process could be mobilized to serve creative goals, I will switch back and forth from Lawrence's works to his life. Although concentrating on the American period, I will begin with an earlier work where projection has been appropriated for creative ends, before Lawrence allowed full expression to (or awareness of) his projective tendencies.

In *The Trespasser* (1912), a thirty-eight-year-old musician spends several idyllic days with a young student on the Isle of Wight. Unable to get his life together thereafter, he returns to his wife and children and hangs himself. That is about the extent of the plot. The writing is mainly taken up with dispensing Wagnerian doom and begetting scenes of exquisite foreplay. The man is withdrawn or impotent or something, and the girl's "passion exhausts itself at the mouth" (T, 55). Practically speaking, nothing below mouth, throat, and bosom exists until their feet—running hot or cold along the beach pebbles—are eventually described. Like his later lovers, this early pair—Siegmund and Helena—are polarized by their elements and enveloped in a living cosmos; but unlike their successors, these are unable to locate either their own or the other's sexual being.

In this early work nature is more sexually distinguished than the characters: sea, sand, and moon are feminine; sun, bees, and birds are masculine. "The water is as full of life as I am," remarks Siegmund, who later tells Helena about a "little virgin bay" that puts him in mind of her; while she had felt how "everything ran with sunshine," and offers that, "I saw the sun through the cliffs, and the sea, and you" (T, 69, 74). But the imagery is so arranged as to suggest that neither is able to incorporate his/her respective cosmic elements and integrate his/her sexual natures. His face is scorched as he sleeps in the sun dreaming of "huge ice crystals," and her face is as "white and shining as the empty moon." The elemental world supplies them with a facilitating environment of primary love. But instead of simply allowing it to hold them, they hold onto it and so clinging remain dwarfed in relation to their cosmic parents—he cleaving to the "great body" of sandy beach, she a "shadow" of inefficiency, cast by the sunshine. While she thinks of the thudding waves as a "great heart beating under her breast," he feels the beach heave under him.

But those living powers remain outside, while the lovers are blocked in their progress (literally losing the path one night) and become increasingly isolated. On their last morning together, she "retreated toward a large cave . . . into the gloom . . . shivering at the coarse feel of the seaweed beneath her naked feet" (T, 148). But the "black pool that confronted her" was "festooned thick with weeds that slid under her feet like snakes," and she lacks the courage to proceed. Anticlimactically, they return to their embracing and farewell kisses; and the imagery suggests that if she does not get beyond her own virgin bay, neither does he find a way to encounter her in the treacherous shoals of that virginity.

Although the theme—that vital connections between man and woman are inseparable from the living cosmos—persists in Lawrence to the end, indeed grows ever more pronounced with the years, it is neither clear why this is so, nor how this theme came to exert such a hold on his imagination. Surely a man and a woman can love without the universe also participating? Not so, says Lawrence. And although he may have his reasons, they are more often asserted or represented than solidly established. In Lawrence's later vocabulary, Helena would be responsive to the outer sun but not to her inner one, and she would thereby miss the dark sun of living connection. A more responsive character to these suns is Juliet (in "Sun," 1926), whom the sun gets to know in "the cosmic carnal sense of the word" (CSS II, 538−45). Ordered for reasons of health to leave the damp New York winter, she sails into the Mediterranean world to inhabit

a house above the bluest of seas, with a vast garden, or vineyard, all vines and olives steeply, terrace after terrace, to the strip of coast-plain; and the garden full of secret places, deep groves of lemon far down in the cleft of the earth, and hidden, pure green reservoirs of water; then a spring issuing out of a little cavern.

In the morning the "sun lifted himself naked and molten, sparkling over the sea's rim," and, watching, Juliet desires to go out naked and lie in the sun: "She sat and offered her bosom to the sun, sighing, even now, with a certain hard pain, against the cruelty of having to give herself." Gradually she feels the "sun penetrating even into her bones; nay farther, even into her emotions and her thoughts":

Something deep inside her unfolded and relaxed, and she was given. By some mysterious power inside her, deeper than her known consciousness and will, she was put into connection with the sun, and the stream flowed of itself, from her womb. She herself, her conscious self, was secondary, a secondary person, almost an onlooker. The true Juliet was this dark flow from her deep body to the sun.

In awakening and revitalizing those elemental centers which civilization had numbed in Juliet, the fiery sun is clearly a benign projection. If it is cruel, it is only to be kind; if it trespasses, it is only to foster inner discovery. Unlike the burned doll of Paul Morel's childhood, Juliet's "burning" occurs within a radically changed emotional perspective: from malicious satisfaction to restorative healing.

As a great primitive projection of male power—cruel and fertile, impersonal and empathic—the sun is fundamental to Lawrence's art and indispensable to appreciating his creative energies. Just as, for example, burning the doll quickened Paul Morel's inner flame of self, so the sun's purgative burning through of Juliet's cultural façade frees her inner organic being. Whatever Paul had projected onto the burning doll—envy, helpless rage, and so on—rebounds after his release as something more benign, pleasing, manageable. Not only does he enjoy a liberating experience, but also the doll itself takes on a new life as a symbol: the immolated doll marks the dawn of imaginative power, and if Paul gains a new sense of freedom from it, so may the figure of woman standing behind it.

In any case, with her "gold-dusky son rolling his orange over the red tiles," Juliet ripens beneath this sun into a new being. Mythically, the mother-son configuration evokes the sacred marriage of Demeter and Eros; psychoanalytically, it recalls the polymorphous-perverse state of diffuse sexuality—Love's body—where the child is equally hers and her emerging self in an ambience of primary love. Creatively, it permits a new beginning: poised between culture and nature, between the old mechanical existence and new life, or going off with a ruddy peasant. "She had seen the flushed blood in the burnt face, and the flame in the southern blue eyes, and the answer in her had been a gush of fire." In an earlier version, the affair is realized, but Lawrence more realistically decided to withhold any transparently wishfulfilling end, no doubt preferring to let the reader grapple with the issues and carry forward his own resolution.

In "Sun" the transition to wholeness can be accomplished by having the reader (via Juliet) deftly select and reject various components of the story, but in *St. Mawr* we have seen that the process is far more ambiguous and treacherous. Once again the journey is both external and internal, with a central female character who serves as delegate for the reader's quest. But as Juliet's journey is eastward to greet the rising sun, Lou Witt's is westward with the solar path, and her guiding star is St. Mawr, looming "like a bonfire in the dark." His ambiguous burning had cruelly/kindly "split some rock in Lou" that disrupts her life and rescues her from ennui.

St. Mawr, the horse who burns like a "bonfire in the dark," links the fiery sun of the heavens to the inner sun of the solar plexus. Cowan has traced the many ways in which the horse abounds in Lawrence's work (AJ, 87–96)—as centaur, hobby horse, gored victim in the bull arena, Ursula's fierce vision at the end of *The Rainbow*, and where, as a symbol he "roams the dark underworld meadows of the soul" (A, 98). As St. Mawr he is a Jungian archetype of the nonhuman psyche and the "strong animal life of man" (EP, 108), a numinous "incarnation of the transcendent and immanent mystery of being" (AJ); apocalyptically, he signals the end of an era, the known, Christian world. In order to save the wild animal from gelding—civilization's toll—Lou takes him to America and deposits him on a ranch. The animal's mysterious consciousness absorbed, she continues her quest for the "new mystic man." Failing that, she will live for "something that matters, way, way down in me" (SM, 157). The movement from a decaying and artificial wasteland to a living desert, with its absolute natural beauty and its terrible "undertone of savage sordidness," is also a movement from outer to inner, from desiccated mental consciousness to vital blood consciousness (SM, 150). Mythically, as Cowan shows, this quest leads to the "solar plexus of the cosmos, the navel of the world," where "an unlocking and release again of the flow of life into the body of the world" can occur (AJ, 68).

That Lou has arrived at this holy place in the unlikely *Las Chivas* ranch she purchases is foreshadowed by the imagery. To her New England predecessor who had operated the ranch, "On still, glittering nights, when the frost was hard, the smell of goats came up like some uncanny acid fire" (SM, 143). And a key passage reveals a vital link with the earth's molten sun-center, in a wildflower

tangle of long drops of pure fire-red, hanging from slim invisible stalks of smoke-colour. The purest, most perfect vermillion scarlet, cleanest fire-colour, hanging in long drops like a shower of fire-rain that is just going to strike the earth. A little later, more in the open, there came another sheer-fire red flower, sparking, fierce red stars running up a bristly grey ladder, as if the earth's fire-centre had blown out some red sparks. [SM, 150]

Just as the earth has an inner sun corresponding to the outer sun, so the human being has a corresponding solar plexus. The sun's beneficent effects on Lou and Juliet comprise both a restoration/healing of burned/destroyed female objects and a crucial rebalancing of the characters' vital centers. Repudiating their former attachments and their narrowly conscious selves, they become more radiantly alive and receptive to the new and undefined realities of Lawrence's circumambient universe as they open themselves up to the elemental/instinctual sources that the virginal lovers in *The Trespasser* had avoided like the terrible Medusa threat of incest/castration.

2   Lawrence Exposed

Lawrence was a living paradox to those who knew him. Just as his fiction could blend cruelty with empathy, he could be considerate, graceful, generous, modest, and at the same time insulting, willful, and superior. But perhaps most perplexing were his sudden outbursts, which, spontaneous or calculated, would always strike without warning. Since these often appear to be eruptions directly out of the unconscious, it is not always easy to determine what they meant at the time. Nonetheless, when taken together, they reveal a personal analogue to the projective tendency we have begun to discern in his art. Like the serpent who can "take poison in his mouth," Lawrence must tolerate the taste of his own venom, if only through his mastery over the "fierce incongruities" of his art.

In an informative, though far from objective, firsthand account of traveling with the Lawrences in Mexico during the early months of 1923, Witter Bynner records several such incidents. Two may be accounted for without much difficulty. During his first bullfight Lawrence suddenly jumped out of his seat and cried, "Stop it!" after watching the bull disembowel the picador's horse. Lawrence turned on the spectators, excoriating them in Spanish, and then abruptly left. At first he apparently had identified with the bull and wanted it to be spared, but then the attack on the horse—to him a special animal—created an intolerable conflict and possibly dredged up primal scene affects. In any case, this episode as reworked in *The Plumed Serpent* is projected as a perversely sexual act which the crowd unforgivably sanctions.

The second incident occurred some weeks later during an

evening at Chapala. Lawrence, again jumping to his feet, snatched from Frieda's hands photographs of her children which she had been showing to Bynner, and tore them up, grinding them into the floor with his boot. From what we know of and may surmise from Lawrence's former experiences with mothers and children, we may guess at his jealousy and fears. Perhaps he also resented Frieda's taking advantage of this susceptibility—if indeed she did. Afterwards, Lawrence went to the distraught Frieda in her bedroom, and was heard saying calmly, "It was better." Yet the children could not be so easily obliterated nor bullfights halted by his denunciations. Indeed he returned to the bullfight arena on a later visit, while Frieda was in Europe with the very children he had symbolically stamped out. Thus it may be inferred that while his actions were impulsive, they did not receive the stamp of permanency. They were also arguably appropriate.

Not so nearly apt were three other outbursts. One involved Lawrence's annoyance at Frieda's habit of allowing her cigarette to hang from her mouth. One evening as she was sitting at a corner table in the hotel restaurant, he stood up and shouted at her to "take that thing out of your mouth!" Not to be silenced, he continued, "There you sit with that thing in your mouth and your legs open to every man in the room!" Frieda was speechless as Lawrence stalked out. On another occasion shortly thereafter, a young American school superintendent named Fred Leighton joined up with the party in Mexico City and arranged a meeting between Lawrence and a government official which did not come about. "We are sitting as usual in the Lawrences' room," Bynner recalls, "watching him write while he talked, hearing him talk while he wrote, when all of a sudden he laid his open notebook upside down on the bed with an air of finality."

"Leighton," he announced as though an icicle spoke, "I have had enough of you."

"What—what do you mean?" stammered Fred.

"I do not need you any more," was the answer. "You have done all you can for me. So please leave." [WB, 32]

Later at Chapala, an even more remarkable incident took place. A group of orphaned shoe-shine boys had endeared themselves to the party, both on the beach and in the water where various games were played. Lawrence warned his friends against bodily contact with the urchins and had them ordered from the hotel restaurant during their meals. But they returned, and on a later occasion Lawrence went out for the police, had them all rounded up, and lodged a complaint against them. Lawrence's friends paid their fines and in a couple of days the boys were free again. Similarly, Frieda's dangling cigarette reappears, as does Leighton. Nothing really changes out there.

Accordingly, one might infer that Lawrence's three outbursts were clearly symbolic, and if purposeful, also veiled. But their import may become clearer if we infer that Lawrence was dealing with things on the inside through things on the outside. This process may be described as projection, all the more so in that it was the tension-relieving act itself, rather than the result, that mattered. If projection relieves anxiety as it is intended to do, then we can also infer that the anxiety stemmed more from internal threats than from external dangers. The examples make this dramatically clear. No real dangers were present in the environment; projection operated in such purity as reality seldom offers. At this point one could declare such material irrelevant, or perhaps rationalize it, or even convert it into a weapon to put in his place an already embattled figure—in which case one would be aiding and abetting the splitting process itself. Or one could explore the dangers projection deals with by linking it to the instinctual drives of the oral-sadistic phase, and then one could determine how these threatening drives are expressed in paranoid or homosexual fears. That would also be a valid way to proceed.

But none of these signals our present direction. We are highlighting the classical defense mechanism of projection to determine how it may have served Lawrence *developmentally*, in ways that extend beyond tension-reducing, among which we had better restrict ourselves to those of perception and creativity—though ultimately the concept of healing also comes into play.

3   Projection As a Stage in Creativity

It is difficult to recognize the personal component in Lawrence's feelings toward England and the war because they coincided with a widely shared malaise. The characters of *Women in Love* and "England, My England" inhabit G. B. Shaw's *Heartbreak House*, just as *St. Mawr* passes through Eliot's *Wasteland*. The "dark beast

slouching to Bethlehem to be born" is Lawrence's feathered serpent. Thus his highly individualized chant—England is dying,
Europe is dead—is easily drowned in the larger chorus. White
America, too, is the "death continent"; likewise is Mexico initially
so perceived. A train delay starts Lawrence storming against the
railway service, the government, and the Mexican race. Arriving in
Orizaba, he is seized with a sudden urge to leave. "Don't you feel it
through your feet?" he tells Frieda. "It exudes from the platform.
The place is evil." The Mexican churches arouse a sense of "cynical barrenness, cynical, meaningless, an empty, cynical, mocking
shell." "The heart has been cut out of the land. That's why hearts
had to be cut out of its people." The Aztecs, Cortes, Diaz all
add up to the same "wholesale, endless cruelty." "It goes on and
will always go on. It's a land of death. Look at this dead soil all
around us—the dagger-fingered cactus—the knife-edged sun! It's
all death" (WB, 35, 38, 36, 40).

It's all death and it's all coming at him from out there; clearly the
environment *is* triggering responses in Lawrence, but their intensity and unqualified nature are highly personal. He is subjectively
perceiving the consequences of his own destructive projections,
at this point a clearly morbid process; yet his involvement in the
land, its people, and their myths continues. He will even insist on
his having a deeper empathy for the Indians than Mexico's contemporary painters (WB, 29); but the "big bright eyes" of these
same Indians, he will also insist, "look at you wonderingly and
have no centre to them" (PS, 81). Their centers, it seems, have
also been destroyed or at least thwarted, and as Lawrence begins
working his subjective observations into the creative process, it
grows clear that his earlier projections served to destroy the environment in the sense of an erasure: blotting out or defocusing
prior to the radical redesigning and redefining of experience that
will be reborn as the Phoenix work of art. The cruel principle
that emerges from a close study of Lawrence's art is that what
is to be created must first be destroyed. Because this kind of
projection is only a preliminary phase in a process that culminates in restoration, it will be more fully examined below as
projective-identification.

Soon he has taken flight from his browbeaten companions and
found an unspoiled place in the lake resort of Chapala. It is there
that the "trail ends," he wrote Murry, and there that a new vision of

Mexico quickens into life through the pages of *The Plumed Serpent*. The novel itself is about the eclipse of present-day Mexican civilization and the rise of a new religion. The fact that the embodiments of this new religion—specifically Don Cipriano—revert to the Aztec dagger in the swift execution of would-be cowards, suggests that not all the destructive projections have been transformed but in their sadistic fury are like the return of the repressed. This is not to say that the far more mysterious creative process itself has failed, because Lawrence is remarkably consistent in allowing the flaws in his cherished religious revival. Rather it is to surmise that the failure to fulfill intentions means that attempts at mastery through creativity will continue.

Lawrence's projective tendency has been noted before. Cavitch, for example, states that Lawrence would "explore his own reality by projecting it onto other countries, other places, other settings, in works that promise or fail to suit his requirements for self-realization" (NW, 30). While favoring a narcissistic circularity, this is basically true, though projection plays a preliminary role in the creative process. What is initially projected are very likely primitive affects of love or hate along with self-components, to be represented in the Lawrencean cosmos as, for instance, "the knife-edged sun." Once projected onto the environment, the threatening impulse is eliminated, but the outside world may turn persecutory unless further measures are undertaken. In order for the impulse—first manifested as part of the environment—to be defused for later representation in art, it must be reincorporated into the receptive creative self: into the artist's creative womb, as Ehrenzweig has it. In other words, that which was once ego-alien must now either be changed into an ego-syntonic form, or else the ego itself must undergo modification. "All the time, underneath," writes Lawrence, who also used the concept of male womb, "there is something deep evolving itself out of me" (CL, 273).

In a broader sense, what constitutes the ego-alien for Lawrence is not easy to determine—he was so ambivalent about so much. For him to claim he was born hating his father, and in so saying to echo his mother, suggests that a classical oedipal position was validated and even fostered by the parent (CL, 69). But he must have needed to respect his father: indeed, to love the authority he had been authorized to hate. Consequently, he would in time come to resent his mother's deprecating the figure every son must struggle against and come to terms with through identification. But so real is the mother even in death and so strong is her hold on her son that his self-preservative drives could feel ego-alien. To live is to live separately from the all-important mother, and that would demand a totally new basis for living.

In addition, because she is all-important, she is both esteemed and envied—ambivalently experienced. The lust of hate and the lust of love, Lawrence says in another context, both seek to consume and possess the object's soul (ST, 90). To retain his identificatory ties with her and to postpone as long as possible the solution to the primitive equation of male sexuality/female harm, he downgraded or even repudiated his emerging phallic drives, which would have conflicted with her ideals and his own early identity.[1] If these repudiations were split off and projected, they might stand a chance of being reintroduced as part of a developing masculine identity, and being accepted more or less consciously as a gift of the cosmos. But the process entails a regression to the sources of personality, to the very "core of chaos, fierce with incongruities," without suffering inner collapse (P, 259). If successful, he may be rewarded by the dark gods with that portion of "strange sapience" emanating from the dark gods of maleness.

In any event, the need to assimilate within the personality feminine components of creativity and at the same time to disengage himself from other feminine ties, concurs with the need to consolidate a more resolute masculine identity in order to enter further stages of selfhood. Once in Mexico City, Lawrence voiced this concern, with comical results. Usually managing to avoid public occasions, he found himself called upon to speak at a PEN banquet and revealed what was then uppermost in his mind: "I said that the most important thing to remember, was that we are all, first and foremost, men together, before we are artists; that to be a man is more important. But they didn't understand. They one and all protested that it was more important to be an artist" (LB, 163 – 64). Perhaps, unlike Lawrence, they were able to take their maleness for granted. Hence, by having to create so much, Lawrence ended the greater artist if not the greater *hombre*.

Thus Lawrence's basic dilemma: unable to completely give up his mother, whose importance in his life was so overwhelming as to compel him to play out his ambivalence with Frieda, he could regress to what Freud in his paper on "Mourning and Melancholia" referred to as a "narcissistic identification" with the lost object—i.e., live the mother's unlived life. This in turn would mean hating male sexuality as embodied in his father. Yet to reject the mother outright would be also to reject much of what was best in himself.[2] If the creative process is summoned, it must involve the total personality—that is, not only the agreeable components, but also those that include the unresolved conflicts with which we have become familiar. A preliminary step toward creative resolution implies projection by splitting-off the unacceptable; but what is also needed is to disassemble those early relationships into manageable components. To assimilate the "good" parts of the mother into the personality (e.g., those affirming the basic quality of life, as well as those related to creative drives), the "bad" feminine parts of the self must be externalized. This, Lawrence frequently portrays as a caul hardening into a shell or husk to be shed entirely for the rebirth into masculine selfhood. This great inner struggle is played out principally in America.

Among Lawrence's principal emotional concerns in America are assimilating the good aspects of the mother relation, laying her unhappy ghost to rest, and shedding his symbiotic membrane. They serve as necessary prerequisites for his own emotional maturation and that of his art. Looking back on America, he will view it as "a lovely stretch of one's youth," but it almost killed him along the way (CL, 1153). Recovering in Mexico City from a near-fatal illness, he composes a fictional fragment, his last imaginative treatment of himself in the New World. After many years abroad, his self-character in "The Flying Fish" is summoned home to England by the "death of his sister, who was twenty years older than he and named *Lydia*, like Lawrence's mother," writes Cavitch (NW, 190). The death of this woman, Cavitch continues, represents Lawrence's release from his mother's dominance as his "anima, or feminine identification."

4 Projective Identification

... through learning repression, the child creates a receiving womb in his own un-conscious. There the split-off material is "buried alive" like the seed of the corn in the womb of the earth. Unconscious dedifferentiation will transform the material and make it acceptable for later introjection—in unrecognizable symbolic form—into consciousness.—Anton Ehrenzweig, HO, 217

The test of a first-rate intelligence is the ability to hold two opposed ideas in the mind at the same time, and still retain the ability to function.—F. Scott Fitzgerald

Perhaps because no other ego-capacity exists, the task of recon-ciling unbearable contradictory feelings falls to creativity. Once modern Mexico has been effectively "demolished," it can be re-imagined by the myth-making faculty. Not only is Mexico reborn in the novel, but also Lawrence as ego-ideal in Don Ramon, as phallic-sadistic son in Cipriano, and as a fusion with Frieda in Kate Leslie, the center of the novel's consciousness. Bynner's book continually demonstrates how Lawrence's and Frieda's experi-ences and reactions in Mexico are fused into that character, ap-parently because he needs to have his male world validated through the eyes of a woman (WB, 122). Supposedly, she will also experience a renewal of sorts by acquiring the knowledge along with the potency that issues from her sexual bonding with Cipriano. But at the end she is still hesitant, and her ambivalence may pinpoint Lawrence's own doubt about having succeeded in harnessing and projecting so many wildly contradictory forces within the creating self.

Whenever Lawrence projects his own destructive drives onto the environment and then reincorporates them as preexisting ele-mental forces or under some other guise, the process amounts to projective identification.[3] This technical but useful concept tem-porarily involves two phases: the first a cleaning-out, an emptying; the second a filling-in and occupying, or reintrojection. For ex-ample, Lawrence was exceptionally tolerant toward Frieda's oc-casional promiscuity, but he panicked at the sight of her, legs spread, a "thing" (cigarette) drooping from her mouth—these seemingly sexual overtures having evidently acquired a forbidden meaning. It would follow then that Frieda may have been invested by Lawrence with his own displaced homosexual wishes and he panicked at her flaunting them. Thus the fear of dangerous passive wishes is countered by his aggressively attacking Frieda and even humiliating her publicly. Yet that scene will soon be followed by one of heterosexual intimacy.

Crossing over briefly into fiction, one finds Cavitch on the right track in his reading of *Women in Love* (NW, 66 – 70). Birkin's overt sexual attraction for Gerald is relegated to the now-famous Cancelled Prologue, whereas in the novel proper, which depicts a neutralized bond of blood-brotherhood, the disavowed homosexual wishes flow into the character of Gudrun, who consummates a sexual relationship with Gerald. However, it seems gratuitous to go further and assert that Lawrence loves his homosexual side in Frieda, or that anal intercourse in the novels is really only displaced homosexuality; such a conclusion assigns a more fundamental role to the homosexual component than is warranted. Like heterosexuality in this respect, homosexuality is secondary to and an outgrowth of earlier drives and libidinal ties. Among various psychoanalytic views on the subject, one maintains that the homosexual act aims at incorporating (concretely and belatedly) a hitherto absent or deficient masculine identity by taking in orally, anally, or howsoever, the member of the other, who embodies an idealized masculinity. However Lawrence fantasied about this option, and he must have in order to free up the material for creative purposes, its actualization was not within his emotional repertory: he was no E. M. Forster (CL, 316). The need to overcome the conflicts in becoming a complete male was more urgent if not necessarily more basic than the need to love a male, and it was the former that prevailed over the latter.[4]

Because in Lawrence various potential identificatory positions persist, they offer clues to the projective processes in his writings, as we have just seen. But it is one thing to have a deficient sense of masculine selfhood—which most close readings of Lawrence accept and which has been most admirably captured by Norman Mailer—but it is quite another thing to feel helplessly thrust out into an unloving and unintelligible universe, and this Lawrence could never abide.[5] Because all of nature is locked into mutual influences of attraction and polarity, everything assumes affective powers. The sun, for example, can be assigned an honorary male gender and perform regenerative functions through its penetration and incorporation. The ancient view of the "vitality of the cosmos" predisposes man to take into himself more and more of

its "gleaming vitality"; "by vivid attention and subtlety and exert-
ing all his strength," he "could draw more life into himself . . . till
he became shining like the morning, blazing like a god" (EP, 50). In
"Sun" the awakened individual is female; in *The Man Who Died*,
male. In both instances the sun can be studied as a transformed,
reintrojected impulse.

Well before his cosmic theories were formulated, *The Trespasser* conveys the belief that natural objects—or rather particles,
substances—are, as we have seen, integral to the complete self:
"The sand was warm to his breast, and his belly, and his arms. It
was like a great body he leaned to. Almost, he fancied, he felt it
heaving under him in its breathing. Then he turned his face to the
sun and laughed." Childlike between the elemental parents, the
male experiences a benign sense of separateness with oppositions
minimized, but the sexual prototypes in nature have been clearly
designated. The beach functions as an ideal holding environment,
its flowing substance yielding to the creative explorations of the
hands; conversely, the sun stands apart, absolute and indestruc-
tible, its future role of reinforcing maleness as yet unspecified—
cosmic not yet carnal.

Earlier it was noted that *The Trespasser* is one instance among
many of Lawrence's collaborative *modus operandi*. Closer scru-
tiny of events around the time of its writing enable us to trace the
dynamics of projective identification. It would be helpful to recall
Greenacre's insight that the artist's distinctive way of relating to
the world includes his tendency to invest peripheral and partial
objects—natural elements, for example—with great affective
meaning.[6] As well as demonstrating this tendency, Lawrence has
attempted, not too successfully, to describe it in reference to the
cardiac plexus of his pollyanalytic system, which combines a
blissful sense of union with the beloved and an objective realization of separateness. This comes about through the "adding of
another self to the own self," and through the "mode of dynamic,
objective apprehension, which in our day we have gradually come
to call *imagination*, a man may in his time add on to himself the
whole of the universe, by increasing pristine realization of the universal" (FU, 40). Projective identification accounts for some of the
internal dynamics of this mystifying process, which feeds into the
artist's creative romance with the world—and like the noble par-

ents of the adoption fantasy must share in the child's need for exalted self-estimation.

In the summer of 1909, during his first year of teaching at Croydon, Lawrence spent a holiday at the Isle of Wight, where Helen Corke, a fellow teacher of recent acquaintance, had also vacationed.[7] But she had been with a married man who had committed suicide soon after returning to his family, all pretty much as it would be told in *The Trespasser*. Her lover was a musician, and older than Lawrence, whose slight degree of artistic success, provided, along with the sexual frustrations of the musician, a common ground of sympathy. The following winter, when Helen Corke told Lawrence about the summer interlude and let him see her account, he "took the record to his lodging and read with growing excitement," she recalls. "He slept little that night; before morning he felt convinced that he had the complete blue print for a second novel." As he begins to work on the project, an unusual situation develops: "He had had no contact with Siegmund living, and Siegmund dead was beyond the range of his observation. He could only study Siegmund through Helena." Perhaps this mode of apprehension is how the "adding of another self to the own self" may take place. Through woman he may reach man; through the mother relation one step removed, he may find the father.

"I've never really had a father," he told Jessie Chambers (PE, 88). He may have been right in the loving, sharing, trusting aspects of the relationship, which were mutually avoided after a certain impasse. More accurately stated, his mother never let him have a father, and so by going through the female to reach the male, he is in effect gaining permission to achieve that which had been withheld. If this can be done indirectly, through the writing process, then the homosexual threat can be reduced and, in more than one sense, circumscribed. Thus an image of ideal maleness must be projected onto the character, who now exists only in the mind of the woman who knew him. And so from the familiar to the unfamiliar are corrective advances undertaken. The Siegmund figure both draws on the conflictual inner self of the artist/son and serves as a stand-in for the missing father relation—which is now set off in a conflict-free zone where prior barriers to identification cannot interfere. And now the repressed or prohibited positive feelings toward the discredited parent may be projected onto the relative vacuum that "Siegmund" (as father) occupies. Eventually, along with the creative work, these feelings can be assimilated into the artist (as son). The success of these labors is not apparent in that early novel, but may be felt in one of his best early stories, "Odour of Chrysanthemums." In it a miner, like Morel a discredited husband and parent, is killed in the mine and upon being returned home, stretched out, undressed, and washed down, awakens powerful feelings of guilt and sympathy.

A rapprochement may have also been taking place within the father's sphere of preeminent interest to the son—that of sexual activity. It is perhaps fitting that Lawrence's first sexual affair is veiled in secrecy, inasmuch as he had not by then found a way to admit "that," as he referred to it embarrassedly with Jessie Chambers, into consciousness (PL, 109). He would manage to do so only through a long and circuitous path winding through the mystical centers of the body, awakening the dark gods, and finally out into the open daylight of phallic reality. But it was during the Croydon period (probably early in 1909) that Lawrence was sexually initiated, and it was also probably with an Eastwood acquaintance, Alice Dax, one of the models for Clara Dawes in *Sons and Lovers* (PL, 112). What can safely be inferred is that the incomplete sexual experience as presented in the early works is associated with the incomplete male identity. Thus when the self-outcast Siegmund is on the beach with the girl, whose breast is bright as the "breast of a white bird," they are presented as a "pair of wild, large birds inhabiting an empty sea." The sea is feminine, and together they are like a bosom resting on the sea—that is, sexually undifferentiated. Alone, when he is exploring a "small, inaccessible sea cave," he is like a "white bee" creeping into a "white virgin blossom." Bee and bird may be taken as partial self-representations (Helena thinks in complementary terms of the sunshine as a bee). Later, while hugging the "warm body of the sea-bay beneath him," he thinks, "it is like Helena." His hand plays over the warm pebbles and then "burrows under the surface," finding the "cold mystery of the deep sand also thrilling." "He pushed in his hands again and deeper, enjoying the almost hurt of the dark heavy coldness." And he comes to realize that although he is held in the warm body of beach, "under all, was this deep mass of cold, that the softness and warmth merely floated upon."

Beyond breast-love is genital-love, and he can't get to it any more than she. The environment can hold him, but it can only be so facilitating, and then he must venture forth himself. Besides, it can be inferred about this early work that Lawrence is more interested in using creativity to explore maleness than to realize the female. And so although all the components for sexual actualization are hovering about, the important work of mature organization does not occur. Helena embarks on a journey to the snakelike seaweed realm of the sea-cave, only to pull back. Hence the novel's impasse. It is only very gradually that woman's full genital nature is allowed into the works, but we do see it happening with Juliet and with Lou. The internal world is always discovered in terms of the external, for the external, acting as facilitator, holds and permits the anxiety-reducing act of symbol-formation. Nature "soothes" and "holds" Lou while she prepares both for the encounter with the unknown wild spirit of the place and for her battle against the ratlike pull into the nonbeing condition of dirt.

In the end Lou has been restored to a near-mythic status as virgin priestess. She waits in a "temple for the spirit of Pan," as Isis awaits her Osiris in *The Man Who Died*. In Isis we can see how this process culminates. The resurrected god-man finds in her "the deep-folded, penetrable rock of the living woman" (MW, 207). In "Pomegranate," and other poems ostensibly about fruit, the poet in Lawrence anticipated these developments:

> . . . the setting suns are open.
> The end cracks open with the beginning:
> Rosy, tender, glittering
>   within the fissure.

The "positive woman," with her own kind of strange sapience, whom Lawrence strives to create must be more than an extension of primary love's early environment or the externalization of his early feminine identifications, but less than the dreaded, fanged, and phallic woman. To whatever relative degree he can succeed in this, the male in him can also come into his own. But his own spontaneous impulses and intuitions—with their analogy to the brooding sapience of the serpent—must, as he acknowledges in his remarkable essay, "On Human Destiny," serve human consciousness. Only then can the thought-adventure advance.

8

Sun

In the interior of every animal the hottest part is that which is around the blood and veins; it is in a manner an internal fountain of fire, which we compare to the network of a creel, being woven all of fire and extended through the centre of the body, while the outer parts are composed of air.—Plato, Timaeus

Inside the earth were fires like the heat in the hot red liver of a beast. Out of the fissures of the earth came breaths of other breathing vapours direct from the living physical under-earth, exhalations carrying inspiration. The whole thing was alive, and had a great soul, or anima. . . . —Etruscan Places, 49

1   Cosmic Centeredness

Traditionally the artist has viewed the sun as a cosmic body and energy-force whose fiery element finds its counterpart in the blood, the heart, and the sanguinary humor; more particularly for Lawrence, the sun also symbolizes the fierce masculine regenerative power whose counterpart is the solar plexus and phallus. Lawrence treats elements of the cosmos like substances that nourish the self and the creative imagination. As natural substances evoke the abiding world of primary love, so cosmic elements represent the originally split-off drive and self-fragments that may yet be reappropriated for equally valid creative ends. Consequently, both the benign and the lethal flow into the creative mix and transmute. As before, a psychic alchemy may be delineated in order to get at the mysterious ways in which body/self and environment/cosmos cross-fertilize and nourish one another. We will continue the line of inquiry begun as projective-identification and delve more deeply into the dynamic processes wherein the solar body is broken down into elements and substances that can be idealized, transformed, and reinternalized, for what Lawrence projects onto the sun is what he most fundamentally needs. Here the twin creative motives announced at the beginning of this study—to remake the self whole and hale, and to revise the sex relation—are inextricably joined.

We have seen that only when Lawrence's turbulent inner world is sundered into self and other, male and female, does the creative imagination awaken to repair self damage and help install missing psychic agencies. The balance of heaven and earth—symbolized in the Rainbow, Phoenix, and Quetzalcoatl—incorporates the sun into unified symbols of wholeness, and presupposes the binding up of some earlier breach. Interestingly, the actual separate sun is ambivalently experienced and often contested by Lawrence. His "greatest experience from the outside world" came in New Mexico: "There I saw the brilliant, proud morning shine high up over the deserts of Santa Fe, something stood still in my soul, and I started to attend." But it is in Old Mexico where the sun comes into its own and "part of the horror of the Mexican people came from . . . the untempered cruelty of the flat-edged sunshine." This literal sun Lawrence also sees and lets be.

But behind the flat-edged physical sun of our noonday consciousness is the "nameless Sun, source of all things," a "vast dark protoplasmic sun from which issues all that feeds our life" (MM, 76). This is the dark sun of the Aztec blood sacrifice and the Hopi snake dance: the sustaining "sun of existence" (MM, 64). Being nonmaterial, it corresponds to and sympathetically influences the "earth's innermost dark sun" and the dark sun at the center of the individual (MM, 70). The "pristine cosmos" (MM, 65) is in continual, circular interaction with the "pristine consciousness" (FU, 8). In the mysterious round dance at Taos, the Indians are giving "themselves again to the pulsing, incalculable fall of the blood, which forever seeks to fall to the center of the earth, while the heart like a planet pulsating in an orbit, keeps up the strange, lonely circulating of the separate human existence" (MM, 48 – 49). In between the sky (with "its fire, its waters, its stars") and the "reddened body" of the earth (with "its invisible hot heart, its inner waters and many juices") is the growing seed of organic life—be it of corn or of man—"like a seed that is busy and aware." Both a subject and a master among cosmic influences, this man "partakes in the springing of the corn, in the rising and budding and earning of the corn. And he eats his bread at last, he recovers all he sent forth and partakes again of the energies he called to the corn, from out of the wide universe" (MM, 60 – 61).

Compressed into this marvelous passage are the major themes of this study. The cosmic identifications and influences reverberate from the Family Romance, while the situating of man between sky and earth points to Primal Scene schema. But the casting forth of the seed, its germination and growth, its harvest and promise of nourishment, is an apt summation of projective identification. Behind it, too, is the configuration both of the dying-reviving god of nature and of the self in creativity. The Aztecs were not altogether alien to Lawrence, who also has to cut the heart from his potential subject-matter before it can throb with renewed life. And closely related is the service which projective identification may render to creative needs. Lawrence's perceptions of Indian rituals are often so penetrating and so essentially just as to border on the uncanny. It is as if he finally found, after all his wanderings over the earth's surface, those phenomena that very nearly coincided with the promptings of his psychic system.

In preparing readers for the snake dance, he draws a distance from the "funeral cortege" of tourists in their black-hooded cars crawling across the desert like beetles. He makes us feel that we too are initiates at a sacred rite, and not mere spectators:

[The snake-priests] were the hot living men of the darkness, lords of the earth's inner rays, the black sun, the earth's vital core, from which dart the speckled snakes, like beams.

Round they went, in rapid, uneven, silent absorption, the three rounds.
. . .

Then, in the intense, secret, muttering chant the grey men began their leaning from right to left, shaking the hand, one-two, and bowing their body each time from right to left. . . .

But the crowd was on tenterhooks for the snakes, and could hardly wait for the mummery to cease. [MM, 72]

Only after the ceremony when the snakes are to be set free, does Lawrence rejoin the tourists: "We must clear away." Nonetheless, a change even in the onlookers is hinted: "We recoiled to the farther end of the plaza" (MM, 75).

Have the onlookers "exchanged spirits" with the snakes, as had the men of the snake clan who had washed and soothed the snakes below in the kiva? The snakes are both "more rudimentary, nearer to the great convulsive powers" in the "earth's dark centre," and "emissaries to the rain-gods" of the sky. By exchanging spirits with them, man participates more fully in the cosmic cycle of renewal and so acquires something of their strange sapience. They are indeed living symbols, and their ritual of incorporation may well be the goal of the Lawrencean quest. Their secret knowledge lies in the transmission of the nonhuman sources of vital energy into the human sphere. Their strange sapience waters the roots of the imagination.

So much for the creative import. The psychoanalytic underpinnings are just as important, for the scene is also a ritual about the incorporation of phallic potency. It is as if Lawrence's most private needs had been magically externalized and legitimized. The witnessed process of projective identification also addresses Lawrence's incomplete maleness, and thus his powerful empathic response to these rituals. Their doing and redoing performs for him things he needs to have done. The snakes brought out of the earth—literally incorporated orally by the Hopi dancers—are like Lawrence's primitive identifications which must be revived to serve as prototypes of masculinity and be connected with his disturbed family relationships, especially with his father. Replanted on English soil, the dark gods function through Mellors as well as Lawrence was able to let them. In a carnal sense, his dark sun performs for Connie what the cosmic sun had performed for Juliet in "Sun." And insofar as sex has been restored to human dimensions, the literal sun is also restored to its natural function of lighting the day. It is probable that only after America was Lawrence able to return to his native village and resurrect his father's discredited image fully enough for his final affirmative works. Internalized and reintegrated, the sun finally becomes a psychic agency, like an ego-ideal:

Conscience
is sun-awareness
and our deep instinct
not to go against the sun.
    [CP, 527]

Let us examine how these processes actually work together creatively as projective identification. In "Pan in America," Lawrence draws on his experiences in Taos to bring home his title thesis (P, 22—31). Nearby their "little ranch under the Rocky

Mountains, a big pine tree rises like a guardian spirit." This is the same "demonish guardian" as in *St. Mawr*, whose "non-phallic" existence predates the "ithyphallic column" of ancient Greece:

Long, long ago the Indians blazed it. And the lightning, or the storm, has cut off its crest. Yet its column is always there, alive and changeless, alive and changing. The tree has its own aura of life. And in winter the snow slips off it, and in June it sprinkles down its little catkin-like pollen-tips, and it hisses in the wind, and it makes a silence within a silence. It is a great tree, under which the house is built. And the tree is still within the allness of Pan. At night, when the lamplight shines out of the window, the great trunk dimly shows, in the near darkness, like an Egyptian column, supporting some powerful mystery in the over-branching darkness. By day, it is just a tree.

It is just a tree. The chipmunks skelter a little way up it, the little black-and-white birds, tree-creepers, walk quick as mice on its rough perpendicular, tapping; the bluejays throng on its branches, high up, at dawn, and in the afternoon you hear the faintest rustle of many little wild doves alighting in its upper remoteness. It is a tree, which is still Pan.

And we live beneath it, without noticing. Yet sometimes, when one suddenly looks far up and sees those wild doves there, or when one glances quickly at the inhuman-human hammering of a woodpecker, one realizes that the tree is asserting itself as much as I am. It gives out life, as I give out life. Our two lives meet and cross one another, unknowingly: the tree's life penetrates my life, and my life the tree's. We cannot live near one another, as we do, without affecting one another.

The tree gathers up earth-power from the dark bowels of the earth, and a roaming sky-glitter from above. And all unto itself, which is a tree, woody, enormous, slow but unyielding with life, bristling with acquisitive energy, obscurely radiating some of its great strength.

It vibrates its presence into my soul, and I am with Pan. I think no man could live near a pine tree and remain quite suave and supple and compliant. Something fierce and bristling is communicated. The piny sweetness is rousing and defiant, like turpentine, the noise of the needles is keen with aeons of sharpness. In the volleys of wind from the western desert, the tree hisses and resists. It does not lean eastward at all. It resists with a vast force of resistance, from within itself, and its column is a ribbed, magnificent assertion.

I have become conscious of the tree, and of its interpenetration into my life.

Interpenetration suggests a continuation of the intense interaction with the mother who breathed him "like an atmosphere" (CL, 70). It is carried on subsequently with the environment by means of projective identification and in the interest of continuing growth.

As shown earlier, Taos had drawn Lawrence as one of the great nodal points of psychic geography ("the Indians say Taos is the heart of the world" [P, 100]). It will serve also as his entrée to the great solar plexus of Mexico. But it draws and holds him after a pattern of primitive bonding: the pine tree appeals to the counter-balancing resistance of the spinal ganglion and renders him defiant, bristling, and "turpentiney." Together, pueblo and pine are life-sustaining.

Following these processes further, one reaches their natural culmination. When the ancient pine tree becomes a "big camp-fire of logs," "a man rises and turns his breast and his curiously-smiling bronze face away from the blaze, and stands voluptuously warming his thighs and buttocks and loins, his back to the fire, faintly smiling his inscrutable Pan-smile," and in his "Pan-voice" saying:

"Aha! Tree! Aha! Tree! Who has triumphed now? I drank the heat of your blood into my face and breast, and now I am drinking it into my loins and buttocks and legs, oh tree! I am drinking your heat right through me, oh tree! Fire is life, and I take your life for mine. I am drinking it up, oh tree, even into my buttocks.

And "when the fire is extinguished," the "man says to the woman, 'Oh, woman, be very soft, be very soft and deep towards me, with the deep silence. . . . Let me come into the deep soft places. . . .'"

Thus the final stage of these processes, and perhaps their goal throughout, becomes all that is implied by sexual potency: the incorporation of the masculine spirit and the blood-consciousness or solar-plexus brand of sexually reuniting with woman.

2   Identity of the Sun

Born with a caul.
A black membrane over the face,
And unable to tear it,
Though the mind awake . . .
  —*"Men in Mexico,"* CP, 408

Those familiar with Lawrence's fiction recognize a pattern which is varied time and again: that of the Woman Who Rides Away. It occurs at least a dozen times, so often that one may surmise it grew out of the author's most profound emotional experience. It is also true that the woman's riding away inevitably signifies a death—either her actual death or that of mental consciousness which is always associated with the industrialized Western world. We also notice that Lawrence himself continually rode away—usually by ship or by train—from Western culture, and that regardless of who leaves whom, he was traumatically affected by his mother's slipping away from him in death. In *Sons and Lovers*, first the mother departs from her son, then the son departs from her home. His action is a sort of compromise between the impossibilities of libidinal fusion and death wishes. The compromise is expressed by means of identification. Paul Morel's separating from home reenacts her separation from him.

By this act, Lawrence minimizes the overwhelming loss, because by taking her action—i.e., her death—inside, he is also taking *her* with him. Earlier discussions have revealed how his identifications with her could serve as an important, sustaining part of his ego, but also as something that prevented him from experiencing a fuller life, which could only result from further development into masculine selfhood.

But he could only accomplish this by breaking from the feminine perimeters of his mother's personality.[1] These he often discredits as the tomb, attributes to the caul of civilization, or demeans as "the glassy envelope, the insect rind, the tight-shut shell of the cabbage, the withered walls of the womb." The fear that encases him is perhaps that of losing the precious, protective tie with the mother and becoming enveloped in the common masses—symbiotically or homosexually. After the blind man runs his hands over the face of the effeminate Bertie Reid, his brittle, narcissistic ego crumbles "like a mollusc whose shell is broken." The feminine skein around the self, often signified as repressive puritanism or mental/white consciousness, can only be shed when replaced by something more suitable. This process begins in Lawrence's work when the dark gods enter from below. It is intimated as early as *The Rainbow* (1915), made explicit in *Kangaroo* (1923), and played out in full costume in *The Plumed Serpent* (1924–26). But also below is the animated dirt-life of obscene insects in his nightmares, the black ants and pack rats in *St.*

Mawr—"the peculiar undercurrent of squalor, flowing under the curious *tussle* of wild-life"—that impede the quest for new centers. And if this "vast and unrelenting will of the swarming lower life" succeeds temporarily in blocking the necessary regression to a new beginning, it is because the underlying emotional threat is maternal engulfment or homosexual fears of attack from behind (SM, 152 – 53). These anxieties are displaced onto the environment. But originally the swarming-insect and biting-rat world may have also been projections of unacceptable drives and wishes, which block a line of sexual development unless they can be modified and assimilated by reintrojection.

It may seem strange that this lower world came into its own on the deserts and steep slopes of the American Southwest, which Lawrence found to be so vividly alive. His disgust with a society viewed as teeming insects or vermin had already been vented during the war years, but apparently the projections could be better sorted out in a remote, natural setting. Moreover, the American desert was alive with real beasts, unlike the half-dead "white monkeys" of the great industrial and cultural wastelands. On a purely subjective level, however, experiencing nature as a wasteland is to risk encountering the dreaded results of one's most lethal projections: *my aggressive wishes have destroyed the world*. Thus, the wasteland as a mental construct can be seen as the projection of primitive, world-destruction fantasies emanating from the earliest phase in infancy—sometimes called paranoid-schizoid—and re-emerging in psychosis. In art such states are evoked in Munch's *The Scream*, Picasso's *Guernica*, Kafka's *The Trial*, Strindberg's *To Damascus*, and so on. It is often a crucial phase in an artist's total development, but the authentic work of art never yields completely to the psychotic impulse. In Lawrence's case, the fact that the desert has that "curious *tussle* of wild life" beneath suggests that it will eventually come into bloom of its own latent power; the nature-god will stir in the tomb, the long-dead Etruscans will quicken to his imagination, the grimy Midlands will beget a pastoral romance. Not only does the early holding environment nourish the springs of creativity, but it also never lets him down. This view is in relation to the mother; in relation to the self, the view shifts to narcissism. The infant's early images of the world—primordially, the mother's responsive face—are mirror-images of himself in the sense that they reflect his own needs, wishes, and fantasies of omnipotent control. Only gradually do the claims of objective reality take hold. For Lawrence, the sense of a living, responding universe beyond the pervasive sense of decay, dissolution, and desolation of the experiential world may be a narcissistic defense against world-destruction fantasies, but it is likely one constructed from a very strong tie of primary love and attachment to the mother.

To his friends he was a vivacious—and at times death-haunted—enigma. Casting his seed in the valley of death, he was both questing knight and ailing king, with the ailments projected yet also contained, so that the wasteland is reciprocal with the healing quest. Thus the environment remains to a degree a subjective object, inexhaustively rich and varied, never in the work of art totally alien or hostile, but a product of apperception as much as of perception. To the extent that Clifford Chatterley, an emblem of our modern wasteland, is not fully realized with empathy or with the mythic embellishment of the ailing king, the shadow of arbitrariness falls over him like a split-off self-image that has not been reintrojected.[2]

If the potency of the sun seems at times unfairly selective, its implications as an overdetermined symbol can stand a further probing. So far we have pursued projective-identification with the woman. We may assume that in such a mental state normal consciousness would be suspended so that, through her, the lower orders may enter under the guise of the dark gods: through her, the paternal phallus may be incorporated. Or to pursue the logic of Primal Scene schema, *in* her it can be discovered and retrieved. Serving masculine development, the sun burns the feminine self into a dry hull which can be shed by the emerging male.

However, the emphasis given to the solar plexus means that both sexes have their inner sun. In its elemental capacity the sun is a Janus-like symbol. It drinks our blood in order to nourish us (the unconscious is not hampered by contradictions). In this polarity, "the sun is asserting himself in drinking up the life of the earth" like a lion, and sympathetically warming "the worlds, like a yellow hen sitting on her eggs" (EP, 69). In the human realm, woman may be sacrificed to the sun ("The Woman Who Rode Away") or be restored by its life-giving heat ("Sun"). By awakening woman to fullness of being, the sun brings to life the natural world; by internalizing the sun, the man and woman alike share in the

awakening and fructifying of the natural/human world. Or negatively, the man may become the blade itself in releasing blood for
sacrifice to the cruel sun of Mexico.

The sun is not exactly phallic, though it is a fertile and impregnating power: for a man must look upon the sun and be with it "as
a woman is with child" (EP, 237). For a man to be impregnated by
the sun is to be first of all female, or to be in the feminine position:
thereby comes to life the phallic self. The sun is not exactly an object, nor is it a principle, though it is a life-energy source. The
instincts come closest to it, especially as Freud was to polarize
and elevate them into Death and Eros. As cosmic energy, the sun
brings about a natural development, which in the human sphere
takes the form of sexual differentiation. So much is Lawrence's
own meaning. A psychoanalytic reading further suggests that the
ostensibly natural generating processes are overdetermined by
psychological ones, and that these processes may be understood
as projective identifications, i.e., a means of reshaping disavowed
drives and their representations for reintegration. The sun is then
a "subjective-object" that signifies the process whereby the masculine self is internalized through the feminine self: to assume
father Sun's power, the son must first be penetrated by it.

After making love to Ursula, Birkin is "like an Egyptian Pharaoh
. . . seated in immemorial potency, like the great carven statues of
real Egypt" (WL, 310). But if genital performance elevates Birkin,
the males in later works tend to be both dark and lowly: the nameless ruddy peasant in "Sun"; the Gypsy, the humbled man who
died with his orange-black cock; and Mellors, with his "red face
and red moustache." Signifiers of the sun, they radiate from the
"core of vital potency" in a universe which knows no personal
gods. "Man all scarlet was his bodily godly self" (EP, 42): an "aristocrat of the sun" (CP, 526).

The dark gods enter from below, but they also enter through the
dark sun in man and in his cosmos. They arise from a culture behind the Greco-Hebraic world which has constituted our own:
a sun behind our sun. The hallmark of this prehistoric world—
often metonymized as "Egypt"—is that it has no supreme god,
only idols and living symbols through which man is rendered one
with the divine cosmos. When Lawrence discovered the Southwest Indians, traveled through Old Mexico, or explored the Etruscan caves, he found intimations of his Egypt, of something worth

sacrificing mental consciousness for. "The American Indian sees no division into Spirit and Matter, God and not-God. Everything is alive, though not personally so. . . . The Indian, like the old Egyptian," seeks to "conquer the cosmic monsters of living thunder and live rain" (MM, 65).

To get back in touch with this prehistoric, animistic world is also to get in touch with the barely differentiated state of primary love and attachment; only then can a new beginning unfold.[3] The sun beams like a beacon on the other side of the terrifying zone of rat and insect fears, and lights up a possible path. If the New Mexican sun can gather his soul to a state of attentive stillness, the "hard, fierce, finite sun of Mexico" can begin burning through the mother's old ego-shell legacy (FF, 782).

Gethin Day in that late fragment, "The Flying Fish," distinguishes between the "yellow sun which is the common day of men," and the "sun behind the sun" of the "Greater Day," because in Mexico the "ordinary day" had begun to "lose its reality to him. . . . It had cracked like some great bubble, and to his uneasiness and terror, he had seemed to see through the fissures the deeper blue of the Greater Day where moved the other sun shaking its dark blue wings." Such darker intimations may accompany the rejuvenated, tender and phallic reality of Connie and Mellors. That a death of sorts had to come first is reasonably certain. For Lawrence, there is no smooth continuity: "The consciousness of one branch of humanity is the annihilation of the consciousness of another branch." The stream of the Indian's vital being can only be understood in terms of the death of our consciousness. And so it happened that Europe had left him with a "dull sort of hopelessness and deadness," whereas in New Mexico the "sun and air are alive, let man be what he may"; thus "a new part of the soul woke suddenly and the old world gave way to a new" (P, 142). Apparently so long as he could remain in touch with surroundings capable of evoking primary love, new beginnings were possible. Yet he never settled in, continually returning to the grave of Europe only to realize, "here they've killed the very sun, the very air" (WB, 339—40). Like the pre-Copernican sun, he is always in motion, dying and reviving. And like his *persona* Gethin Day, he would like to unify Gē, "earth," with the solar *Day*, but instead finds himself moving, as in the German suffix *hin*, "away from" earth.

Fittingly, Lawrence's last imaginative work, *The Man Who Died*, begins on a desert that could be American as well as Mediterranean, with a cock crowing in a new day, his cry so loud and splitting that it reaches even a lifeless form sealed in a tomb. The cock "gave a wild strange squawk, rose in one lift to the top of the wall," and the man in the tomb who wanted to rest in "the place where even memory is stone dead," stirs, "his hands rose and begun pushing away at the bandages. . . ." The naturalistic source of this resurrection is itself partly buried in the repeated verb *rose*, both flower and act, and like the flower both virginal and genital. But if the Man Who Died has not really died, what has?

Gradually he comes to realize, "I have outlived my mission." It is the "teacher and the saviour [that] are dead" in him now, and with them his public life and his life of self-importance. Mary Magdeleine gazes at the Man who has risen and sees that the enthusiastic celibate whom she had worshipped as her messiah has not risen. But this disillusioned, middle-aged man has not yet risen either. Having crucified his flesh, he is instinctually dead. Only gradually does it begin to dawn on him, as it had on Gethin Day, that "the body, too, has its little life, and beyond that, the greater life." His virginity had been a form of greed; in the future he will resist the temptation of asexual worship. His past he now repents. "I tried to compel them to live, so they compelled me to die. It is always so with compulsion."[4]

He sojourns with the peasant who owns the tied-up cock. "The sun and the subtle salve of spring healed his wounds" and restored his strength. Thus the sun operates on him as it had on Juliet in "Sun": it touches and quickens the vital blood centers, healing the much-abused body. But if we consider that what had also died and not been reborn was the early feminine ego-structure—i.e., the shell left in the tomb—then the next step would be for him to acquire a phallus. Of course just as any male child, he has always had a penis to urinate with. But the phallus encompasses both the child fantasies of the adult organ and its mythical fertile property. Lawrence's character may be said to possess a merely external appendage, for which he is implicitly reproached by the counterparts in nature and in the cosmos—the orange-black cock and the sun—for not being vitally connected and so for not completing the whole order of existence. As Lawrence has it in *John Thomas and Lady Jane*, "the penis is a mere member of the physiological body," but "the phallus, in the old sense, has roots, the deepest roots of all in the soul and the greater consciousness of man."[5]

This paradoxical condition requires some explanation. Sagar's account of Lawrence's discovery in the spring of 1927 of the Etruscan tombs is excellent background (AD, 210). There he found not only the seeds of his story—with the cycle of life, death, and rebirth symbolized by the "mysterious egg" in the hand of a frescoed man who had died, along with a temple of Isis—but he also found a beautifully preserved record of the joyous vision he had sought to establish in his utopian Rananim. "To the Etruscans all was alive. . . . They knew the gods in their fingertips." Elsewhere in *Etruscan Places* he evidently associates the "egg of resurrection within which the germ sleeps as the soul sleeps in the tomb, before it breaks the shell and emerges again," with the carefully observed scene in a shop window of a "toy rooster escaping from an egg," which undoubtedly stimulated memories and creative fantasies. A friend's remark in passing the window became Lawrence's first title, "The Escaped Cock," for his story of resurrection (AD, 216 – 19). But before Lawrence can allow the bird to escape to the heavens, it must be caught, or at least its virtue seized.

The process of acquiring a phallus, that is, of awakening a new center or of internalizing the genital function, appears in an appealing collection of American Indian tales grouped under the Trickster cycle.[6] Whether or not Lawrence heard any of them, their parallels suggest that the mythopoeic imagination has transcultural similarities. Trickster in his various protean capacities is after all a fertility figure who has a great time mismanaging his penis. When he isn't using it as a center pole for his tent, he coils it up and puts it away in a box he carries on his back. Once he sends it over the water to greet some women who are swimmng. In many ways it is a magical and detachable object, the occasion for humor, confusion, experimentation, and enjoyment. Lawrence's story— humorous in its sexual puns and amoral in its religious license— is also about the making of a fertility god, and is likewise about the acquisition and use of that problematic organ.

In his story, when the pallid, wormlike Man leaves the peasant and takes under his arm the cock, "whose tail fluttered gaily behind," the Man is assuming his place in the life cycle both of nature and the Phoenix. The black-orange bird is also the microcosmic sun at dawn, the little dark sun which must live at the center of one's self. One morning, finding his cock battling the rooster of a henhouse, the Man offers to leave him to the hens if he prove victorious, as he is certain to. By restoring the cock's freedom (as Lou had restored St. Mawr to his natural element), the Man achieves a new sympathetic rapport with the natural order. Finding comes paradoxically through letting go—the opposite of compulsion.[7]

He wanders into Egypt—the ancient and mythical country Lawrence had so long dreamed of—and into the temple presided over by "Isis in Search": she of the "subtle lotus, the womb which waits submerged and in bud, waits for the touch of that other inward sun that streams its rays from the loins of the male Osiris." It becomes the mythic task of Isis and her Osiris to encompass the life of the little people in the "circle of the greater life." But they will do so naturally, as man and woman, sexual beings whose attachments and departures are nevertheless cyclically governed. LeDoux has shown how the story should be read not as a reworking of ancient myths—at least not simply so—but chiefly for its human meaning. He remarks that among the ancient female-deities, it is the male who dies, while the female survives, "waiting and dormant, through the dead winter, to be renewed in the spring by the revived male."[8] Yet here the actions of renewal are reciprocal. The Man, now becoming Osiris, is "anointed with oils and spices, as for a funeral, for to become a whole man he must die again, to himself, to his self-consciousness"; the efforts at healing exhaust the priestess. But he is soon able to reawaken her and animate her dormant womb. This reciprocal, interpenetrating process begins on the other side in *Lady Chatterley* when Mellors performs a healing function for Connie and is then renewed by her. The elemental forces within nature—discussed earlier in reference to the lovers in *The Trespasser* as the cosmic parents, and identifiable as primitive projections and/or drive representations—have become by degrees absorbed and humanized in these late works, and almost totally so in the novel.

Returning to the resurrection story: as the woman must also fertilize the man to make the process truly reciprocal, so Isis anoints the wounds of Osiris and chafes his scars; she looks into the wounds of his feminine past, the "scar deep in the soft socket above the hip" where "his blood had left him, and his essential seed." As he winces she "put her palm over the wound in his right side," so near to the great sympathetic center of the solar plexus which must come alive for the sex act to engage the circuits of tenderness as well as those of sensuality. Next,

> she put her breast against the wound in his left side, and her arms around him, folding over the wound in his right side, and she pressed him to her, in a power of living warmth, like the folds of a river. And the wailing died out altogether, and there was a stillness, and darkness in his soul, unbroken dark stillness, wholeness.
>
> Then slowly, slowly, in the perfect darkness of his inner man, he felt the stir of something coming. A dawn, a new sun. [MW, 206]

At last, "powerful and new like dawn," he bends over the "deep-folded, penetrable rock of the living woman," until in ecstacy he puns, "I am risen!"

"Magnificent, blazing indomitable in the depths of his loins, his own sun dawned." The resurgence of nature follows and with it new life in the priestess Isis. Osiris recognizes that "this is the great atonement, the being in touch," and promises his seasonal return.

Projective identifications underlie the creative process in this work, especially in the transition from the prototypal sun to the eponymous cock. These two images are carefully joined at the outset by the "animal onrush of light" that first awakens the entombed figure. Thereafter the text can be read as the necessary internalization of maleness. The story can also be read on an oedipal level, but since this chapter dawned with the sun, we may also end it there.[9] To "re-establish the living organic connections with the cosmos, the sun and earth, with mankind and nation and family," Lawrence concludes on his deathbed at the end of *Apocalypse*, "start with the sun, and the rest will slowly, slowly happen."

So even at the end, one starts again.

9

Creative selfhood

I do not maintain that every image of an erotic encounter is a primal scene repre-
sentation, but I believe that such images may have specific traits which label them as
"primal scene material." First among these traits is the characteristic double identi-
fication, which may be either simultaneous or alternating . . . —Henry Edelheit[1]

But it is the fight of opposites which is holy.—C, 18

By now, we have seen something of the formation of the artist out
of the matrix of early development. In order to get closer to Lawrence's inner turmoil, we have paid less attention to analysis of
fully formed fictional characters than to interpretations of imagery
and symbol, of memory and motif. And by rolling aside the stone
of infantile narcissism we have been able to explore the cavernous
early relationships with the mother. Their delineation may now in
summary reveal the continuum along which the self develops.

The infant's whirl of primordial sensations resolves itself into
partial representations—fluids, substances, and various fragments—of its own organism and of the mother at the so-called
preobject stage. Out of such diffuse and oceanic experience
emerges a fantasy of primary harmony which may carry the first
inklings of a creative romance with the world. During this era of
dual-unity the mother has been referred to in psychoanalytic par-
lance as the cosmic object or the holding environment in order to
better approximate the child's felt experience prior to his achieving total-object comprehension of her as a separate person with
her own individual self, needs, and relationships. Gratified wishes
may contribute to idealization, frustrated wishes to projection;
respectively, they may form the earliest building blocks for divine
or demonic versions of the Family Romance fantasy.

In Winnicott's view the "good-enough mother" serves as an instinct barrier to the child, who must neither be left fully at the
mercy of his own impulses nor solely to the slings and arrows of

his environment until he is better able to fend for himself. In "Dance Sketch" (see fig. 5), for example, the female is both a shield over part of the male's lower body and a restraining force in the way her arm encircles his loins and pulls away from his forward-thrusting shoulders.

One could speculate about the pivotal ways in which Lawrence's mother may have been rather too good in protecting him from his libidinal impulses, his normal aggressive wishes, and his emerging phallic drives, or not good enough in protecting him from her own impulses, and one could speculate in vain. But it can be shown that as the maternal shield against instinctual drives was internalized and developed into an ego-structure, Lawrence acquired a vividness of being and an intensity in relatedness that would later be conveyed as distortions of surface, as deficiencies in reality-testing, and as a fluidity of self-object boundaries that approximate Freud's "identity of perception" in which the dreamer is fused with the dream. And so they may fuse at the profound level we have often cited as primary harmony. But to stop short of their flow into those creative adaptations sustained by correspondences and interpenetrations, both of which affirm distance as "star polarity" between self and surroundings, would be to short-circuit a complicated sequence. Like everything else for Lawrence, creativity was dualistic, serving needs to be vitally connected, along with the needs of separation and individuation.

The artist in Lawrence sees in a "curious rolling flood of vision, in which the image itself seethes and rolls" (EP, 72). And that remarkable expansion of creative energy which lifts and sustains one in his works implies the security and support of a holding environment similar in effect to the way Shakespeare's plays "seem to be reflecting a larger concord on which they repose as on a quiet."[2] In Lawrence's words, it may be the "eternal stillness that lies under all movement, under all life, like a source, incorruptible and inexhaustible" (CL, 241). This vision of Greek sculpture, however, he would later reject as too idealized, in favor of a less concentrated and self-conscious organicism cued by the Etruscans, among others. But its power may still be felt in the counterbalancing stillness and Apollonian chasteness that recent critics have cited in Lawrence's own works.[3]

This buoyance and acuity of creative vision is signaled in a nature sketch Paul Morel shows Miriam, who wonders why it appeals to her. "It's because," Paul explains,

there is scarcely any shadow in it; it's more shimmering protoplasm in the leaves and everywhere, and not the stiffness of the shape. That seems dead to me. Only this shimmeriness is the real living. The shape is dead crust. The shimmer is inside really. [SL, 152]

This quality applies to Lawrence's works of shimmering, pulsating life, but the sharp outline of form is there too, not as dead crust but as living flesh.

In this connection, one thinks back to the peculiarities attendant on Lawrence's birth, especially his mother's mistreatment by and rage toward his father, and the questions whether he might have been a "preemie." Such a possibility could provide a physiological basis for his (1) hypersensitivity to the environment, "monitoring every tender moment of nature around him: the many birds coming and going under the trees, the huge shadows straying up the wild high mountains, and the light of the desert below us," as his friend Joseph Foster observed (JF, 237); and (2) for his extraordinary capacity for controlled regression which in one story ("Glad Ghosts") carries him back to a virtual intrauterine state: "I must have gone far, far down the intricate galleries of sleep, to the very heart of the world . . . beyond the strata of images and words, beyond the iron veins of memory, and even the jewels of rest, to sink in the final dark like a fish, dumb, soundless, and imageless, yet alive and swimming." And there "at the heart of the ocean of oblivion" comes the woman ghost "to answer my deep with her deep." Such connections must remain speculative; it may have only been his psychological hatching-out that was traumatically premature.

But insofar as these early capacities owe a substantial debt to the intimate bond with an ambivalent mother, then his somewhat later relationships—entertaining a distinct Family Romance fantasy and centering on the sharing of a literary project—would mark a second phase of separation-individuation, a rapprochement through collaborative partnership. If at one time he had felt so close to the mother that either her powers were also his or that he shared in them, then the illusory belief that he was able to procreate or participate in procreation begins to be manifested perhaps as its realistic likelihood grows more dubious. Illness, whatever its organic basis, evidently functioned to regain the lost symbiotic bond. The child's falling ill may also have mimicked his experience of the mother's withdrawal into childbirth, so that creativity eventually becomes a miming of procreativity. But to whatever degree the rage felt over the mother's formidable powers to intrude or withdraw is turned inward against the self, the propensity to illness remains an organic danger. Thus the self acquires a continual dying/reviving, injuring/healing, structural identity. The compulsive nature of this process suggests the trauma if not of premature birth then of premature separation, exacerbated by the mother's pregnancy, the birth of a sibling, and the ongoing marital conflicts.

The strength of these early alliances would work to inhibit and postpone sexual drives as well as heighten the emerging negative side of the Oedipus complex, while early double identifications with both parents would provide an impetus for subsequent creative work. Creativity and symbol-formation have been able to unify or bind-up antagonistic object-relationships as well as to provide outlets for conflicting drives or wishes and divisions within the self. A degree of mastery is discerned in the works' progression toward oedipal or genital issues, accompanied by what critics agree is an insouciance of style. Yet it appears that the mother's probable inhibiting of the son's phallic development heightened her own dangerous role as a phallic, castrating woman. Of this threat she must be divested without sacrificing her good side. This goal entails a necessary phase of growth; the pathway is narrow and perilous, littered with the bodies of life-denying characters, male as well as female, like so many broken dolls.

At the triadic stage mother is woman rescued into love but in such a way as to accommodate her marital disappointments, the son's necessary sense of belatedness, the birth of other siblings, and the father's highly equivocal presence. In *Lady Chatterley*, the oedipal mother divested of her lamia's fangs and harpy's beak—or if we prefer, the post-oedipal love object—comes into her own to conduct a full-fledged romance with her (belatedly) assertive phallic lover as he grafts onto himself the paternal image. The binding-up of conflicting ties, loyalties, and desires through symbol-formation demonstrates the emerging ego's capacities for creative solutions. The double or often multiple representations in the composite symbols of Rainbow, Phoenix, and Plumed Serpent eloquently testify to the dynamic balance of multiplicity within unity. This symbolic mode endows with emotional richness many Lawrencean characters who are both unlike and similar to the way we imagine their creator to be. In any kind of psychological or close reading of his text, there is a very real danger of assigning Lawrence's ego to one character rather than of identifying his varied components and drives with the totality of his created world. In this respect the work of imagination may be closer to a dream than to literal or allegorical representations of reality.

Thus the present study has tried to bring all the writings into an alignment with the life, especially those in which his most compelling images and symbols appear. Even so, certain steps along the way may look more like leaps into the unknown. It is a hazardous enterprise from any viewpoint. Implicitly assumed, for example, has been the proposition that when certain elements recur in various contexts—such as composite symbolism, burning/breaking imagery, a plot motif like that of the woman-who-rides-away, or a characterological preference like the woman's sexual stillness—one may justifiably look beyond the confines of textual explication for psychoanalytic insight into creative strategies. The extent of relationship between deep-seated emotional trauma and compulsive-repetitions on the one hand, and creative rhythms on the other is a question that need not be—probably cannot be—answered. But connections can be noted and recognized as genuine. Although a creative working out should never be construed as a therapeutic working through, we can surmise certain resolutions of universal early conflicts.[4]

2   The Creative Process As a Phoenix Cycle

In *The Hidden Order of Art*, Anton Ehrenzweig bases his three stages of the creative process on a correspondence between Kleinian object-relations theory and the myth of the dying-reviving god. Because that prospectus coincides with this study's emphasis on self-remaking, it is included here (see Table 3). But its forward direction must be modified to depict a spiraling around the subjective and objective poles of origins—the Family Romance and the Primal Scene.

Plotted in this way, Lawrence's creative process is inseparable from content and vision; it gives inner unity to the single piece of fiction and binds the oeuvre as a whole. An overview reveals how the larger pattern corresponds to the smaller: (1) In *Sons and Lovers*, the all-important love-object is lost, and the son's drift toward darkness/death is interrupted only at the very end by the quickening of his step toward the dawnlike "city's gold phosphorescence." (2) Subsequently, in *The Rainbow* and *Women in Love*, Ursula begins "dark and unrevealed . . . like a seed buried in dry ash" (R, 437), and gradually becomes "individual, self-responsible, taking her own initiative" (CL, 273). The self is first reborn as female. To balance the creation of the positive woman, there follows a series of negative-polarized works (*Aaron's Rod*, etc.) building up the phallic powers in the positive man. (3) The theme of resurrection in the late works prepares us for the meeting of the regenerated male and female, and *Lady Chatterley's Lover* makes possible a symbolic reunion with the all-important love-object on a new level of consciousness. The thread which joins the bolts of loss/renewal, of restoration/reunion, is that of differentiation, first between self and other, then between male and female. And although this seems to be the direction recapitulated by a given individual work, it is also the overall direction of the whole, of which the individual works may be seen as stages.

A look at the middle phase may clarify this pattern. Making *The Rainbow* and *Women in Love* from the whole cloth of an earlier work-in-progress referred to as *The Sisters* has been studied in great detail, but an observation by Roger Sale touches on the deeper interstices of Lawrence's creative activity.[5] The situation of the two sisters resembles that of Ursula and Gudrun in the "beginning of *Women in Love*, and their situation is like Paul Morel's at the end of *Sons and Lovers*." If by this, Sale means that Ursula and Gudrun are facing the prospect of marriage as Paul Morel had attempted and failed to do, then interesting possibilities are raised. If their creator is presenting the same conflicts by switching genders and doubling his characters, he has also followed a familiar pattern in reverting from male to female by means of the Ernst Kris formula, "regression in the service of the ego." This is a first step in any creative process, as well as in a developmental process where identification with mother precedes the one with father.[6] Setting and atmosphere have also briefly adjourned in spirit to the mannered world of Jane Austen. And Birkin, especially in the abandoned draft of the novel known as the Cancelled Prologue, is an important bridge: like Paul Morel, he "ran from death to death" and "studied women as sisters" (P2, 99, 104). Traumatized and regressed, Birkin is fascinated by the "male physique" and feels for women only a "fondness, a sort of sacred love, as for a sister," though it is textually unclear why he finds himself in this anomalous state.

Let us further suppose that part of the impetus for the two-sisters device came from Lawrence's elopement with Frieda around that time. The anxiety of this leap into the unknown may have activated regressive adaptive measures. Perhaps this strange new bond between him and Frieda is represented as being built on the safely narcissistic bond of the two sisters, like that "peculiar fusion of soul" (CL, 69); or on Gethin Day's tie to his older sister Lydia—bonds of likeness which precede a more mature libidinal connection. The only way to exceed these old bonds is through differentiation: one of the pair must become externalized as the "positive woman," while "phallic reality" must emerge in the other.[7]

The degree to which this actually caused a personal conflict for Lawrence cannot definitely be ascertained, but it was at least partially recorded in terms of creative issues in the letters of 1913–14. "I've written more than half of a most fascinating (to me) novel . . . I love and adore this new book" (CL, 193). Here an apparent fusion with a substitute love-object illustrates the manic absorption and dedifferentiation in the second phase of creativity. Soon finding something ailing in the book, he decides to "theorize myself out . . . and make it into art now." So far, the sustaining self of the creator seems to be diffused throughout the work. "It is a queer novel, which seems to come by itself . . . it hasn't got hard outlines" yet, but a theme is emerging. It will be about "*the* problem of today, the establishment of a new relation, or the readjustment of the old one, between men and women" (CL, 200). There is still some hedging of bets here, perhaps because "the old one" included sons who became their mothers' lovers, and the new one is as yet uncertain in its outcome.

What eventually takes place is not that the character of the two

Table 3

A. Kleinian Phases of Early Development	*B. Myth of the Dying/Reviving God*
1. Schizoid-paranoid (persecutory). Includes: projection, splitting and fragmentation of objects, destructive drives, etc., directed at the mother's breast or womb, or at oneself. Oral gnawing, anal attacks, fecal scattering.	1. The nature god is dismembered, burned, torn-up, scattered.
2. Manic. Child merges with mother and incorporates her generative powers; dedifferentiation and fusion with the breast.	2. Burial in the grave, like the seed of corn, the sun swallowed into earth.
3. Depressive and Reintrojective stage. Giving up object, mourning process, step in separation-individuation. Reintrojection of split-off material in unrecognizable symbolic forms (by means of repression and transformation): $\doteq$ projective identification.	3. God is mourned and reborn in the new year.

C. Creative Process	D. Applied to Lawrence
1. Heroic self-surrender of the creative mind; death, dissociation faced; hollowing out of the void.	1. The primordial oneness of the cosmos (the Cosmogonic Egg) is split into duality and multiplicity; loss of early self-object wholeness; immersion in the "flux of corruption" to the "core of chaos, fierce with incongruities." [P, 259]
2. Receiving and burying the torn-up fragments in the creative womb, unconscious envelopment in the work. Boundaries between inner and outer, space and time dissolve. Mystical, oceanic oneness as the mind prepares a creative-womblike receptacle in the inner world into which it can deposit split-off parts of the self. "These "repressed and dedifferentiated images are safely contained, melted down and re-shaped for re-entry into consciousness."	2. All-consuming holocaust in which bird and nest are fused and consumed. Ashes of destruction are regathered and internalized. Wishes for union with the lost maternal object and sharing in her procreative powers are subjected to reworking in timeless realm of the creative unconscious; a new egg is molded. "Light is within the grip of darkness, darkness within the embrace of light, the Beginning and the End are closed upon one another" [C, 49]; "Germs of the known and the unknown" fuse.
3. Secondary elaborations; depths are reintegrated with surface functions; detachment, work becomes independent object; otherness.	3. "Something deep evolving itself out of me." Emergence of the young Phoenix, the newly formed symbol which unifies the earlier sundering into dualism and death of self by recapitulating the processes within his own being. Resurrection and eternal recurrence as part of the elaboration of meaning; mythic sense of time gives "depth coherence" to human beings interacting with their own histories: the symbol (Phoenix) becomes the literary work (e.g., *The Man Who Died*), affecting the reader as "strange sapience."

sisters is changed—they remain Ursula and Gudrun—but that the single work in which they had started out is differentiated into two separate novels. One ends with "woman becoming individual, self-responsible, taking her own initiative" (Ursula); the other, with Birkin coming into his own as Lawrence's first fully realized male. Thus the separation of male and female, as a stage in the ongoing process of differentiation and self-definition, is conducted in the sphere of creativity. In the late works, a further phase of differentiation into specific genital sexuality is tenuously achieved, which apparently makes possible a more complete reunion with the lost object. And again the self is differentiated via the work: as cued by its title, *Lady Chatterley's Lover* is a "tender and phallic" novel that discovers a safer syntax for the son-lover and affirms in its own way that elusive goal of genital primacy.

3   From Primary Love to Genital Love

Since the writers who have insisted on how fierce, disruptive and antinomian an energy sexuality (potentially, ideally) is, are mostly men, it's commonly supposed that this form of imagination must discriminate against women. I don't think it does, necessarily.—Susan Sontag[8]

Rampant narcissismo—or . . . just me being a boy again? . . . How do I ever get to be what is described in the literature as a man? Or—could it be?—is this boy's life a man's life after all? Is this it?—Philip Roth, My Life As a Man

In her valuable and fair-minded study, *D. H. Lawrence and Feminism*, Hilary Simpson makes the interesting point that while remaining "incontrovertibly masculine," the phallus comes to "embody the 'feminine' qualities of tenderness and sensitivity" (pp. 124, 133). Thus it functions occasionally for Lawrence as a third term (that of Reconciler) beyond male and female gender boundaries. Since its celebration is most fully observed in *Lady Chatterley's Lover*, a final consideration of that work will reveal something of how Lawrence blended not only male/female polarities, but also primary/genital love.

Apparently psychoanalytic thinking has varied as to whether genitality should be considered a separate and distinct function unto itself or whether it should be seen as the culmination of earlier drives. Perhaps the issue cannot be decided on theoretical grounds alone. Lawrence's near-obsessive concentration on genital functioning has produced its critical backlashes. He has been upbraided for neglecting the welfare of Connie's unborn son, for encouraging sensual indulgence, and perhaps most tellingly, for the "element" in Mellors of "bullying which, despite the emphasis on tenderness, and the numerous episodes of real tenderness, characterizes" his treatment of Connie (AD, 195). Clearly, Lawrence overloads the genital function in ways already suggested, and it is unfortunate that the pastoral form encourages perfected types which conflict with other aims—both literary and personal. And even if we take Clifford Chatterley as the "presiding devil" over the fallen world from which the lovers flee, he is obviously also a part of creation, dehumanized and mechanical-minded as he may be (AD, 196). For Daniel Weiss, he "represents the total dilapidation of Lawrence's Oedipal longings" in "fondling the housekeeper's breast."[9] But although such a reading of the work may be too diagrammatic, one senses that Chatterley, the trivial conversationalist and writer, externalizes a negative cluster of Lawrence's early and late self-representations. The miners are seen as only "crude raw phenomena," and he feared their looking "at him now he was lame" (LCL, 14–15). Thus does Lawrence both associate himself with and distance himself from his mother's prejudices and defensive aloofness, his own humiliations before the miners when collecting his father's pay, his defective body-images, and phobias about the seething masses.

Sir Clifford's regression, however, is to the nurturing mother of the oral stage, if we choose to view it that way, while Mellors is out in the woods with the lady of the house, conducting an oedipal romance. Better yet, these categories should be dropped entirely. Clifford Chatterley extrudes into the novel like a foreign growth, which, even though reintrojected into consciousness, cannot be finally integrated into the work. A "smashed" doll who cannot burn toward a Phoenix rebirth, he is set apart in his impotent omnipotence, a spoiled autarch, a profound embarrassment and distraction from the beauty of the phallic dancers Lawrence memorialized so clearly in *Etruscan Places*. Half-machine but still half-man, even in his wheelchair he casts a long shadow over this modern pastoral. His epigraph might come from a late poem: "Death is not Evil, Evil is Mechanical" (CP, 713). Thus he may be that part of Lawrence which remained smashed and could not be reborn. One almost suspects Lawrence would have liked to save Clifford, but it was too much. In any event Lawrence is right under the circumstances to remove his lovers as far away as possible from him. Given Lawrence's favoring of opposing pairs, it is likely that the also evil magic of industrialism which Clifford represents elicits in part the strong countermagic of the copulating lovers.

But even organs can interfere with the organic, and perhaps more apposite is the way in which genital sexuality is partially overdetermined by the author's drives to retain a preserve of primary love. Such an aim would have its negative as well as its positive side. One of the preconditions for primary love is that the environment yield to the individual's needs—even when they are destructive—and that, in turn, no counterdemands be made on him. Such at times is Mellors's treatment of Connie—his bullying manner, his disregard of foreplay, his blunt speech. But while these do not nearly determine the relationship, they do seem necessary for something like basic trust to be grounded. Here also are some of the roots of Lawrence's antifeminism and the basis for many other discordant impressions honest readers have taken from his texts.

More positively, primary love contributes something worthwhile to genital sexual love, and this Lawrence perceived quite clearly and radically. It is conveyed by the natural surroundings, the woods, the animals, and particularly the flowers with which they decorate their naked flesh in diametric opposition to the fig leaf of shame and guilt. It is perhaps an obvious comment, but the implication is that genital love can come into its own only when it can rest on what the early relationship with the mother provides as a "holding" or facilitating environment.[10] One supposes that much of Lawrence's travels—almost always accompanied by a genital love-object—were aimed at his getting right with the early environment. But instead of a Rananim to colonize, what he found in Old and New Mexico, in occult books, and in the Etruscan caves were the nutriments for his creative imagination. Only then could he go home and dream of Newthorpe transformed into a shining Egyptian city. Only then could primary love blend with other forms of Eros. And only then could an ecology of sex blend with an ecology of nature to secure its true balance. Below Lawrence's mystical Egypt lies "the land of Mesopotamia, where Paradise was, or the Park of Eden, where man has his beginning" (P2, 506). This site of humanity's Primordial Scene is bounded by two rivers, the Euphrates and the Tigris, and the sexual act is the Communion of their circuit, where the two blood streams meet. This comes about through that "blood-column" and "bridge to the future," the phallus, the absolute center of the universe. Is this delusional, phallic narcissism, misguided mysticism, or a development of genital primacy out of the primeval waters of primary love? Or is it that the phallus, apparently being a late acquisition for Lawrence, retains the enviable prerogatives of the paternal phallus and acquires the age-old, magical properties of myth?

4   The Ambiguous Nature of Genital Primacy

For mature individuation is not a burden, but an achievement; symbiosis is not ultimate unity, but the deepest incapacity to grow. And love is only meaningful when it is given by one who does not dissolve in the giving, but has a self and a personal history with which to respond to and reach the other.—Gerald J. Gargiula[11]

"I would like to have all the rest of the world disappear," she said, "and live with you here."

"It won't disappear," he said.—LCL, 256

In recent years scholars have been turning to *The Rainbow* and *Women in Love* as Lawrence's best works. Certainly these contain a richness of texture and a complexity of theme which critics love to grind through their mills. And one would not want to advance literary judgments on such psychological grounds as the achievement of genital primacy—though it is such a rare accomplishment that it ought to be applauded at least when done well. Moreover, one treasures courage and clarity of vision. In Lawrence's final work genital sexuality is portrayed with such eminence, as when forget-me-nots intertwine pubic hair, that one scarcely dares wonder how so much previous dissonance could ever have been so naturally harmonized. And if the cost of Sir Clifford's "laming" is high, it is perhaps on balance, not too high.

The shift from the other two novels to his final "tender and phallic novel" is from any viewpoint a significant one; and eventually, regardless of one's perspective, it must affect the work's overall value. In our present narrow perspective, this shift is keyed in part by the fact that for all his quicksilver presence, Birkin has no more history than Topsy, whereas Mellors is rooted in the real world of time and suffering, by his own past.[12] A similar shift affects the women. One of Lawrence's chief complaints with Thomas Hardy was that he could only create deficient, negative women, for Lawrence's conscious task to a great degree was to create a positive woman.[13] This he manages first with Ursula. Yet for all her "becoming individual, self-responsible, taking her own initiative," she is strangely bodyless and is made to enthuse excessively over the "marvelous flanks," "strange fountains" and loins "deeper than the phallic source" of Birkin's body. He scarcely does the same for her.

But Connie corrects this imbalance. Her body is very much in the picture—from her scrutinizing its deathlike pallor in her mirror, to its lapsing from life, and to her gradual reawakening in the sexual encounters with Mellors. It is *her* ass that gets praised and caressed rather than his.[14] And what had been perfunctorily and evasively described in *Women in Love* as Birkin's having taken Ursula in the "mystic fountains of corruption" is subjected to the light of common speech: "'tha's got such a nice tail on thee,' he said, in the throaty caressive dialect." The "beautiful curving drop of her haunches ... fascinated him today. How it sloped with a rich downslope to the heavy roundness of her buttocks." He "exquisitely stroked the rounded tail, till it seemed as if a slippery sort of fire came from it into his hands. And his finger-tips touched to two secret openings to her body, time after time, with a soft little brush of fire."

"Tha're real, tha art! Tha'rt real, even a bit of a bitch. Here tha shits an' here tha pisses: an' I lay my hand on 'em both an' like thee for it. I like thee for it. Tha's got a proper, woman's arse, proud of itself. It's none ashamed of itself, tis isna."

He laid his hand close and firm over her secret places, in a kind of close greeting.

"I like it," he said. "I like it! an' if I only lived ten minutes, an' strokes thy arse an' got to know it, I should reckon I'd live *one* life, sees ter! Industrial system or not! Here's one of my lifetimes." [LCL, 268]

The acknowledgment that *nascimur inter feces et urinas* is a necessary component to the greater realization, "Th'art good cunt, though, aren't ter?" (LCL, 212 – 13). Connie exists in the flesh as Mellors exists in time; they are rooted in this life.

In exchange for renouncing the magical birth-properties of the male child's anal zone and for this belated celebrating of woman's body, there is the "mystery of the phallus," which Connie duly recognizes and which has been found offensive, not without reason, to some feminists. Yet one may just as easily come to the conclusion that Lawrence has sacrificed much of his previous sexual mystique in his "fight for the phallic realities" over the "cerebration unrealities" (CL, 1045). The old power-supremacy drives have died away on the same soil out of which genitality will flower. The dark gods have receded, but so has the Devouring/Phallic Mother. There is Mellors's early indifference to Connie's forepleasure, but thematically when she comes to him at his rabbit hutch and becomes distraught over the chicks, she is lapsing away from her old life. In this pastoral context, only nature can heal her oversocialized condition, and Mellors is cast as the natural man. To deny this is to deny fiction its right to formal conventions—which is not to say that they too cannot be examined. Let us agree anyway that at such moments Connie may be the passive party, while at others she is the active party, taking responsibility for her sexual destiny over against the norms of society.[15]

But it is too easy to turn polemical here when what clearly matters is that as a Lawrencean male, Mellors does not entirely give up his maternal side. The care of the game allows him to display plenty of tender mothering, a crucial quality Connie recognizes:

"I'd love to touch them," she said, putting her fingers gingerly through the bars of the coop. But the mother hen pecked at her hand fiercely, and Connie drew back startled and frightened.

"How she pecks at me! She hates me!" she said in a wondering voice. "But I wouldn't hurt them!"

The man standing above her laughed, and crouched down beside her, knees apart, and put his hand with quiet confidence slowly into the coop. The old hen pecked at him, but not so savagely. And slowly, softly, with gentle fingers, he felt among the old bird's feathers and drew out a faintly-peeping chick in his closed hand.

"There!" he said, holding out his hand to her. She took the little drab thing between her hands, and there it stood, on its impossible little stalks of legs, its atom of balancing life trembling through its almost weightless feet into Connie's hands. But it lifted its handsome, clean-shaped little

head boldly, and looked sharply round, and gave a little "peep."
   "So adorable! So cheeky!" she said softly. [LCL, 134−35]

Within the context of the Lawrence family, the inference is that the child's pets—disgusting, messy little animals to the mother—may have been the magical, fantasy children of his anal period. Thus, once she can be made to recognize them as real living things, as Connie does, the child can move on to the phallic-genital stage, as Mellors instantly does. "'Lie down,' he said softly." This may explain the viability of the gamekeeper as a character from the earliest to the latest novel. His premature demise as a homosexual threat in *The White Peacock* when the youth Cyril comes to him is revised by the belated developmental processes of identification and sexual differentiation when Connie comes to Mellors. To produce a true male and a true female may well be the final achievement, as well as the dissolution of the bisexual artist as such.

Moreover, other strata of pregenital traits can be found in Mellors's background. He had loved his colonel in the cavalry; he had practiced anal intercourse with his wife; and he still carries with him a great deal of sadistic misanthropy. Still his organic concerns suggest that bisexuality is subordinated and better integrated than are Sir Clifford's obsessions with male literary chat and modern machinery, which represent his bisexual power drives as manifested exclusively through mental consciousness. Clifford presides over a realm of sexual debasements, where sex is like a mere food-hunger, a purely conscious mode of conversation, or a shamefully private thing ("We don't want to follow a man into the W. C., so why should we want to follow him into bed with a woman?" [LCL, 34]). And his relationship with Connie as a kind of sisterly male is uncannily familiar: "Their interest had never ceased to flow together over his work. They talked and wrestled in the throes of composition" (LCL, 18). It is the old baby/book-sharing impulse externalized and properly placed in the pregenital section of the novel, just as Mellors's manly love for his officer will be relegated to his military past. Finally, the author's own oscillating bisexual identifications are creatively fulfilled in the story's sexual dialectics and in the reciprocal empathy of Connie and Mellors.

It is now recognized that as part of the novel's general program to effect a restoration of healthy sexuality, one of the scenes between Connie and Mellors involves anal sex. Because buggery was and still is a criminal offense in England, Lawrence is circumspect in his treatment. But the purpose to effect once and for all a "phallic hunting out" of all our hidden shames seems valid, and is so recognized in most recent criticism. Kermode ingeniously connects this episode, the seventh sexual encounter, with the opening of the seventh seal, one of seven ganglia which in occultism were "centres or gates of 'dynamic consciousness.'" The seventh episode is crucial as well as occult because it marks the symbolic death of the postulant and her initiation into life. It is also significant for the male, in that it entails *coitus reservatus*, the preferred act of such occult groups as The Brethren of the Free Spirit, and is believed to be identical to that performed by Adam in Paradise. Thus, as Kermode states, "the act is anal, Adamite" (SA, 26 – 29). But although the Lawrencean pastoral has both occult and polymorphous perverse underpinnings, these are not its final determinants.

In his earlier sexual theories, Lawrence believed the exchange between the sexes heightened the partners' sense of gender identity ("I am pure male, she is pure female" [P, 468]). This balanced polarity, however, yielded to male dominance / female submission in the leadership novels of the middle period, where the dark gods may be said to have irremediably darkened Lawrence's reputation among many feminists. But the late works chart another more complex mingling between the sexes. Not only does the phallus assume an androgynous cast, but also Connie tells Mellors that he is unique among men because he has the courage of his tenderness. She later describes her love for Mellors as one combining tenderness and sensuality—the same coalescence of feelings Freud finds in mature sexual love.

But other sexual attitudes remained more constant. As early as 1915 Lawrence had written to Russell that the "great living experience for every man is his adventure into the woman." It is to "venture in upon the coasts of the unknown, and open my discovery to all humanity" (CL, 324, 318). It is true that the expression of such a need may lead to the use of woman, but it need not lead to her exploitation or suppression. Mutuality and singleness—albeit in peculiar Lawrencean forms—are to be preserved.

In the same letter to Russell, however, Lawrence also affirms that the "ultimate passion of every man is to be within himself the whole of mankind—which I call social passion" (CL, 324). It is this second drive which seems to have encouraged the prophet in him and to have activated those chauvinistic and fascistic yellows in the rainbow of his art. For this drive to be relinquished Lawrence must renounce not only much of his elitism but he must also overcome his fear of and contempt for the masses. The reign of bisexual autocracy must yield. The physician must heal himself. The prophet must descend from his Mt. Pisgah of grandiosity and become low—grow common. Only in this manner can he reach the Promised Land of fatherhood and permit tenderness to become central to his being; only in this manner can he conceive himself as Mellors, the quintessential private man—still Lawrencean enough to be filled with intense likes and dislikes, but in the end, private. The "core" of his life, he tells Connie, is having a "right relation with a woman" (LCL, 245).

But the real test of these assertions centers on Connie's pregnancy. Lawrence is as much threatened by impregnation as his virgins are by defloration. The latter may violate an incest taboo, but the former is even more strongly resisted. Here life and fiction converge, for pregnancy is tied to loss of the mother, and impregnating is tied to becoming the scorned father at the steep price of the son's bisexual eclipse. And it is true that Connie's pregnancy is followed by the lovers' temporary separation, just as the lovers—in their mythical dimension as Isis and Osiris in *The Man Who Died*—separate after the goddess has conceived the god of the new year.

For Lawrence to love in a mature way he must forgive his parents; otherwise the early bonds are not loosened. And for Mellors to love Connie in a mature, relatively selfless way, he must accept without succumbing to the fecundating powers of life within Connie. This is his test. In a larger psychological sense, it is the climax of their relationship:

> "And say you're glad about the child," she repeated. "Kiss it! Kiss my womb and say you're glad it's there."
> But that was more difficult for him.
> "I've a dread of puttin' children i' th' world," he said. "I've such a dread o' th' future of 'em."

"But you've put it into me. Be tender to it, and that will be its future already. Kiss it!"

He quivered, because it was true. "Be tender to it, and that will be its future."— And that moment he felt a sheer of love for the woman. He kissed her belly and her mount of Venus, to kiss close to the womb and the fetus within the womb.

"Oh, you love me! You love me!" she said, in a little cry like one of her blind, inarticulate love cries. And he went into her softly, feeling the stream of tenderness flowing in release from his bowels to hers, the bowels of compassion kindled between them.

And he realized as he went in to her that this was the thing he had to do, to come into tender touch, without losing his pride or his dignity or his integrity as a man. [LCL, 336]

As Hilary Simpson shows, the "new masculinism" of Lawrence à la Mellors embodies traditional feminine values of compassion, gentleness, and tenderness;[16] but there is also in the male's "dark thrust of peace . . . such as made the world in the beginning" a continuing alliance with the primary-love bond (LCL, 207).

The macrocosm of Lawrence's creative universe—which re-enacts the cycle of (1) death, (2) fusion of nest and flames, and (3) rebirth—corresponds not only with the microcosm of the Phoenix symbol, but also with the developmental curve of the Osiris man-who-died figure, and with various other plots. This comes about because the unifying Phoenix may be in turn a self-form, a libidinal wish for fusion with an object, the gratification of that wish, and its dissolution in the emergence of a new life directed toward separation-individuation. In a restricted psychoanalytic sense it is a transitional fantasy geared to master separation and loneliness by building bridges to an external reality. The Phoenix fuses both instinct and symbol, both Freudian libido and Jungian archetype. To proceed further and take the breakdown of creative processes provided by Ehrenzweig as also being *norma-tive*—i.e., as representing the essential phases through which a given work must pass—would lead to formidable difficulties almost at once. But if we were to entertain the possibility for only a moment, we might agree that Lawrence's struggle through these phases is not only singularly heroic, but testimony to his lasting importance.

Of more immediate interest is Ehrenzweig's formulation that one way to understand the artist's early identifications with the mother is to interpret her incorporated breast as his creative womb, both the repository for his own reintrojected projections, which may assist in future developmental tasks, and the source of dedifferentiated images and depth coherence in the ongoing creative tasks. In this light the artist's bisexuality becomes more comprehensible, and the record in his works of sexual striving or early conflicts blends into the *données* for various themes and patterns. The capacity for repeated hatchings-out from the symbiotic union is the other side of the coin of traumatic repetition. According to Margaret Mahler, the toddler in his "elated escape from fusion, from engulfment by mother, is exhilarated by his own abilities, continually delighted with the discoveries he makes in his expanding world, and quasi-enamored with the world and his own grandeur and omnipotence." The world, she writes, is his oyster; and "his love affair with the world" first dawns. For the artist, for Lawrence, it seems to be continually rediscovered, as Louise Kaplan suggests in quoting Lawrence's poem, "New Heaven and Earth," from his *Look! We Have Come Through* sequence: "I touch, I feel the unknown!/I am the first comer!/Cortes, Pisarro, Columbus, Cabot, / they are nothing, nothing!/ I have found the other world!"

Thus poised at this early peak of separation/individuation, the child looks forward to completing his identification with the parents. So also did Lawrence, but although making forays in both parental directions, he goes all the way in neither. Yet, it cannot be said that he fails. A clue to the later direction his art will take may be found in his brief essay, "Aristocracy" (1925). There the sun is summoned along lines earlier discussed: "The sun, I tell you, is alive, and more alive than I am ... it is the Holy Ghost in full raiment, shaking and walking, and alive as a tiger is, only more so, in the sky." To meet the sun is to come finally into one's own: "He who has the sun in his face, in his body, he is the pure aristocrat." So much for revitalization and masculinization along the earlier specified cosmic lines. But Lawrence thrusts his thought further: "He who has the sun in his breast, and the moon in his belly, he is the first: the aristocrat of aristocrats, supreme in the aristocracy of life. Because he is *most alive*." To have the male sun and the female moon inside oneself is not only to embody a Primal Scene of cosmic proportions but also to affirm a persisting bisexual identification. Only, one may add, is the sun higher than the moon, which now resides in the solar plexus, the womb of creativity.

Appendixes

Appendix 1

On Symbol Formation

Thinking about symbolism within psychoanalysis begins at the very beginning when Freud in his famous Chapter 7 of *The Interpretation of Dreams* (1900) includes symbols under the heading of Indirect Representations. Ernest Jones retains this unconscious determinant and stresses the primitive nature, the condensation of several ideas within one image, and the "flow of significance . . . from the more essential to the less essential." The individual represses the affects of symbols and quite often may not be aware that he is using symbols at all. The number of symbols is great, but the number of ideas symbolized is small. These are *ideas of the self* ("the whole body or any separate part of it") *and the immediate blood relatives, or of the phenomena of birth* ("giving birth, begetting, or of being born oneself"), *love* ("more strictly sexuality . . . including excretory acts"), and *death*.

This appears sound enough, but I agree with Kubie's (1953) strictures against Jones for separating symbols from metaphors, similes, and other seemingly conscious literary representations. "There are no such discontinuities in nature as those who put symbolism of dreams in a category of its own would seem to imply," according to Kubie. This means not only that metaphors and similes may have unconscious components, but also that symbols may exist on conscious, preconscious, and unconscious levels.

Kubie's work has proven to be valuable for a study of Lawrence. "Early in its formative process, every concept and its symbolic representatives develop two points of reference, one internal with reference to the boundaries of the body, and one external." This "dual anchorage" forms the basis for acquiring knowledge and serves as a "bridge between the inner and outer world." Of the many implications of this view, two stand out for our purposes: (1) The "infant experiences his psychic needs as changes in his vague sensory precepts of the parts, the products and the requirements of his own body." Thus the "first learning concerns itself entirely with bodily things," and all "expanding knowledge of the nonbodily world must relate itself automatically to that which has already been experienced in the bodily world." And (2) "Every conceptualization of the outer world comes into relationship with evolving conceptualizations of the body world" in such a way that *"each can be and is used to represent the other."*

To return to the English school of object-relations for additional insight is also to turn to larger issues of creativity. With characteristic audacity, Melanie Klein (1930) introduced the crucial affect of *anxiety* into the process of symbol-formation and hypothesized its appearance in the infant at around three months. As a result of destructive fantasies aimed at the mother's body (which may house feces, paternal phallus, and children), it is only through a process of symbolic equation with other objects that anxiety may be reduced, the persecutory fears allayed, and gestures of restoration or reparation instituted. Thus symbol-formation begins in a total fantasy world and gradually serves integrative and healing processes both within the emerging self and with object relations. Klein considers it the basis for all future talent.

Important subsequent contributions by Hannah Segal (1952, 1957, 1964, 1975) and Marion Milner (1955, 1957) have built on Klein's ideas. For Segal the earliest symbolic equations, based on mechanisms of introjection and projection, become "fully formed symbols in the depressive position" (1957). By this time, the early representations of the mother into good and bad images have fused into a whole object, and the infant has undertaken important steps along the route of separation-differentiation. The accompanying affects are "guilt, fear of loss or actual experience of loss and mourning, and a striving to recreate the object." The "symbol is used not to deny but to overcome loss." Modifications in thinking from the omnipotent toward the realistic follow along with the inhibition of the early instinctual aims.

The ego takes an active hand in internalizing, restoring, and preserving the original object within its own sphere, safely removed from primitive instinctual assaults. These internally created symbols can be cast again onto the external world and endow it with meaning. Likewise, anxieties over earlier conflicts can be lessened by symbolizing them. The symbol itself, Segal concludes, means "throwing together" and integrating "the internal with the external, the subject with the object, and the earlier experiences with the later ones." This interplay coincides with Kubie's "dual anchorage" and the child's gradual establishment of ego boundaries. Along the same lines is Winnicott's classic paper on "Transitional Objects and Transitional Phenomena" (1951), in which he assigns a positive role to illusion. The transitional object, the child's "first Not-Me possession," fills the emergent spaces between himself and the mother from whom he is gradually separating; it may symbolize the breast or the (illusory) maternal phallus, but the real point lies in its being an object in its own right. At an earlier stage, the infant believed its hunger needs created the mother's breast, giving it the "illusion that there is "an external reality that corresponds" to its "own capacity to create." The mother's task is "gradually to disillusion the infant." Meanwhile otherwise neutral objects are relinquished; but the larger task of "reality-acceptance is never completed," for "no human being is free from the strain of relating inner and outer reality." This "intermediate area of experience which is not challenged" is filled in later life by religion, culture, and the arts. Thus as the element of illusion in the work of art allows the beholder to create his own meaning, the same would apply to symbols.

Appendix 2

On the Relation of Aggression
to Creativity and Sexuality

*. . . love consists of new editions of old traces and repeats infantile reactions. But this
is an essential character of every love. There is no love that does not reproduce
infantile prototypes. The infantile conditioning factor in it is just what gives it its
compulsive character which verges on the pathological.—Freud*[1]

*I do love her. If she left me, I do not think I should be alive six months hence. . . . I
didn't know life was so hard. But really for me it's been a devilish time ever since I was
born. But for the fact that when one's got a job on, one ought to go through with it, I'd
prefer to be dead any minute. I can't bear it when F. is away. I could bang my head
against the wall, for relief. It's a bit too much.—Lawrence,* CL, 134

It is easier to ask why the sense of the lost mother must be revived within a genital
relationship than it is to find an answer. Lawrence's refusal to idealize sex did not
rule out his own mystical embellishments. His women characters are consistently
drawn from the upper levels of society, and even a plain woman like Clara Dawes
has dignity and sensitivity. By and large, his women are more refined and in a problematic sense more civilized than are his men. It is not difficult to trace this idealization to his superior mother, but if idealization is to be more than a universal
pigment, we must look behind it to the feelings of envy and awe over the mother's
procreative and nutritive powers, which have previously been associated with
mastery through identification. And behind both identification and idealization,
we can assume there exist fears of loss bound up either with helpless dependency
and abandonment, or with retaliation over aggressive wishes. Idealization readily
feeds on envy and resentment as well as on fear, and since the object in question
which draws forth so much feeling is also incestuous, idealization serves as a barrier to the genital function. Thus when images of the lost-mother relation are resurrected in other relationships or when she is felt as a rudiment for fictional women,
the accompanying idealization apparently must be offset by devaluing strategies
such as the short-circuiting of foreplay, verbal or physical abuse, indifference to

certain forms of female orgasm (as if the woman's deriving of too much pleasure from the act signifies that she is *getting more out of it* than the man and is thus *taking something away from him*), and the ultimate antiidealizing mode of anal penetration. Such a great life-struggle does Lawrence seem to make of sexuality that it is no wonder he locates the operations of the great macrocosm in its microcosmic circuits—and thereby manages to retain his idealization on a "higher" plane of meaning.

Of course what the agent intends to be a necessary devaluing can only be felt as cruelty or hostility by the object, and rightly so. There seems to be no getting around this. If we were proposing the sexual relationship in Lawrence's work as a model to follow, there would be problems; but if we see it primarily as a means of presenting some of the complexities that can accrue within an otherwise pleasurable, genital relationship, further exploration of it may be more profitable. One reason for the disrupting forces' not being fatal to the relationship is the sense one has of its being "held," either by an early bond of basic trust with the mother or by the earlier primary love.

But so deeply conflicted over women is Lawrence that his conscious attitudes are racked by contradiction and only rarely relieved by paradox; one can indulge in playing one passage off against another *ad infinitum* without resolution. His own "superiority" is contingent on woman's recognition of it, which is not the same as her being made inferior—though the difference is neither one that feminists would accept nor one that could readily be defended. He objected not to women's thinking but to their having "learned to think like men" (RE, 180). And while he would insist that this robs them of their "blood individuality," we may infer also that in making their egos resemble men's, he is robbed of loving them, for he can only genuinely love what is differentiated from him; everything else would be narcissism.

And the love of Narcissus for his own watery image led to his death—suitably by starvation, for had he disturbed the water's surface, he would have touched otherness and formed an object-relation. The unexpected but apt relationship of Death Drive, Ambivalence, and Narcissism has been examined in a paper so titled by K. R. Eissler,[2] and the danger of redefining narcissism to accommodate a primitive love-bond is that the influence of aggressive drives might be minimized. Yet to speak of Lawrence as a man obsessed is to recognize the strong ambivalence in conflicts between love and hate. To speak of his dangerous swerves toward fascism and sexism is to recognize in the sphere of object-relations and their representations an extension of self-hatred symbolized by Clifford Chatterley as a (partial) self-representation. And to include Melanie Klein's paranoid-schizoid stage by way of the resourcing process does at least provide a framework for further investigations into primitive drive development.

Although aggression may be enlisted in the attempts at anti-idealizing an object whom one loves and upon whom one depends, it would be a mistake to so limit our views of its operations. One must consider a role for aggression nearly equal to that of love. Lawrence saw himself as a "priest of love" (CL, 173), and would prefer to view his struggles in that light, or as Frieda saw him: "tender and gentle and fierce" (NI, 34). At the same time it is possible to recognize in his life a battleground between those giant forces Freud eventually named as Eros and Thanatos.

Winnicott distinguishes between aggression and anger. The former is an attribute of life itself—the tendency to kick in the womb, thrash away with one's arms, gum-chew the nipple. It is a "primitive expression of love," which "includes an imaginative attack on the mother's body," and it may naturally lead to an early sense of guilt, responsibility, and reparation. Somewhat similarly, Anna Freud uses the phrase "aggressive love."[3] Anger, on the other hand, is an affective transformation of the drive, often a response to frustration, which may lead the child away from the guilt and toward the splitting of love and hate along separate lines.

What follows may look like a strange compilation of theory and inference, but perhaps by now a greater degree of reconstruction of Lawrence's earliest development is possible.

A close reading of Winnicott's papers reveals that aggression is necessary for normal emotional development because it leads to concern and to fusion both of drives and of object-and-self-representations. Frustrations of aggression lead to anger and object- or self-splitting as defensive measures. With aggression as the norm, anger becomes more problematic. And since we are by now familiar with a great deal of splitting in Lawrence at almost every turn, we are justified in probing beyond aggression to anger.

Available information about Lawrence's early nursing tells us two things above all: his own sickly condition and his necessarily divided but devoted mother, who as late as his twelfth year would share his sickbed to wean him from his illness. She would not only fill the bill of Winnicott's good-enough mother, she would perhaps fill it too well, a too-good mother. The role of aggression as set forth by Winnicott is integral to emotional well-being, for it not only allows an instinctual discharge but it also sets in motion a natural healing sequence and allows the externally destroyed object to be gradually recreated and instituted internally during periods of absence. We first came upon this process in its derivatives in the genital sphere as a condition of sexual love. The lost object must be located and reawakened.

In attempting to minimize the infant's periods of deprivation, the too-good mother imposes another kind of deprivation. When normal aggression is not given its due, it may become bottled-up as frustrated anger with which the too-good mother cannot easily deal. Such a mother may be acting out of her own needs for a type of symbiotic or libidinal relationship, or she may be responding to the unstable condition of the infant; or, as for Mrs. Lawrence and her son, it may be both. Lawrence seems to be in agreement when he took into account his mother's "unfulfilled desire" and her secret Don Juan dreams of a Dionysian son-lover, and also when he overheard his mother say, "He has seemed to be part of me" (P, 181 – 89; CL, 69). The mother's loving him not only as a lover, but also as part of herself—symbiotically, narcissistically—opens the way for a final reconstruction of the events surrounding Lawrence's birth. One can only wonder whether his being born hating his father (which he wasn't), is not instead a way of saying he was conceived in hate—the mother's for the father. If so, his task as Don Juan hero might then become entangled with restoring to the mother her lost innocence, through some incomprehensible magical deed. In any case, her loving him as part of herself does suggest that the part of herself unconsciously felt as lost or cut off is what he will make up for or restore. Whatever this may have originally been for the mother, it seems clearly to have been related to the painful—physically and emotionally—wounding experiences with her miner husband, against whom she vigorously turns her children. One wounding episode which stood out in the family memory was her being shut out of her own house while pregnant with young Bert. Although she is portrayed as swooning deliriously among her flowers in the moonlight, it was shown that this lyrical segment could not have actually occurred. We are also informed as the scene gets under way that "the child boiled within her" as the quarrel was replayed like a "brand red-hot down on her soul" (SL, 23). The son is infused with her anger as part of that "peculiar fusion of soul," so Lawrence will later stress (CL, 69). The reconstructed account goes as follows: Locked out, Mrs. Lawrence's anger shifted from her husband to his child, "which she had not wanted" (SL, 37), and by emotionally ridding herself of what she cannot actually rid herself, she ejects the child from her womb in retaliation for her spouse's ejection of her: Lawrence's birth was not only surrounded by parental anger, it may also have been premature.[4] This accounts in part for his initial frailty, a "puny little specimen" that looked like a "skinned rabbit" to a neighbor, and for his disposition to infection. (N, 21; PL, 12). However, the act of birth, regardless of its timing, restores him to the mother as part of herself, and her fiery moral will blows his faltering flame into fierce vitality. "This fierce and overpowerful love had harmed the boy who was not strong enough to bear it," so Frieda puts in, but she gives a clue to how he did bear it by offering that "he was almost dead but fought his way back with the fierce courage and vitality that was his" (NI, 56, 44).

Aggression in the service of survival—certainly this is important too. But the terms of this survival dictated that the mother be spared. It appears consistent with the line of reasoning thus far to assume that if normal aggression had not been allowed direct discharge, it may have been turned inordinately against the self, thereby contributing to the tendency to fall ill; and it may have, through its turning into anger, resulted in splitting and conflicts over ambivalence. Thus when Paul Morel slips his dying mother a lethal dose of morphine, he is doing more than attempting to anticipate her imminent loss; he is asserting his power over a love-object by showing that if he is to recreate it he must first be able to destroy it. Processes such as these, which lay down the conditions for future love relationships, emerge more clearly in the fiction, especially *Lady Chatterley*, and in his ties to Frieda.

To recapitulate: if the infant is able to "destroy" the object by virtue of his aggression, he can then recreate it internally. If the object resists its own "destruction" or takes on overwhelming meaning, or imposes its own claims, or any of these is so perceived, angry tensions can build up, creating a situation of danger which then may induce repeated acts of object destruction and defensive formations of identifications with the (dangerous) aggressor; splitting of self or object may easily result. Creativity is then called upon not only to complete by reparation and restitution a process begun by aggression but also to bind up splits in object- and self-representations. And it is this added burden of accommodating anger in Lawrence's creative work that may show up as cruelty, will-to-power fantasies, etc., not to mention the mixture of sadism and indifference to women that has understandably proven so troublesome to many of his sympathetic readers, but which together have just as often endowed his works with searing portraits of *homo in extremis*. It is not, however, that Lawrence has too little a sense of woman as a self in her own right, but more likely, to the contrary, too great a sense, and one that appears to be highly colored by early emotional experience. Thus, even minor, sexually neutral acts of self-assertion may be interpreted as seething, self-seeking female will and so elicit fierce responses—or be typically represented as variations on the devouring lamia or castrating harpy type.

From this perspective, dependency and idealization would be complicating issues, and as we move from the earliest dyadic structure to the later triadic structures, we can incorporate into this theoretical developmental scheme images of the quarreling and copulating parents. Here again, Winnicott appears to be on the mark, and we may ask with him, What happens when a child's parents quarrel in front of him "when he is fully occupied over some other problem"? And the answer, identical to the one offered at various points throughout this study, is identification with both parents: "He manages only by taking the whole experience into himself in order to master it."[5]

And then the outcome, insofar as we are able to recognize it in the creative sphere, is in the composite symbolism, or else in the "good" male and female images often in juxtaposition with hateful self-representations. These may appear as Bertie Reid in "The Blind Man," Banford in *The Fox*, Clifford Chatterley in opposition to the "good" lovers, and so on. A more extensive listing of characters might well indicate that Lawrence did not play favorites with his anger, that he did not structure it along lines of gender. But when his self-hatred is directed toward a female object, he risks being cast, rightly or wrongly, as antifeminist. Yet his judiciously phrased formulation of adult sexuality as warmhearted fucking should be seen as mediating between coldblooded aggression and hotheaded anger.[6]

To arrive at such an undramatic conclusion after the deployment of so much critical ingenuity may be a disappointment. Perhaps one would hope for a richer polemical yield from the tapping of such deep roots. Yet when one attempts to sort out questions of sexism and narcissism from essentially nonideological regions of the mind, designated as the unconscious, a few faltering steps toward truth need not be discounted.

Appendix 3

On Maturation versus Development

... affect must quicken percept. . . . —René A. Spitz, 1972

The fact that more sophisticated art forms begin with life *in media res* assumes that eventually they will get around to accounting for life *ab initio*. Consequently, every artist creates a new beginning when he produces a work of art, and every such act of creation is also necessarily a re-creation. This will sound axiomatic, but it should take on added meaning now that we know something of the available polarities of those beginnings and have Ehrenzweig's dynamic sequence of this reshaping process. We should also be able to perceive a bit more clearly how the sources of life serve as the resources of art.

The idea that creative processes and emotional development are intimately, perhaps inseparably, bound together has never been far from the focus of this study. Yet the nature of this relationship is intensely obscure. Certainly it would be a misguided application of psychoanalysis to place creativity merely in the service of psychosexual development, if only because it would circumscribe the area far too narrowly. On the other hand, Lawrence's emotional development and evolving reality-sense are patently discernible through the works. Clearly the two proceed hand in hand, and it would be a mistake to view him as a fixed entity, as does Dorothy Van Ghent when she asserts that the yellow pollen streaks Mrs. Morel retains on her face following her rapturous interlude among the lilies is an instance of the "phallic reality" which Lawrence was only able to deal with adequately some fourteen years later in *Lady Chatterley's Lover*.[1] For even though he was enjoying a richly varied kind of phallic experience with Frieda during the writing of *Sons and Lovers*, he had not re-sourced his own life thoroughly enough or worked through his conflicts sufficiently well to deal with phallic reality in the fullness of imagination that he eventually would attain.

This leads to an important distinction within psychoanalysis between maturation and development. René Spitz, in a provocative paper we shall shortly come to, notes that *maturation* is innate as "part of the newborn's congenital equipment";

development is "the product of the constantly changing requirements of onto-
genesis, of the unpredictably shifting adaptive demands imposed or withheld by
the surround." Peter Blos has nicely illustrated this distinction by stating that
whereas puberty is an act of nature, adolescence is an act of man. The two may
come to have rather separate agendas and not proceed hand-in-glove at all; yet
Spitz maintains that there may be "organizers of the psyche"—which he desig-
nates in the title of his paper as "Bridges"—to harmonize the biological process
with various psychic forces and environmental influences.[2]

Lawrence, for example, was probably biologically ready for sexual functioning
from puberty on, and was prepared to initiate a sexual relationship at least by 1909
when he was living away from home in Croyden. But he had by then split women
into spiritual/physical extremes, and apart from a few furtive initiatory episodes
apparently involving Alice Dax, he finds himself diffidently inquiring of Jessie
Chambers whether she thinks any girl might give him "that" without marriage
("*difficult*," she thinks [PE, 167]). With Frieda three years later he gets not only "that"
but a lasting human relationship within marriage and an extremity of passion he
refers to as the very "*hinterland der seele*" (CL, 132). These words are more positive,
no longer pointing to something outside the boundaries of self, but still discretely
veiled in a foreign phrase and still somewhat foreign to consciousness. In 1924,
during the American period, he writes a story about a wealthy American woman's
infatuation with a bullfighter; however, when it came to sex she would have, as the
title puts it, "None of That." Here the earlier position is disavowed by shackling it to
the life-denying woman obsessed with power over others and in the end the victim
of gang rape. After years of sexual euphemisms and circumlocutions both poetic
and occult, it is only in the last three years of his life, into his forties and under the
pressure of dying, that phallic reality with the attendant four-letter words appears
and the novel "says shit! and fuck! in so many syllables" (CL, 1036). And if the final
irony is true—that Lawrence was personally impotent during this time—one can
only wonder and ask oneself this question: if Lawrence was able to deal with his
relationship to his mother only after her loss, i.e., as an absent object, could he deal
with phallic reality only when it too was becoming an absent object?

In any case the jarring latitude between development and maturation used to
strike me, as it must have struck others, as remarkable in a writer who was not
intimidated by sociocultural amenities and conventions. Quite the opposite, in
fact. The only unforgivable offense for Lawrence is for one to deny life, and it was
the changing nature of social existence that he was so long at pains defining. So it
does seem valid to expect other more obscure processes affecting his protracted
struggle toward genitality. Some of these we have described as projective identification in the service both of art and self, and a pattern of illness, emotional injury,
and self-reconstitution via play or re-sourcing.

Spitz in his context is also somewhat uncertain about the components of those psychic organizers he calls bridges that exist between the growing organism and the developing self. He suggests that they must blend "percept" and "affect" long enough for anticipation to come into play and for meaning to unfold. His bridges are adaptive and forward-looking. As considered here, creativity resembles a psychic organizer and may function analogously. But it is a movable feast on the psyche's calendar, for it manages to break out of time frames and specific phases on behalf of adaptive roles throughout life. And because it can operate retrospectively as well as affect others, it is perhaps a multilevel, two-way bridge. As countless individuals traffic across its constructions, many of its original purposes and more private functions may be easily and properly overlooked.

The awkward fact that Lawrence managed most fully to assimilate phallic reality into his art at a time of personal sexual hiatus suggests that creativity was no psychic organizer in a predictable sense. This fact allows us to direct our attention toward creativity's larger role in the life-and-death struggle being waged within his physical being from very early on and manifested but intermittently in the finished piece of work. Throughout, though, creativity was on the side of life, of Eros. And in its more intrapersonal campaigns—whether to preserve a bond with the all-important mother, sustain life separately from her, or achieve the necessary differentiation into selfhood and object-relation—creativity marshaled the available energies for this task in a similar manner to Spitz's psychic organizer. Unshackled for creative use, these energies in turn may well have enhanced emotional development. So the task of assigning a clear-cut priority may be neither possible nor ultimately relevant. In the end the loss of sexual potency must have been symptomatic of the organism's gradual defeat. But the emergence of phallic reality in the art may have been symptomatic also, of the final, fierce triumph of Eros.

Notes

1 Fantasy

1 For example, Anthony Storr's *The Dynamics of Creation* (New York: Atheneum, 1972).

2 Otto Rank, *The Myth of the Birth of the Hero* (New York: Alfred Knopf, Vintage Book, 1959); Ernst Kris, *Psychoanalytic Explorations in Art* (New York: International Universities Press, 1952); Phyllis Greenacre, "The Family Romance of the Artist," *Psychoanalytic Study of the Child* 13 (1958):9−36; Linda Joan Kaplan, "The Family Romance: Theoretical and Clinical Implications," *Psychoanalytic Review* 61 (1974):169−202.

3 For Wordsworth, see Greenacre above; for Shaw, see Daniel Dervin, *Bernard Shaw, A Psychological Study* (Lewisburg, Pa.: Bucknell University Press, 1975).

4 Lawrence employs the idea of psychic geography in his second draft of *Studies in Classic American Literature*, published as *The Symbolic Meaning*. Links between psyche and geography are explored in Chapter Four, Body; Michael Balint, *Thrills and Regressions* (New York: International Universities Press, 1959); and *The Basic Fault* (London: Tavistock, 1968).

5 In a similar vein Judith C. Ruderman writes that "throughout his career [Lawrence] shows evidence of unresolved pre-oedipal conflicts beneath the oedipal overlay" ("*The Fox* and the 'Devouring Mother,'" *D. H. Lawrence Review* 10 (1977):252. See also her book, *D. H. Lawrence and the Devouring Mother* (Durham, N.C.: Duke University Press, 1984).

6 In *Journal of the American Psychoanalytic Association* 23 (1975):334−62.

7 Leo Bersani, "Lawrentian Stillness," in *A Future for Astyanax* (Boston: Little Brown, 1976), pp. 156−85.

8 "*The Plumed Serpent*, and the Mexican Revolution," *Journal of Modern Literature* 4 (1974):455−72.

9 Hillis Miller, "D. H. Lawrence: *The Fox* and the Perspective Glass, *Harvard Advocate*, Dec., 1952, p. 137; David J. Kleinbard, "Laing, Lawrence, and the Maternal Cannibal," *Psychoanalytic Review* 58 (1971):5−13; Edmund Bergler, "D. H. Lawrence's *The Fox* and the Psychoanalytic Theory on Lesbianism," in *A D. H. Lawrence Miscellany* (Carbondale: Southern Illinois University Press, 1959); Judith G. Ruderman, "*The Fox* and the 'Devouring Mother,'" *D. H. Lawrence Review* 10 (1977):251−69; James Twitchell, "Lawrence's Lamias: Predatory Women in *The Rainbow* and *Women in Love*," *Studies in the Novel* 11 (1979):23−42.

10 George H. Ford, *Double Measure* (New York: W. W. Norton, 1965).

11   This viewpoint is supported in Charles Rossman, "'You Are the Call and I Am the Answer': D. H. Lawrence and Women," *D. H. Lawrence Review* 8 (1975): 255–329.

12   An intermediate stage in this process occurs in the destructive oral sensuality of Ursula and Anton in *The Rainbow* (p. 479). There is her "beaked mouth" and her "fierce, beaked, harpy's kiss" that overpower the hapless male.

13   Paul Delaney, *D. H. Lawrence's Nightmare* (New York: Basic Books, 1978).

14   Ibid., p. 280.

15   Ibid., p. 210.

16   Barbara Hardy, *The Appropriate Form, An Essay on the Novel* (London: Athlone Press, 1964).

17   Hilary Simpson, *D. H. Lawrence and Feminism* (DeKalb: Northern Illinois University Press, 1982), p. 35.

18   Géza Róheim, *The Gates of the Dream* (New York: International Universities Press, 1952), p. 534.

19   Helm Stierlin, *Psychoanalysis and Family Therapy* (New York: Jason Aronson, 1978).

2   Reality

1   William Niederland, "Early Auditory Experiences: Beating Fantasies and the Primal Scene," *Psychoanalytic Study of the Child* 13 (1958):471–504.

2   Sigmund Freud, "The Sexual Enlightenment of Children," *Standard Edition* 9.

3   Robert Bak, "The Phallic Woman: The Ubiquitous Fantasy in Perversion," *Psychoanalytic Study of the Child* 23 (1968):15–36.

4   Edoardo Weiss, "The Phenomenon of 'Ego Passage,'" *Journal of the American Psychoanalytic Association* 5 (1957):267–81.

5   Aaron Esman, "The Primal Scene, A Review and a Reconsideration," *Psychoanalytic Study of the Child* 28 (1973):49–83.

6   Paul Delaney, *D. H. Lawrence's Nightmare* (New York: Basic Books, 1978), p. 249.

3   Symbol

1   Henry Edelheit, "Mythopoiesis and the Primal Scene," *Psychoanalytic Study of Society* 5 (1972):212–33.

2   Henry Edelheit, "Crucifixion Fantasies and Their Relation to the Primal Scene," *International Journal of Psycho-Analysis* 55 (1974):193–204.

3   Sister Mary Francis McDonald, "Phoenix Redivivus," *Phoenix* 14 (1960): 187–206.

4   Douglas J. McMillen, "The Phoenix in the Western World from Herodotus to Shakespeare," *D. H. Lawrence Review* 5 (1972):238−67.

5   Louis Ginzberg, *The Legends of the Jews*, vol. I (Philadelphia: Jewish Publication Society of America, 1909).

6   D. W. Winnicott, "Transitional Objects and Transitional Phenomena," *Collected Papers* (London: Tavistock Publications, 1958).

7   Ginzberg, *Legends of the Jews*.

8   McDonald, "Phoenix Redivivus."

9   L. D. Clark, *Dark Night of the Body* (Austin: University of Texas Press, 1964).

10   R. T. Rundle Clarke, "The Origin of the Phoenix," *University of Birmingham Historical Journal* 2 (1950):105−40.

11   Alice Baldwin, "The Structure of the Coatl Symbol in *The Plumed Serpent*," *Style* 5 (1971):138−50.

12   Richard Ellmann, *Ulysses on the Liffey* (New York: Oxford University Press, 1972).

13   Frank Kermode, *D. H. Lawrence* (New York: Viking Press, Modern Masters Series, 1973).

14   Sigmund Freud, *The Freud/Jung Letters*, 169F (Princeton: Princeton University Press, 1974).

15   A closer look at some of the historical references discloses the fascinating interplay between the mythical and the psychological, especially as they converge on reproductive concerns. At the close of his remarkable life-span the Phoenix builds a nest of fragrant boughs—"cassia and sprigs of incense, which he fills with perfumes," according to Pliny. He then deposits himself on "that pyre which shall be at once his tomb and cradle," in the words of Claudian, and either awaits the "golden hairs" of Phoebus Apollo or sets the nest afire with the friction of his wings. Tacitus has him first shedding a "genital substance," while other versions play up the olfactory aspect. In Hebrew accounts, his "excrement is a worm, whose excrement in turn is the cinnamon used by kings and princes." Sometimes the fiery death is seen as an acceleration of the natural processes of decay, and the repugnance of putrifying flesh is transformed in the still-moist nest of ashes as the newly born worm rises "with wings full of fragrant perfume." Behind such imagery and transformations may be anal fantasies of copulation and birth. There evidently are many strata of meaning in this myth, but Claudian most eloquently expresses the most abiding motif:

> Never was this bird conceived nor springs it from any mortal seed, itself is alike its own father and son, and with none to recreate it, it renews it outworn limbs with a rejuvenation of death and at each decease wins a fresh lease of life. . . .

He who was but now the sire comes forth from the pyre the son successor; between life and life lay but that brief space wherein the pyre burned.

Whether for Lawrence it stood for maternal-hatching or self-begetting, it was clearly preferable to biological paternity, which he resented for many years. "I didn't ask him to be my father," he told a chum in his youth. "I had nothing to do with it" (George Neville, *A Memoir of D. H. Lawrence* [New York: Cambridge University Press, 1981], p. 60).

16 Ginzberg, *Legends of the Jews*.

17 Their discussions were a "vivid re-creation of the substance" of their reading, according to Jessie Chambers. A "mutual exchange" is how Lawrence put it (PE, 93, 148). For more on Lawrence's creative collaborations, see "A Literary Trespasser," in Hilary Simpson's *D. H. Lawrence and Feminism* (1982); and my paper, "D. H. Lawrence and Freud," in *American Imago* 36 (1979):93 − 117.

18 Géza Róheim, *The Riddle of the Sphinx* (London: Hogarth Press, 1934), p. 225.

19 D. W. Winnicott, "Aggression in Emotional Development," *Collected Papers*, 1958.

20 Lawrence Kubie, "The Drive to Become Both Sexes," *Psychoanalytic Quarterly* 43 (1974):349 − 426.

4 Body

1   The following papers are all by William Niederland: "Narcissistic Ego Impairment in Patients with Early Physical Malformations," *Psychoanalytic Study of the Child* 20 (1965):518 − 33; "Clinical Aspects of Creativity," *American Imago* 24 (1967):6 − 34; "Psychoanalytic Approaches to Artistic Creativity," *Psychoanalytic Quarterly* 45(1976):185 − 212.

2   James Joyce, *Ulysses* (New York: Random House Edition, 1961), p. 391.

3   Caroline Spurgeon, *Shakespeare's Imagery* (1935; reprint ed., Boston: Beacon Hill Press, 1961).

4   Phyllis Greenacre, *Swift and Carroll* (New York: International Universities Press, 1955).

5   Richard Ellmann, *Ulysses on the Liffey* (New York: Oxford University Press, 1973).

6   Sigmund Freud, "A Difficulty in the Path of Psychoanalysis," *Standard Edition* 9.

7   Michael Polanyi, *Personal Knowledge, Towards a Post-Critical Philosophy* (New York: Harper and Row, 1958).

8   John Wheeler, "The Universe As Home for Man," *American Scientist* 62 (1974): 683 − 91.

9   Leonard Barkin, *Nature's Work of Art, The Human Body as Image of the World* (New Haven: Yale University Press, 1975).

10 James M. Pryse, *A New Presentation of the "Prometheus Bound" of Aischylos* (London: John Watkins, 1925).

11 William I. Grossman and Bennett Simon, "Anthropomorphism, Motive, Meaning, and Causality in Psychoanalytic Theory," *Psychoanalytic Study of the Child* 24 (1969):87.

12 Lawrence Kubie, "Distortion of the Symbolic Process in Neurosis and Psychosis," *Journal of the American Psychoanalytic Association* 1 (1953):59 – 86. (See Appendix 1, "On Symbol Formation.")

13 Sigmund Freud, *The Ego and the Id, Standard Edition* 19.

14 Joseph D. Lichtenberg, "The Development of the Sense of Self," *Journal of the American Psychoanalytic Association* 23 (1975):453 – 84.

15 Heinz Kohut, *The Analysis of the Self* (New York: International Universities Press, 1971).

16 William York Tindall, *D. H. Lawrence and Susan His Cow* (New York: Columbia University Press, 1939).

17 Thomas H. Miles, "Birkin's Electro-Mystical Body of Reality: D. H. Lawrence's Use of Kundalini," *D. H. Lawrence Review* 9 (1976):194 – 212.

18 Frederick Carter, *D. H. Lawrence and the Body Mystical* (London: Garden City Press, 1932).

19 Henry Edelheit, "Crucifixion Fantasies and Their Relation to the Primal Scene," *International Journal of Psycho-Analysis* 55 (1974):193 – 204.

20 Frank Kermode, *Shakespeare, Spenser, Donne*, chap. 1 (New York: Viking Press, 1971); Rosemary Reeves Davies, "The Eighth Love Scene: The Real Climax of *Lady Chatterley's Lover*," *D. H. Lawrence Review* 15 (1982):167 – 76.

21 These associations will likely lead to questions about masturbation, which was for Lawrence the outcome of mental consciousness, of sex-in-the-head dominating the body. But it was possibly connected also with the primal scene experience and hence with creativity. On the latter, see Evelyn Shakir's article, " 'Secret Sin': Lawrence's Early Verse," in *D. H. Lawrence Review* 8 (1975).

22 Ernst Kris, *Psychoanalytic Explorations in Art* (New York: International Universities Press, 1952).

23 Apparently the regressed state of the illness involved both sensory-motor controls and affective states, if one can so infer from a neighbor's account of a sixteen-year-old Lawrence recuperating from pneumonia, which had come about following his mother's depressive withdrawal after the death of her son Ernest. Thus the illness, while entailing a regression, served to draw the

mother out of herself by restoring an earlier object-relation—not with the lost son but with the still living one. "He seemed like a jackknife opening and shutting," Jessie Chambers's sister recalls. "'I can't—I can't keep still a moment. I am twitching all over. Look, I can't control myself!' He giggled as his knees shot up and down. 'You hold me. She can't.'" Whereupon his mother protested he was too big and heavy to be held, although in *Sons and Lovers* at this time she had moved into bed with him during the worst phases.

24   Knud Merrild, *A Poet and Two Painters* (New York: Viking Press, 1939).

25   James M. Pryse, *The Apocalypse Unsealed* (New York, 1910).

26   Joseph Foster, *D. H. Lawrence in Taos* (Albuquerque: University of New Mexico Press, 1972), pp. 222 – 39.

27   Noah D. Fabricant, "The Lingering Cough of D. H. Lawrence," in *Thirteen Famous Patients* (New York: Chilton, 1960); see also John White, "Psyche and Tuberculosis: The Libido Organization of Franz Kafka," *Psychoanalytic Study of Society* 4 (1967):185 – 251.

28   Peter Balbert, "The Loving of Lady Chatterley: D. H. Lawrence and the Phallic Imagination," in *D. H. Lawrence: The Man Who Lived* (Carbondale: Southern Illinois University Press, 1980), pp. 143 – 58.

29   Mark Spilka, "What Happens to a Pagan Vitalist When the Juice Runs Out?" in ibid., pp. 105 – 20.

30   Donald M. Kaplan, "Freud and the Coming of Age," *Bulletin of the Menninger Clinic* 40 (1976):335 – 56.

31   Julian Stamm, "Creativity and Sublimation," *American Imago* 24 (1967): 82 – 97.

32   T. S. Eliot, "Tradition and the Individual Talent," in *Selected Essays* (New York: Harcourt, Brace and Co., 1950).

33   Northrop Frye, *Spiritus Mundi, Essays on Literature, Myth, and Society* (Bloomington: Indiana University Press, 1976).

5   Play

1   D. W. Winnicott, "Transitional Objects and Transitional Phenomena," first appeared in *The International Journal of Psycho-Analysis* 34 (1953):89 – 97, and reappears in his *Collected Papers* (London: Tavistock Publications, 1958). A volume of papers stimulated by his concepts has recently appeared: *Between Reality and Fantasy*, ed. Simon Grolnick et al. (New York: Jason Aronson, 1978).

2   Fiction and fact agree on the arrival of a younger sibling when Bert (or Paul) was under two. For Bert it was Ada Lettice with whom he remained close for most of his life; for Paul it was Arthur (the same surname as Lawrence's father). The "symbiotic phase" has become almost standard in psychoanalytic usage

since the work of Margaret Mahler (cf. *The Psychological Birth of the Human Infant* [New York: Basic Books, 1975]). This earliest period refers to the child's attachment to the primary parent up to his birth as human being between ages 2 and 3. The doll episode which occurs when Paul is 3 or 4, may signify the early steps in his hatching out from the dual-unity with mother. The fact that it may be happening a bit late may have to do with her close-bonding and his fragile health.

I have so far been unable to corroborate the doll-episode's authenticity. Ada Lawrence describes a kindred episode involving the elaborate burial ceremony of a pet rabbit complete with "coffin to a small grave at the bottom of the garden" (quoted in Edward Nehls, *D. H. Lawrence: A Composite Biography* [Madison: University of Wisconsin Press, 1957], pp. 12 – 13). But it would have had to be Emily, the more reticent older sister, to recall the other episode—if it had happened. The grief-sessions have been corroborated by Ada: "My brother was a delicate and sensitive child and became morbid frequently, so that it was difficult to approach him. Sometimes, for no apparent reason, he would burst into tears and irritate mother, who would say 'Bless the child— whatever is he crying for now?' Bert invariably sobbed, 'I don't know,' and continued to cry" (Ibid., p. 17).

3   This connection was first noted in William H. New, "Character As Symbol: Annie's Role in *Sons and Lovers*," *D. H. Lawrence Review* 1 (1968):31 – 43.

4   Harry T. Moore, *The Priest of Love*, rev. ed. (Carbondale: Southern Illinois University Press, 1974), p. 125. Lawrence concludes a paragraph in a famous letter written shortly before his mother's death with a bewildering *non sequitur*: "Ugh—I have done well—and cruelly—tonight." This may refer to his mother or to Jessie Chambers, whom he spoke of being cruel to and wronging in the preceding paragraph.

That Lawrence both knew his mother was dead and felt she was still alive is observable in his writings; and L. D. Clark in "Lawrence and the American Indian," *D. H. Lawrence Review* 9 (1976):310, suggests that in the aftermath of her death he felt "like a composite ghost of his mother and himself." His poem "All Souls" conveys the dual-unity sense via the imagery of the doll-burning episode:

The naked candles burn on every grave.
On your grave, in England, the weeds grow.

But I am your naked candle burning,
And that is not your grave, in England,
The world is your grave.
And my naked body standing on your grave

Upright towards heaven is burning off to you
Its flame of life, now and always til the end.

    [CP, 233]

5   Cf. Albert Rothenberg's "Janusian Thinking and Creativity," *Psychoanalytic Study of Society*, 1976, for a theory which may be able to accommodate such dualistic thinking processes; cf. EP, 68.

6   Keith Cushman, "D. H. Lawrence at Work: The Making of 'Odour of Chrysanthemums,'" *Journal of Modern Literature* 2 (1971–2):367–92.

7   During the war, Lawrence attacked his friend Russell for being *"full* of repressed desires" and having a "perverted blood-lust." For awhile Russell may have burned inwardly from this assault almost to the point of self-destruction. The doll association arises with a comment from Lawrence that he was "glad" but also "sorry," and felt like "going into a corner to cry, as I used to when I was a child." Later he admitted to quarreling "with something in *myself."* He would similarly attack Russell's sometime mistress, Lady Ottoline, for willfulness, adding, "I'm too much like that myself." Both she and Russell are treated and abused like self-objects, still inhabiting the sphere of play (cf. Paul Delaney, *D. H. Lawrence's Nightmare* [New York: Basic Books, 1978], pp. 145–46, for the episodes quoted from above).

8   Italics for "it" are Lawrence's, emphasizing the neuter or doll quality of the lifeless body.

9   "I don't so much care what the woman *feels*—in the ordinary usage of the word. That presumes an ego to feel with. I only care about what the woman *is*—what she IS—inhumanly, physiologically, materially . . . what she *is* as a phenomenon (or as representing some greater, inhuman will), instead of what she feels according to the human conception." The choice of female to represent his view of character is noteworthy as is the interest in the nonliving, phenomenological aspect, which perhaps must precede the animation or re-animation in the creative process. Also there is the sense of conflation—of two wills coexisting. "There is another ego," he writes further down, "according to whose action the individual is unrecognizable, and passes through, as it were, allotropic states . . ." (letter to Edward Garnett, 6 May 1914, CL, 282).

10   Alan Friedman in "The Other Lawrence," *Partisan Review* 37 (1970):239–53, explores the "kind of illumination that goes beyond what the art of the novel, the rise of the novel," etc. can provide. He searches for a distinctively Lawrencian unconscious (neither Freudian nor Jungian) where the "entire significance of very extended narrative passages condenses on moments that transcend (downward) the confining muddle of daylight feeling and consciousness and carry us to another domain of psychic life, a physical and impersonal Underself."

11 Delaney, *Nightmare*, p. 5.

12 Arnold Modell, "The Transitional Object and the Creative Act," *Psychoanalytic Quarterly* 39 (1970):240 – 50. In more speculative terms, Anthony Storr considers creativity from the viewpoint of play and adaption in *The Dynamics of Creation* (New York: Atheneum, 1972). And in a very valuable contribution, James W. Hamilton shows how certain fantasies function like transitional objects and nourish the creative process. Behind all the Phoenix symbols and accompanying the doll-burning episode in Lawrence is very likely some singular transitional fantasy serving the needs of separation-individuation ("Transitional Fantasies and the Creative Process," *Psychoanalytic Study of Society* 6 (1975):53 – 70).

13 Marian Tolpin, "On the Beginnings of a Cohesive Self: An Application of Concept of Transmuting Internalization to the Study of the Transitional Object and Signal Anxiety," *Psychoanalytic Study of the Child* 26 (1972):316 – 54.

14 René A. Spitz, "Bridges: On Anticipation, Duration, and Meaning," *Journal of the American Psychoanalytic Association* 20 (1972):721 – 35.

6 Origins

1 Harold Stewart argues persuasively that the reason for Jocasta's complicity in saving Oedipus is in order to enact the curse on Laius and thereby reveal her hatred of him for frustrating her sexual needs and wishes ("Jocasta's Crimes," *International Journal of Psycho-Analysis* 42 [1961]:424 – 30). See also Matthew Besdine, "The Jocasta Complex, Mothering and Genius, I and II, *Psychoanalytic Review* 55 (1968):259 – 77, 574 – 600. Helm Stierlin's generic term, "delegated mission," would apply to Mrs. Lawrence's indirectly fulfilling her needs through her children.

2 The first of these comes from L. D. Clark's "D. H. Lawrence and the American Indian," *D. H. Lawrence Review* 9 (1976):305 – 73; the second from Daniel Weiss's *Oedipus in Nottingham* (Seattle: University of Washington Press, 1962).

3 James Cowan, *D. H. Lawrence's American Journey* (Cleveland: Case Western Reserve Press, 1970), p. 68. The added quote is by Joseph Campbell.

4 An unassimilated digression, according to L. D. Clark in *Dark Night of the Body* (Austin: University of Texas Press, 1964), p. 42; but for Cowan, it is a necessary digression to define the "wild spirit" of the place, p. 96.

5 The mutually exclusive ideas of virgin/wife or purest/scarlet may be a continuation of that Janusian mode of creative-thinking introduced by Albert Rothenberg and discussed in the alive/not-alive condition of the doll/mother relation. Rothenberg's example is the mutually exclusive ideas of sacred/obscene, yoked together in Eugene O'Neill's *The Iceman Cometh*.

6 Michael Kirkham, "D. H. Lawrence and Social Consciousness," *Mosaic* 12 (1978):79 – 92.

7 Clark, "D. H. Lawrence and the American Indian," p. 310.

8 James Cowan's chapter is entitled, "The Duality of *St. Mawr*"; Keith Sagar, *The Art of D. H. Lawrence* (New York: Cambridge University Press, 1966), pp. 151 – 59.

9 See "Lawrence, Feminism, and the War," in Hilary Simpson's *D. H. Lawrence and Feminism* (DeKalb, Ill.: Norther Illinois University Press, 1982).

7 Projection

1 As a young man Lawrence could only bring himself to discuss his sexual needs with Jessie Chambers by invoking the distancing pronoun "that," as when he considered marrying a girl to give him "that" (PL, 109).

2 L. D. Clark, "D. H. Lawrence and the American Indian," *D. H. Lawrence Review* 9 (1976):305 – 73.

3 This term was first introduced by Melanie Klein and appears throughout her writings as well as those of her followers. It refers to the earliest and hence most primitive stage of infancy, prior to the "depressive position" and beginnings of assimilation of partial representations of the mother into a cohesive whole. The equivalent stage in the creative process is touched on by Lawrence as the "core of chaos ... fierce with incongruities."

4 Without endorsing any psychoanalytic theory about homosexuality, Meyer's study (1973) lends weight to my point. He finds that the homosexual scenes in the fiction "invariably occur after a frustrating humiliation with a woman." Here *post hoc* may mean *propter hoc*. The heterosexual frustration is presumably unconsciously interpreted as an organic or functional deficiency which generates an effort to incorporate a more adequate male identity through a male partner. If not sooner, then later, Lawrence felt that the "homosexual contacts are secondary, even if not merely substitutes of exasperated reaction from the utterly unsatisfactory nervous sex between men and women" (P2, 508).

5 Norman Mailer, *The Prisoner of Sex* (Boston: Little, Brown, 1971).

6 Phyllis Greenacre, "The Family Romance of the Artist," *Psychoanalytic Study of the Child* 13 (1958):9 – 36.

7 Corke's most recent account of these exchanges, quoted below, appears in "The Writings of *The Trespasser*," *D. H. Lawrence Review* 7 (1974):227 – 39.

8   Sun

1   Joyce Carol Oates also sees beyond the critics who assume "that Lawrence is
     venting his sadistic rage" against women characters: "Part of his energies are
     sadistic, of course, but essentially Lawrence is exorcising unclean, muddled,
     pseudo-primitive yearnings in himself" (*The Hostile Sun, The Poetry of D. H.
     Lawrence* [Los Angeles: Black Sparrow Press, 1973]).

2   Barbara Hardy, *The Appropriate Form* (London: Athlone Press, 1964).

3   Balint's term, but also Lawrence's when he spoke paradoxically of America not
     as a young continent but as being "old in senile decay and second childish-
     ness . . . nearer to the end, and the new beginning." In America, moreover, "the
     skies are not so old, the air is newer, the earth not as tired" (SP, 88).

4   Sagar distinguishes an "insouciance which glows through the later prose" in
     contrast to the insistent, incantatory rhythms of *The Plumed Serpent* (AD, 224).

5   See "The Phallic Consciousness," in Hilary Simpson's *D. H. Lawrence and
     Feminism* (DeKalb, Ill.: Northern Illinois University Press, 1982).

6   Paul Radin, *The Trickster, A Study of American Indian Mythology* (New York:
     Schocken Books, 1956). In the phallic phase one may separate early steps from
     the more advanced. If still under the sway of the anal period, the phallus may
     be perceived as a magical possession, a weapon of attack, or an instrument
     of control over an object. Inevitable castration threats foreclose the phallic
     period, and when its drives reemerge in early adolescence they carry with
     them some of the early sadism before they yield to the concerns of tenderness
     and the expressions of sensuality which coalesce for relatively stable genital
     relationships (Blos, 1965). Sagar rightly points out that in Lawrence's late
     works, "the insistence on tenderness, purity, gentleness, beauty is clearly a re-
     jection of the power-principle which dominated *The Plumed Serpent*." "Total
     awareness" must supersede "blood-knowledge" (AD, 192), which for Sagar
     even in *Lady Chatterley's Lover* has not quite been realized (AD, 195 – 96).

7   The disappearance of the cock halfway along is similar to the disappearance
     of St. Mawr midway in the other tale. By returning the animals to their place in
     nature, both characters by means of their sympathetic gesture in effect in-
     ternalize and identify with what the two natural creatures represent. St. Mawr
     is a bonfire in the night; the cock is orange and black. They are suns which,
     once centered in the characters' solar plexus, bring them nearer to wholeness.

8   "Christ and Isis: The Function of the Dying and Reviving God in *The Man Who
     Died*" (*D. H. Lawrence Review* 5 (1972):132 – 48).

9   Gerald Fiderer, "D. H. Lawrence's *The Man Who Died*: the Phallic Christ,"
     American Imago 25 (1968):91 – 6.

9   Creative Selfhood

1   Henry Edelheit, "Crucifixion Fantasies and Their Relation to the Primal Scene," *International Journal of Psycho-Analysis* 55 (1974):194.

2   Jonas Barish, *Ben Jonson and the Language of Comedy* (Cambridge, Mass.: Harvard University Press, 1960).

3   Leo Bersani, "Lawrentian Stillness," chap. 6 in *A Future for Astyanax, Character and Desire in Literature* (Boston: Little, Brown, 1976); Mark Spilka, "What Happens to a Pagan Vitalist When the Juice Runs Out?" in *D. H. Lawrence: The Man Who Lived*, ed. Robert Partlow, Jr., and Harry T. Moore (Carbondale: Southern Illinois University Press, 1980), pp. 105 – 20.

4   For more on the distinction between working out and working through, see Daniel Dervin, "D. H. Lawrence and Freud," *American Imago* 36 (1979): 93 – 117.

5   Roger Sale, *Modern Heroism* (Berkeley: University of California Press, 1973).

6   Ernst Kris, *Psychoanalytic Explorations in Art* (New York: International Universities Press, 1952).

7   Margaret Mahler, *The Psychological Birth of the Human Infant* (New York: Basic Books, 1975).

8   Susan Sontag, "Notes on Art, Sex, and Politics, *New York Times*, 8 December 1976; *Salmagundi* (Fall, 1975; Winter, 1976).

9   Daniel Weiss, *Oedipus in Nottingham* (Seattle: University of Washington Press, 1962), p. 109.

10   Orwell's lovers in *1984*, who in key ways are revisions of the pair in *Lady Chatterley*, discover that genital bonds cannot prevail in a nonfacilitating environment despite their own emotional commitments.

11   From a review of Norman O. Brown's *Love's Body*, in *Psychoanalytic Review*, 1970.

12   A past, it must be noted, which is partly his own, so to speak, and partly a patchwork of Lawrence's earlier fictions, especially *Sons and Lovers* and "The Prussian Officer." Perhaps as a masculine self-representation, he must in part be the result of prior creativity.

13   Hardy thus appears as a worthy rival in the artistic contest of creating women. To a certain extent, Lawrence's pastoral novels may be read as a corrective to or completion of Hardy's fiction. The thrust of Harold Bloom's thesis that the artist chooses his precursor as father-rival in a Family Romance context is borne out here. See his *Anxiety of Influence* (New York: Oxford University Press, 1973).

14   Of this some feminists may disapprove, not without reason. But recently Erica Jong (whose affinities with Henry Miller do render her suspect) has gotten

considerable mileage out of her character's prominently discussed ass. Perhaps it is different when a woman does it—not a double standard in reverse?

15 For a balanced judgment, see Lydia Blanchard, "Women Look at Lady Chatterley, Feminine Views of the Novel," *D. H. Lawrence Review* 11 (1978):246—59.

16 Hilary Simpson, *D. H. Lawrence and Feminism* (DeKalb, Ill.: Northern Illinois University Press, 1982), p. 138.

Appendix 2

1 Sigmund Freud, "Thoughts for the Times on War and Death" (1915), *Standard Edition* 17.

2 K. R. Eissler, "Death Drive, Ambivalence, and Narcissism," *Psychoanalytic Study of the Child* 26 (1971):25—78.

3 D. W. Winnicott, "Aggression in Relation to Normal Development" (1950), *Collected Papers*, 1958; Anna Freud, "Aggression in Relation to Emotional Development: Normal and Pathological," *Psychoanalytic Study of the Child*, 1949, vols. 3—4, pp. 37—43.

4 Beyond speculation and a measure of circumstantial evidence, the prospect of convincing proof is indeed bleak. Inquiries I made in Eastwood and conversations I had with English physicians virtually excluded the possibility of documentary evidence. Contemporaneous ignorance of woman's fertility cycle and the lack of medical records have conspired to keep the inquisitive in the dark.

5 Winnicott, "Aggression in Relation to Normal Development."

6 Just how powerful a hold *fuck* has on the human mind is illustrated in Kate Millett's feminist critique of Lawrence. Where one would expect to see Mellors's, "'Lie down,' he said softly," uttered to a distraught Connie, one finds instead, "Lie down," with *he ordered* extrapolated in Millett's version. Rather than considering this dishonest, one may prefer to believe in some primitive revulsion implicit in the sex act *qua* fucking. However, in another passage Kate Millett quotes from a temporary cessation of Kate Leslie's love-making in *The Plumed Serpent* in such a way as to render the break permanent—a form of critical *coitus interruptus* suitably left for Normal Mailer to complete by re-inserting the phallic text where one would have thought it necessarily had belonged all along.

But what is truly astonishing about these lapses is that until Mailer's counterattack they were unanimously overlooked by reviewers of the Millett book, most of whom accepted her revisionary reading of Lawrence without question.

The temporary withdrawal by Kate's Mexican lover is in order to bring about a shift in consciousness which is presented in sexual terms: her European (mental) consciousness which gravitates toward the frictional, Aphrodite-of-the-foam type of clitoral orgasm is to give way to Mexican (blood) consciousness in the quiet lava-flow or vaginal orgasm. For Lawrence, this is organic and regenerative, but for many feminists at the time Kate Millett was propounding her theories of sexual politics, vaginal sexual experience was anathema, and Lawrence was accused, through his writings, of being indifferent to woman's sexual satisfaction. Although not overlooking the yellows of sexism in the rainbow of his art, one would want to allow his metaphors their freedom. One would also like to clear the air of implied conspiracy a bit more by adding that the arch-villain in this scenario, Freud himself, never distinguished between clitoral and vaginal orgasms nor advocated one over the other. He spoke of *cathexes* only, not of orgasms. In pointing out this misconstruing of Freud's position in a review of *Sexual Politics*, Donald Kaplan goes on to note that in confusing sex with psychosexuality, Millett becomes not literal but literalistic.

How far sexual ideology may be in the mind of the beholder and how dangerous Cyclopean views of human sexuality can be is seen from the difficulty in assigning the following passage:

[The man] began to rely on manipulating her externally, on giving [the woman] clitoral orgasms. Very exciting. Yet there was always a part of her that resented it. Because she felt that the fact he wanted to was an expression of his instinctive desire not to commit himself to her. She felt that without knowing it or being conscious of it (though perhaps he was conscious of it) he was afraid of the emotion. A vaginal orgasm is emotion and nothing else, felt as emotion and expressed in sensations that are indistinguishable from emotion. The vaginal orgasm is a dissolving in a vague, dark generalised sensation like being swirled in a warm whirlpool. There are several different sorts of clitoral orgasms, and they are more powerful (that is a male word) than the vaginal orgasm. There can be a thousand thrills, sensations, etc., but there is only one real female orgasm and that is when a man, from the whole of his need and desire, takes a woman and wants all her response. Everything else is a substitute and a fake, and the most inexperienced woman feels this instinctively.

This of course is fiction. The character is "Ella," a self-projection of another character, "Anna," herself a self-projection of the author (Doris Lessing). But then Lawrence wrote fiction too, and had he written the above passage, he would have made himself even more anathema to the more doctrinaire brands of feminism.

Cf., Kate Millett, *Sexual Politics* (New York: Doubleday, 1970), and Norman Mailer, *The Prisoner of Sex* (Boston: Little, Brown, 1971). And after them a rebalancing of the scales in John Hoyles, "D. H. Lawrence and the Counter-Revolution: An Essay in Socialist Aesthetics," *D. H. Lawrence Review* 6 (1973): 173 – 200; Lydia Blanchard, "Love and Power: A Reconstruction of Sexual Politics in D. H. Lawrence," *Modern Fiction Studies* 21 (1975):431 – 43; Charles Rossman, "'You Are the Call and I Am the Answer': D. H. Lawrence and Women," *D. H. Lawrence Review* 5 (1975):255 – 329; *D. H. Lawrence and Women*, ed. Anne Smith (London: Vision Critical Studies, 1978); Donald Kaplan, "Sugar and Spice Revisited," *Psychiatry and Social Science Review* 5 (1971):12 – 17; L. D. Clark, *The Minoan Distance* (Tucson: University of Arizona Press, 1980), p. 190; Doris Lessing, *The Golden Notebook* (New York: Ballantine Books, 1962), pp. 215 – 16.

Appendix 3

1   Dorothy Van Ghent, *The English Novel: Form and Function* (New York: Holt, Rinehart, and Winston, 1953).

2   René A. Spitz, "Bridges: On Anticipation, Duration, and Meaning," *Journal of the American Psychoanalytic Association* 20 (1972):721 – 35; Peter Blos, "The Initial Stage of Male Adolescence," *Psychoanalytic Study of the Child* 20 (1965): 145 – 64.

Selected Bibliography

1 Works by Lawrence

Aaron's Rod. New York: Viking Press, 1961.

Apocalypse. New York: Viking Press, 1966.

The Collected Letters. Edited by Harry T. Moore. 2 vols. New York: Viking Press, 1962.

The Complete Poems. New York: Viking Press, 1972.

The Complete Short Stories. 3 vols. New York: Viking Press, 1961.

"The Crown." In *Reflections on the Death of a Porcupine*. Bloomington, Ind.: Indiana University Press, 1963.

Etruscan Places in D. H. Lawrence in Italy. New York: Viking Press, 1972.

Four Short Novels. New York: Viking Press, 1965.

Kangaroo. New York: Viking Press, 1960.

Lady Chatterley's Lover. New York: Grove Press, 1957.

Mornings in Mexico. London: Wm. Heinemann, 1956.

Paintings of D. H. Lawrence. Edited by Mervyn Levy. New York: Viking Press, 1964.

Phoenix, The Posthumous Papers of D. H. Lawrence. New York: Viking Press, 1936.

Phoenix II. New York: Viking Press, 1959.

The Plumed Serpent. New York: Alfred Knopf, Vintage Books, 1955.

Psychoanalysis and the Unconscious and *Fantasia of the Unconscious*. New York: Viking Press, 1960.

The Rainbow. New York: Viking Press, 1961.

Saint Mawr and *The Man Who Died*. New York: Alfred Knopf, Vintage Books, 1953.

Sons and Lovers. New York: Viking Press, Viking Critical Edition, 1968.

Studies in Classic American Literature. New York: Doubleday Anchor, 1951.

The Trespasser. New York: Mitchell Kennerley, 1912.

The White Peacock. London: J. M. Dent and Sons, Everyman's Library, 1935.

Women in Love. New York: Viking Press, 1960.

2 Biographical

Brett, Hon. Dorothy. *Lawrence and Brett, A Friendship*. Philadelphia: J. P. Lippincott, 1933.

Bynner, Witter. *Journey with Genius*. New York: Farrar, Straus and Giroux, 1974 (1951).

Carswell, Catherine. *The Savage Pilgrimage*. London: Secker and Warfung, 1951.

Chambers, Jessie ("E. T."). *D. H. Lawrence, A Personal Record*. New York: Knight Publications, 1936.

Corke, Helen. *D. H. Lawrence: The Croyden Years*. Austin: University of Texas Press, 1965.

———. "The Writing of *The Trespasser*." *D. H. Lawrence Review* 7 (1974):227 – 39.

Delaney, Paul. *D. H. Lawrence's Nightmare*. New York: Basic Books, 1978.

Delavenay, Emile. *D. H. Lawrence, The Man and His Work, The Formative Years: 1885 – 1919*. Carbondale: Southern Illinois University Press, 1972.

Foster, Joseph. *D. H. Lawrence in Taos*. Albuquerque: University of New Mexico Press, 1972.

Lawrence, Ada, and Gelder, Stuart. *Early Life of D. H. Lawrence*. London: Martin Secker, 1932.

Lawrence, Frieda. *"Not I, But the Wind . . . ."* New York: Viking Press, 1934.

Merrild, Knud. *A Poet and Two Painters*. New York: Viking Press, 1939.

Meyers, Jeffrey. *D. H. Lawrence and the Experience of Italy*. Philadelphia: University of Pennsylvania Press, 1982.

Moore, Harry T., *The Priest of Love, A Life of D. H. Lawrence*. Rev. ed. New York: Farrar, Straus and Giroux, 1974.

Murry, John Middleton. *The Autobiography*. New York: Julian Messner, 1936.

Nehls, Edward. *D. H. Lawrence: A Composite Biography*. Vol. 1. 1885 – 1919. Madison: University of Wisconsin Press, 1957.

Neville, G. H. *A Memoir of D. H. Lawrence*. New York: Cambridge University Press, 1981.

Zytaruk, G. J. *The Quest for Rananim*. Montreal: McGill-Queen's University Press, 1970.

3   Critical, Contextual, Historical

Baldwin, Alice. "The Structure of the Coatl Symbol in *The Plumed Serpent*." *Style* 5 (1971):138 – 50.

Barish, Jonas A. *Ben Jonson and the Language of Prose Comedy*. Cambridge: Harvard University Press, 1960.

Barkin, Leonard. *Nature's Work of Art: The Human Body As Image of the World*. New Haven: Yale University Press, 1975.

Bersani, Leo. "Lawrentian Stillness." In *A Future for Astyanax*. Boston: Little, Brown, 1976. Pp. 156 – 72.

Blanchard, Lydia. "Love and Power: A Reconsideration of Sexual Politics in D. H. Lawrence." *Modern Fiction Studies* 21 (1975):431 – 43.

Bloom, Harold. *The Anxiety of Influence*. New York: Oxford University Press, 1973.

Brown, Norman O. *Love's Body*. New York: Random House, 1966.

Campbell, Joseph. *The Masks of God*. Vol. 4, *Creative Mythology*. New York: Viking Press, 1968.

Carter, Frederick. *D. H. Lawrence and the Body Mystical*. London: Garden City Press, 1932.

Cavitch, David. *D. H. Lawrence and the New World*. New York: Oxford University Press, 1969.

Clark, L. D. *Dark Night of the Body*. Austin: University of Texas Press, 1964.

———. "D. H. Lawrence and the American Indian." *D. H. Lawrence Review* 9 (1976): 305—72.

———. *The Minoan Distance: The Symbolism of Travel in D. H. Lawrence*. Tucson: University of Arizona Press, 1980.

Clarke, Colin. *River of Dissolution*. London: Routledge and Kegan Paul, 1969.

Clarke, R. T. Rundle. "The Origin of the Phoenix." *University of Birmingham Historical Journal* 2 (1950):105—40.

Cowan, James. *D. H. Lawrence's American Journey*. Cleveland: Case Western Reserve Press, 1970.

Cushman, Keith. "D. H. Lawrence at Work, the Making of 'Odour of Chrysanthemums.'" *Journal of Modern Literature* 2 (1971—72):367—92.

D'Alviella, Count Goblet. *The Migration of Symbols*. New York: University Books, 1956.

Dix, Carol, ed. *D. H. Lawrence and Women*. Totowa, N.J.: Littlefield, 1980.

Ebbatson, Roger. *The Evolutionary Self: Hardy, Forster, Lawrence*. Totowa, N.J.: Barnes and Noble, 1982.

Eliot, T. S. "Tradition and the Individual Talent." In *Selected Essays*. New York: Harcourt, Brace and Co., 1950.

Ellmann, Richard. *Ulysses on the Liffey*. New York: Oxford University Press, 1972.

Ford, George H. *Double Measure*. New York: W. W. Norton and Co., 1965.

Frye, Northorp. *Spiritus Mundi: Essays on Literature, Myth and Society*. Bloomington: Indiana University Press, 1976.

Gilbert, Sandra. *Acts of Attention: The Poems of D. H. Lawrence*. Ithaca: Cornell University Press, 1972.

Ginzberg, Louis. *The Legends of the Jews*. Vol. 1. Philadelphia: Jewish Publication Society of America, 1909.

Goodheart, Eugene. *The Utopian Vision of D. H. Lawrence*. Chicago: University of Chicago Press, 1963.

Gregory, Horace. *Pilgrim of the Apocalypse*. New York: Grove Press, 1957.

Hardy, Barbara. *The Appropriate Form*. London: Athlone Press, 1964.

Holbrook, David. *The Quest for Love*. University: University of Alabama Press, 1965.

Hoyles, John. "D. H. Lawrence and the Counter-Revolution: An Essay in Socialist Aesthetics." *D. H. Lawrence Review* 6 (1973):173—200.

234

Kermode, Frank. "D. H. Lawrence and the Apocalyptic Types." In *Continuities*, pp. 122 – 51. London: Routledge and Kegan Paul, 1968.

———. *D. H. Lawrence*. New York: Viking Press, Modern Masters Series, 1973.

———. *Shakespeare, Spenser, Donne, Renaissance Studies*. New York: Viking Press, 1971.

Kirkham, Michael. "D. H. Lawrence and Social Consciousness." *Mosaic* 12 (1978): 72 – 92.

Kleinbard, David J. "Laing, Lawrence, and the Maternal Cannibal." *Psychoanalytic Review* 58 (1971):5 – 13.

Langbaum, Robert. "Lords of Life, Kings in Exile: Identity and Sexuality in D. H. Lawrence." *American Scholar* 4 (1975):807 – 15.

Le Doux, Larry V. "Christ and Isis: The Function of the Dying God and Reviving God in *The Man Who Died*." *D. H. Lawrence Review* 5 (1972):132 – 48.

Lessing, Doris. *The Golden Notebook*. New York: Ballantine Books, 1962.

Mailer, Norman. *The Prisoner of Sex*. Boston: Little, Brown and Co., 1971.

McDonald, Sister Mary Francis. "Phoenix Redivivus." *The Phoenix* 14 (1960):187 – 206.

McMillen, Douglas J. "The Phoenix in the Western World from Herodotus to Shake-speare." *D. H. Lawrence Review* 5 (Fall 1972):238 – 67.

Meyers, Jeffrey. "D. H. Lawrence and Homosexuality." *London Magazine* 13 (1973): 68 – 98.

———. "*The Plumed Serpent* and the Mexican Revolution." *Journal of Modern Literature* 4 (1974):55 – 72.

Miles, Thomas H. "Birkin's Electro-Mystical Body of Reality: D. H. Lawrence's Use of Kundalini." *D. H. Lawrence Review* 9 (1976):194 – 212.

Miller, Hillis. "D. H. Lawrence: *The Fox* and the Perspective Glass." *Harvard Advocate* (1952):137.

Millett, Kate. *Sexual Politics*. New York: Doubleday, 1970.

Moynahan, Julian. *The Deed of Life: The Novels and Tales of D. H. Lawrence*. Princeton: Princeton University Press, 1963.

Murry, John Middleton. *Son of Woman*. New York: Cape and Smith, 1931.

Oates, Joyce Carol. *The Hostile Sun: The Poetry of D. H. Lawrence*. Los Angeles: Black Sparrow Press, 1973.

Partlow, Robert B., Jr., and Moore, Harry T., eds. *D. H. Lawrence: The Man Who Lived*. Carbondale: Southern Illinois University Press, 1980.

Polanyi, Michael. *Personal Knowledge, Towards a Post-Critical Philosophy*. New York: Harper and Row, 1958.

Pryse, James M. *The Apocalypse Unsealed*. New York, 1910.

———. *A New Presentation of the "Prometheus Bound" of Aischylos*. London: John Watkins, 1925.

Radin, Paul. *The Trickster, A Study in American Indian Mythology*. New York: Schocken Books, 1956.

Ross, Charles. *The Composition of the Rainbow and Women in Love*. Charlottesville: University of Virginia Press, 1979.

Rossman, Charles. "'You Are the Call and I the Answer': D. H. Lawrence and Women." *D. H. Lawrence Review* 8 (1975):255 – 329.

Roth, Philip. *My Life as a Man*. New York: Holt, Rinehart and Winston, 1974.

Ruderman, Judith C. *D. H. Lawrence and the Devouring Mother*. Durham, N.C.: Duke University Press, 1984.

Sagar, Keith. *The Art of D. H. Lawrence*. New York: Cambridge University Press, 1966.

Sale, Roger. *Modern Heroism, Essays on D. H. Lawrence, William Empson, and J. R. Tolkien*. Berkeley: University of California Press, 1973.

Sanders, Scott. *The World of the Major Novels*. New York: Viking Press, 1973.

Simpson, Hilary. *D. H. Lawrence and Feminism*. DeKalb, Ill.: Northern Illinois University Press, 1982.

Smith, Anne, ed. *Lawrence and Women*. London: Vision, 1978.

Sontag, Susan. "Notes on Art, Sex, and Politics." *New York Times*, 8 February 1976 (see also *Salmagundi*, Fall 1975, Winter 1976).

Spender, Stephen. *The Struggle of the Modern*. Berkeley: University of California Press, 1963.

Spurgeon, Caroline. *Shakespeare's Imagery*. Boston: Beacon Hill Press, 1961.

Tindall, William York. *D. H. Lawrence and Susan His Cow*. New York: Columbia University Press, 1939.

Twitchell, James. "Lawrence's Lamias: Predatory Women in *The Rainbow* and *Women in Love*." *Studies in the Novel* 11 (1979):23 – 42.

Van Ghent, Dorothy. *The English Novel: Form and Function*. New York: Holt, Rinehart and Winston, 1953.

Vickery, John B. "Myth and Ritual in the Short Fiction of D. H. Lawrence." *Modern Fiction Studies* 5 (1959):68 – 82.

Wheeler, John. "Our Universe: The Known and the Unknown." *American Scientist* 56 (1968):1 – 20.

———. "The Universe As Home for Man." *American Scientist* 62 (1974):683 – 91.

4   Psychoanalytic and Medical

Ash, Mildred. "Freud on Feminine Identity and Female Sexuality." *Psychiatry* 34 (1971):322 – 26.

Bak, Robert, C. "The Phallic Woman: The Ubiquitous Fantasy in Perversion." *Psychoanalytic Study of the Child* 23 (1968):15 – 36.

236

Balint, Michael. "Early Developmental States of the Ego. Primary Object-Love."
(1937) In *Primary Love and Psycho-Analytic Technique*. New York: Liveright,
1965).

———. *Thrills and Regressions*. New York: International Universities Press, 1959.

———. *The Basic Fault*. London: Tavistock, 1968.

Blos, Peter. "The Initial Stage of Male Adolescence." *Psychoanalytic Study of the
Child* 20 (1965):145 – 64.

———. "The Genealogy of the Ego Ideal." *Psychoanalytic Study of the Child* 29
(1974):43 – 88.

———. "When and How Does Adolescence End?" Paper presented at Chestnut
Lodge, 3 October 1975. *Annals of Adolescent Psychiatry*, forthcoming.

Bradley, Noel. "Primal Scene Experience in Human Evolution and Its Phantasy
Derivatives in Art, Proto-Science and Philosophy." *Psychoanalytic Study of
Society*. Vol. 4, pp. 34 – 82. New York: International Universities Press, 1967.

Dervin, Daniel. "D. H. Lawrence and Freud." *American Imago* 36 (1979):93 – 117.

Edelheit, Henry. "Mythopoiesis and the Primal Scene." *Psychoanalytic Study of
Society* 5 (1972):212 – 33.

———. "Crucifixion Fantasies and Their Relation to the Primal Scene." *International Journal of Psycho-Analysis* 55 (1974):193 – 204.

Ehrenzweig, Anton. *The Hidden Order of Art*. Berkeley: University of California
Press, 1967.

Eissler, K. R. "Psychopathology and Creativity." *American Imago* 24 (1967):35 – 82.

Fabricant, Noah. "The Lingering Cough of D. H. Lawrence." In *Thirteen Famous
Patients*. New York: Chilton, 1960.

Ferenczi, Sandor. *Thalassa*. New York: *Psychoanalytic Quarterly*, 1938.

Fiderer, Gerald. "D. H. Lawrence's *The Man Who Died*: The Phallic Christ." *American Imago* 25 (1968):91 – 96.

Freud, Anna. *The Writings of Anna Freud*. Vol. 6. *Normality and Pathology in Childhood*. New York: International Universities Press, 1965.

———. "Aggression in Relation to Emotional Development: Normal and Pathological." In *Psychoanalytic Study of the Child*. Vols. 3 – 4, pp. 37 – 43. 1949.

Freud, Sigmund.

1900. *The Interpretation of Dreams. Standard Edition* 4. London: Hogarth Press.

1908. "Creative Writers and Day-dreaming." *S.E.* 9.

1909. "Family Romance." *S.E.* 9.

1909. "Notes upon a Case of Obsessional Neurosis." *S.E.* 10.

1910. "A Special Type of Object-Choice Made by Men." *S.E.* 11.

1911. "Formulations of the Two Principles of Mental Functioning. *S.E.* 12.

1914. "On Narcissism." *S.E.* 14.

1915. "Thoughts for the Times on War and Death." *S.E.* 17.

1917. "A Childhood Memory from *Dichtung und Warheit*." *S.E.* 17.

1917. "A Difficulty in the Path of Analysis." *S.E.* 9.

1920. *Beyond the Pleasure Principle. S.E.* 18.

1926. *The Problem of Anxiety. S.E.* 20.

1931. "Female Sexuality." *S.E.* 21.

1933. *New Introductory Lectures. S.E.* 22.

1937. "Analysis Terminable and Interminable." *S.E.* 23.

1954. *The Origins of Psychoanalysis* (The Fliess Correspondence). Edited by Ernst Kris. New York: Basic Books.

1974. *The Freud/Jung Letters*. Edited by William McGuire. Princeton: Princeton University Press, Bollingen Series 94.

Goodheart, Eugene. "Freud and Lawrence." *Psychoanalysis and the Psychoanalytic Review* 47 (1960):56 – 64.

Greenacre, Phyllis. *Swift and Carroll*. New York: International Universities Press, 1955.

———. "The Family Romance of the Artist." *Psychoanalytic Study of the Child* 13 (1958):9 – 36.

Grolnick, Simon, and Barkin, Leonard, eds. *Between Fantasy and Reality*. New York: Jason Aronson, 1978.

Grotjahn, Martin. *The Voice of the Symbol*. New York: Dell, 1971.

Guttman, Samuel A., et al. "Symposium on Symbolism." *Journal of the American Psychoanalytic Association* 9 (1961):146 – 57.

———. "Bisexuality in Symbolism." *Journal of the American Psychoanalytic Association* 3 (1955):280 – 84.

Heimann, Paula. "Certain Functions of Introjection and Projection in Early Infancy." In *Developments in Psychoanalysis*. Edited by Joan Riviere. London: Hogarth Press, 1952.

Henderson, James. "Exorcism, Possession, and the Dracula Cult: A Synopsis of Object Relations Psychology." *Bulletin of the Menninger Clinic* 40 (1976): 603 – 28.

Holland, Norman. "Freud and the Poet's Eye." In *Hidden Patterns*, pp. 151 – 70. Edited by Leonard Manheim and Eleanor Manheim. New York: Macmillan, 1966.

Jacobson, Edith. "Development of the Wish for a Child in Boys." *Psychoanalytic Study of the Child* 5 (1950):139 – 52.

Jaffe, Daniel S. "The Masculine Envy of Woman's Procreative Function." *Journal of the American Psychoanalytic Association* 16 (1968):521 – 48.

Jones, Ernest. "The Theory of Symbolism." In *Papers on Psychoanalysis*. London:

Bailliere, Tindace, and Cox, 1950.

———. *The Life and Works of Sigmund Freud in Three Volumes*. New York: Basic Books, 1960.

Kaplan, Donald. "Sugar and Spice Revisited." *Psychiatry and Social Science Review* 5 (1971):12 – 17.

———. "On Shyness." *International Journal of Psycho-Analysis* 53 (1972):439 – 53.

———. "Freud and the Coming of Age." *Bulletin of the Menninger Clinic* 40 (1976): 335 – 56.

Kaplan, Linda Joan. "The Family Romance: Theoretical and Clinical Implications." *Psychoanalytic Review* 61 (1974):169 – 202.

Kaplan, Louise. *Oneness and Separateness*. New York: Simon and Schuster, 1978.

Kernberg, Otto F. "Barriers to Falling and Remaining in Love." *Journal of the American Psychoanalytic Association* 22 (1974):486 – 511.

Kestenberg, Judith. "On the Development of Maternal Feelings in Early Childhood." *Psychoanalytic Study of the Child* 11 (1956):284 – 91.

Klein, Melanie. "The Importance of Symbol Formation in the Development of the Ego." In *Contributions to Psychoanalysis 1921 – 45*, pp. 236 – 50. London: Hogarth Press, 1950.

———. "Notes on Some Schizoid Mechanisms." In *Developments in Psychoanalysis*. Edited by Joan Reviere. London: Hogarth Press, 1952.

Kohut, Heinz. *The Analysis of Self*. New York: International Universities Press, 1971.

———. *The Restoration of the Self*. New York: International Universities Press, 1977.

Kris, Ernst. *Psychoanalytic Explorations in Art*. New York: International Universities Press, 1953.

Kubie, Lawrence. "Distortion of the Symbolic Process in Neurosis and Psychosis." *Journal of the American Psychoanalytic Association* 1 (1953):59 – 86.

———. "The Drive to Become Both Sexes." *Psychoanalytic Quarterly* 43 (1974): 349 – 426.

Kuttner, Alfred Booth. "A Freudian Appreciation." *Psychoanalytic Review* 3 (1916).

Lichtenberg, Joseph D. "The Development of the Sense of Self." *Journal of the American Psychoanalytic Association* 23 (1975):453 – 84.

Mahler, Margaret. *The Psychological Birth of the Human Infant*. New York: Basic Books, 1975.

Meyer, Bernard C. "Some Reflections on the Contribution of Psychoanalysis to Biography." *Psychoanalysis and Contemporary Science* 1 (1972):373 – 91.

Milner, Marion. "The Role of Illusion in Symbol Formation." In *New Directions in Psychoanalysis*. Edited by Melanie Klein et al. New York: Basic Books, 1955.

———. *On Not Being Able To Paint*. New York: International Universities Press, 1957.

Niederland, William G. "Narcissistic Ego Impairment in Patients with Early Physical Malformations." *Psychoanalytic Study of the Child*. Vol. 20, pp. 518–33. New York: International Universities Press, 1965.

———. "Clinical Aspects of Creativity." *American Imago* 20 (1967):6–34.

———. "Scarred: A Contribution to the Study of Facial Disfigurement." *Psychoanalytic Quarterly* 44 (1975):450–59.

———. "Psychoanalytic Approaches to Artistic Creativity." *Psychoanalytic Quarterly* 45 (1976).

"Panel on Aggression." *International Journal of Psycho-Analysis* 53 (1972):13–19.

Pollock, George H. "On Mourning, Immortality, and Utopia." *Journal of the American Psychoanalytical Association* 23 (1975):334–62.

Rank, Otto. *The Myth of the Birth of the Hero*. New York: Alfred Knopf, Vintage Book, 1959.

Ricoeur, Paul. *Freud and Philosophy*. New Haven: Yale University Press, 1970.

Rothenberg, Albert. "The Process of Janusian Thinking in Creativity." *Psychoanalytic Study of Society* 7 (1976):1–31.

Schneider, Daniel J. *D. H. Lawrence: The Artist as Psychologist*. Lawrence: University of Kansas Press, 1984.

Segal, Hanna. "Notes on Symbol Formation." *International Journal of Psycho-Analysis* 38 (1957):391–97.

———. "A Psycho-Analytic Approach to Aesthetics." *International Journal of Psycho-Analysis* 33 (1952):196–207.

———. "Symposium on Fantasy." *International Journal of Psycho-Analysis* 45 (1964):191–94.

———. "Delusion and Artistic Creativity: Some Reflections on Reading William Golding's *The Spine*." *Psychoanalytic Forum* 5 (1975):390–430.

Shengold. Leonard. "The Parent as Sphinx." *Journal of the American Psychoanalytical Association* 11 (1963):725–51.

Spitz, René A. "Bridges: On Anticipation, Duration, and Meaning." *Journal of the American Psychoanalytical Association* 20 (1972):721–35.

Stamm, Julian. "Creativity and Sublimation." *American Imago* 24 (1967):82–97.

Sterba, Richard. "The Cosmological Aspect of Freud's Theory of the Instincts." *American Imago* 6 (1949):157–61.

Stierlen, Helm. *Psychoanalysis and Family Therapy*. New York: Jason Aronson, 1978.

Stoller, Robert. "Symbiosis Anxiety and the Development of Masculinity." *Archives of General Psychiatry* 30 (1974):1964–72.

Stone, Leo. "On the Principal Obscene of the English Language." *International Journal of Psycho-Analysis* 30 (1954):30–56.

Wiedeman, George H. "Homosexuality, A Survey." *Journal of the American Psychoanalytical Association* 22 (1974):651–96.

White, J. Psyche and Tuberculosis: The Libido Organization of Franz Kafka. *Psychoanalytic Study of Society* 4 (1967):185−251.

Winnicott, D. W. "Aggression in Relation to Emotional Development." In *Collected Papers*. London: Tavistock Publications, 1958.

———. "Transitional Objects and Transitional Phenomena." In *Collected Papers*. London: Tavistock Publications, 1958.

Index

Aaron's Rod, 31, 119, 186
Apocalypse, 83, 86, 180
"Autobiographical Fragment," 17 – 19

Balbert, Peter, 104
Balint, Michael, 3, 7 – 9, 18 – 21, 86. *See also* Primary love
Basic fault, 19 – 21. *See also* Balint
Bergler, Edmund, 28
"Blind Man, The," 92, 210
Bradley, Noel, 49
Brett, Dorothy, 26, 71, 99
Brynner, Witter, 153 – 54, 156

"Captain's Doll, The," 117
Cavitch, James, 157, 159, 161
Chambers, Jessie (Miriam), 29, 36, 66 – 68, 71, 73, 91, 115, 129, 145, 163, 164, 213
"Cherry Robbers," 73
Clark, L. D., 135
Corke, Helen, 67 – 68, 163
Cowan, James, 6, 152
Creativity, 3 – 4, 10 – 11, 19, 30, 33, 46 – 47, 68 – 70, 74 – 75, 83 – 89, 97, 108 – 10, 124 – 26, 143 – 47, 155, 181 – 201, 206 – 11, 212 – 14; as aggression and reparation, 10 – 11, 166 – 67, 172 – 74, 206 – 11; as dual mode, 11 – 13, 39 – 47, 168, 186; as mastery through play, 3, 59, 111 – 26; as natural cycle, 166 – 71; as Phoenix cycle, 185 – 90, 199 – 200; as projecting and identifying, 155 – 65, 169 – 80; as re-sourcing origins, 127 – 47; as self-remaking, 89 – 99, 120 – 26; as separation/individuation, 3, 103 – 7, 193 – 200, 212 – 14; as symbol-formation, 3, 48 – 75, 121, 184 – 85, 203 – 5

Crown, The, 23, 50 – 51, 54 – 55

Delaney, Paul, 21, 123 – 24
Delavenay, Emile, 34
"Demon Justice," 145 – 46
"Discord in Childhood," 44, 65, 72, 145

Edelheit, Henry, 49, 86, 181
Ehrenzweig, Anton, 2, 185 – 87
Eissler, K. R., 80, 207
"England, My England," 125
Etruscan Places, 48 – 49, 178, 191

Family Romance, 15 – 19, 21 – 22, 25, 31, 34, 37 – 38, 40 – 41, 43, 65, 145, 181, 183, 185 – 86
"Flying Fish, The," 159, 176, 187
"Fox, The," 120, 210
Freud, Anna, 208
Freud, Sigmund, 5, 14 – 15, 38, 40 – 41, 49, 54, 63, 65, 70, 73, 77, 80, 83, 158, 175
Frye, Northrop, 110

"Glad Ghosts," 183
Greenacre, Phyllis, 15, 77

"Healing," 101

Incest, 30, 31, 35, 88, 99, 102, 153. *See also* Oedipus complex

Jung, C. G., 4, 70, 199

Kangaroo, 57 – 60, 91, 103, 172
Kermode, Frank, 197
Kirkham, Michael, 134
Klein, Melanie, 3, 160, 188, 204
Kleinbard, David J., 28

Kris, Ernst, 15, 93
Kubie, Lawrence, 72, 80, 203 — 4

Lady Chatterley's Lover, 27, 31, 34 — 35,
47, 77, 88, 94, 97, 104 — 5, 121, 127,
138 — 47, 177 — 78, 179, 184 — 85, 186,
190 — 92, 193 — 99, 207, 210, 212
Lawrence, D. H.: and aggression, 10 —
11, 32 — 33, 95, 206 — 7; and body
(-image, etc.), 44, 76 — 102; and fantasy, 14 — 38, 70, *see also* Family
Romance; and feminism, 190, 195,
197, 199, 210 — 11, 227 — 29; and
homosexuality, 161; and narcissism,
5 — 9, 77 — 82, 90 — 94, 105, 109, 207;
and occult, 74, 83 — 89, 107 — 10; and
his parents, 9, 21 — 22, 35 — 36, 65 — 66,
72 — 74, 89, 91, 100, 128 — 30, 138, 163,
208 — 11, *see also* Primal Scene; and
psychoanalysis, 1 — 9, 74, 85 — 86, 88
Lawrence, Frieda, 24, 26, 28, 33, 38, 44,
66, 67, 96, 97, 99, 110, 154, 158
LeDoux, Larry, 179
Lichtenberg, Joseph, 82

Man Who Died, The, 74, 104 — 6, 120 — 21,
162, 165, 177 — 80, 189, 198
Meyers, Jeffrey, 27
Miller, Hillis, 28
Moore, Harry T., 66 — 67, 115
Murry, John Middleton, 24, 32 — 33, 156

Niederland, William, 3, 90, 93, 95, 107

"Odour of Chrysanthemums," 46, 116 —
17, 119, 164
Oedipus complex, 3, 21, 35 — 37, 70, 73,
146, 157. *See also* Incest
"On Human Destiny," 137 — 38, 165

"Pan in America," 98, 134, 169 — 71
Plumed Serpent, The, 28, 33 — 34, 61 —
62, 66, 91, 103, 137, 153, 157, 160, 172
Primal Scene, 41 — 47, 48, 64, 69 — 70,
71 — 73, 145, 186, 193

Primary love, 3, 7 — 9, 77, 97, 190 — 93,
207. *See also* Balint
"Princess, The," 118
"Prussian Officer, The," 119
Rainbow, The, 15, 23, 26, 29 — 30, 50 — 53,
56, 67, 103, 117 — 18, 123, 152, 172,
186 — 87
Rananim, 24 — 28, 37
Róheim, Géza, 36, 71
Ruderman, Judith, 28, 32
Russell, Bertrand, 24 — 26, 33 — 34,
197 — 98

Sagar, Keith, 178
St. Mawr, 28, 94, 118, 127, 130, 132 — 38,
144 — 45, 146, 151 — 52, 155, 172 — 73
"Scientific Doctor, The," 101
Sea and Sardinia, 32
"Ship of Death," 100
Simpson, Hilary, 190, 199
Sons and Lovers, 16, 24, 29 — 30, 34, 43,
46, 67, 71, 72, 77, 91, 99, 103, 104, 112 —
17, 123, 127 — 30, 141, 146, 151, 164,
172, 182 — 85, 210
Spilka, Mark, 104
Spitz, René, 80, 124, 212 — 14
"Study of Hardy, The," 23, 63, 64, 94
"Sun," 16, 150 — 51, 162, 169, 174

"Tickets, Please," 119
Tindall, William York, 84
Trespasser, The, 8, 16, 18, 148 — 50, 153,
162 — 65, 179
Twitchell, James, 28 — 29

van Ghent, Dorothy, 212

Weiss, Daniel, 2, 191
White Peacock, The, 68, 77, 140, 196
Winnicott, D. W., 3, 59, 72, 111, 122 — 23,
181, 204 — 5, 208
"Woman Who Rode Away, The," 118 —
19, 125, 174
Women in Love, 15, 29 — 30, 40, 47, 67,
118, 123, 186 — 87, 194

Library of Congress Cataloging in Publication Data
Dervin, Daniel, 1935 –
A "strange sapience".
Bibliography: p.
Includes index.
1. Lawrence, D. H. (David Herbert), 1885 – 1930—
Biography—Psychology. 2. Psychoanalysis and
literature. 3. Creation (Literary, artistic, etc.)
I. Title
PR6023.A93Z62366   1984   823'.912 [B]   84 – 2681
ISBN 0 – 87023 – 455 – 2